MW00618280

SOMEONE ELSE'S YESTERDAY

Someone Else's Yesterday

The Confederate General and Connecticut Yankee

A PAST LIFE REVEALED

JEFFREY J. KEENE

BLUE DOLPHIN PUBLISHING

Copyright © 2003 Jeffrey J. Keene
All rights reserved.

Published by
Blue Dolphin Publishing, Inc.
P.O. Box 8, Nevada City, CA 95959
Orders: 1-800-643-0765
Web: www.bluedolphinpublishing.com

ISBN: 1-57733-134-6

Library of Congress Cataloging-in-Publication Data

Keene, Jeffrey J., 1947–
Someone else's yesterday : the Confederate general and Connecticut yankee, a past life revealed / Jeffrey J. Keene.
p. cm.
Includes bibliographical references.
ISBN 1-57733-134-6 (pbk. : alk. paper)
1. Keene, Jeffrey J., 1947– 2. Gordon, John Brown, 1832–1904. 3. Reincarnation—Biography. I. Title.

BL520.K44A3 2003
133.9'01'35092—dc21

2003005904

Printed in the United States of America

5 4 3 2 1

To my beloved wife Anna
for putting up with me,
and to Shannon and Samantha
for their belief in and love of their father.

Any man's death diminishes me, because I am involved in mankind, and therefore never send to know for whom the bell tolls; it tolls for thee.

—John Donne (1571?–1631),
Meditation XVII from
Devotions upon Emergent Occasions

Contents

Foreword

THE PHRASE "NEW AGE" has been bantered about for so many years that it makes one wonder just when this "New Age" will come about. Well, stop waiting and start looking around. The twentieth century was chock full of technological advancements. We went from the infancy of air travel to flights to the moon and back. Communications went from crank operated telephones and primitive radios to mobile phones and televisions you can hold in the palm of your hand. We have come a long way here on Earth, but our spiritual advancement has not kept pace with our technical discoveries.

We are now witnessing the rebirth of spiritual seeking on a scale never seen before. One of the all-time great puzzles through the ages has been what happens after we die. Some people say, "There is only one way to find out: Die." There is an alternative way. This path involves studying the most recent cases involving reincarnation. Ever since 1952 when the Bridey Murphy story hit the media, people in the U.S. have seen a progression of reincarnation cases. Each decade has brought about stronger and stronger cases, including dozens of well-documented histories of children who spontaneously remember past lifetimes.

At the turn of the millennium, a group of cases has emerged that demonstrates a common pattern in how reincarnation occurs. These cases show that facial architecture, personality traits, aptitudes, interests and writing style stay consistent from lifetime to lifetime. Symbols and synchronistic events related to past lifetimes have been observed. People are also found to incarnate in karmic soul groups. In my research, Jeffrey Keene's case is one of the first that I encountered, which demonstrates *all* of these principles of reincarnation. In his story, in which it is proposed that he is the reincarnation of Confederate General John B. Gordon, we observe the following features characteristic of reincarnation cases:

Similar Physical Appearance:	Yes
Similar Personality Traits:	Yes
Consistent Writing Style:	Yes
Karmic Group Identified:	Yes
Past Life Symbols:	Yes (birth date, emergency room visit)
Past Life Memories:	Yes

To add to the credibility and feasibility of the conclusions drawn by Mr. Keene's belief that he had been General John B. Gordon is the fact that he bears markings on his face, in three places, that match wounds received by Gordon in battle. Once he was even rushed to a local hospital emergency room with pain that mimicked a wound Gen. Gordon received 115 years before.

The photographic resemblance between Confederate General John B. Gordon and Jeffrey Keene is, to say the least, uncanny; some even say spooky. Jeff's story is a marvelous collection of hindsight and foresight. You will be carried through history from America's Civil War to the sorrowful aftermath of the terrorist attack on the World Trade Center, where Mr. Keene, a decorated firefighter himself, paid respects to America's fallen. It is a wondrous thing to travel along with someone who has not only seen the past, but who has felt it; someone who has witnessed a modern tragedy of historic proportions, who can also impart insights from past battles, which will help humanity grow beyond its recurring pattern of needless conflict and war.

If you listen closely, you may hear the guns of Antietam mixed with the sound of bagpipes echoing through the masonry canyons of New York. Let his story teach us and let wisdom emerge like a phoenix from the smoking rubble and our broken hearts.

Walter Semkiw, M.D.
Author of *Return of the Revolutionaries: The Case for Reincarnation and Soul Groups Reunited*

Preface

LIKE MOST PEOPLE, I was stumbling through life minding my own business when all at once the world started having its way with me. Suddenly, the extraordinary became the ordinary and strange occurrences throughout my life started to make sense. I found that I had been a friend to some very famous people, people that I was not even aware I had met. I was being given insights that answered some of life's greatest questions. Before too long I found myself on the front page of a statewide newspaper and featured in an Arts & Entertainment Network documentary titled, "Beyond Death." Getting to a point where the word "coincidence" was worn very thin, I decided to accept the fact that I was being guided and opened myself to what life wanted to show me. Long after I had been convinced of a past life, unusual events kept reinforcing my conclusions, so much so that the only reason I could come up with for such revelations was that I am to share them with others.

My story is your story too, for I am not the lone actor on this stage. *Someone Else's Yesterday* is a remarkable journey, an adventure as seen through the eyes of two people; one a Georgian, the other a Connecticut Yankee. Similarities between the two go far beyond coincidence. They think alike, look alike and even share facial scars. Their lives are so intertwined they appear to be one. I know, for I am half of this equation: Jeffrey Keene, born September 9, 1947. The other half, John B. Gordon, Confederate General, died January 9, 1904. I had never given reincarnation much thought, nor had I ever seen a psychic, but both of these elements came together one Halloween night. That one night was to change my outlook on life and my way of thinking forever. That evening started a progression of puzzle pieces floating into place. As each piece gently touched down, it added to a picture, a portrait that reinforced a strong case for reincarnation. My story weaves a tapestry of mystery and history, of love and the horrors of warfare. The journey was and still is a wondrous one, sometimes funny but at other times sad and physically painful. I force my beliefs on no one. I only ask that the readers open their minds to their own experiences, to take a good look at the world around them. As for me, I have no choice but to believe in reincarnation. I lived the story, and every word is true.

PART I

CHAPTER ONE

Not Yet

IT WAS A PEACEFUL QUIET DAY at the Bloody Lane, one of those beautiful days in May you would like to catch in a jar and save for winter. I walked down the fieldstone stairs into the old farm road. I had no idea of the series of events being put into action. Soon, in a few short steps, the line between past and present would become very blurred.

My wife Anna and I were on a vacation to hunt for antiques. Our travels took us through New Jersey, Pennsylvania and then into Maryland. While in Maryland, we stopped in Sharpsburg, where the battle of Antietam had been fought during the Civil War. I was not a student of the Civil War. For that matter, I had never even read a Civil War book. I had watched a couple of shows from the Ken Burns Civil War series on the local Public Broadcast System and, while we were in the area, felt compelled to visit this battlefield. Our first stop was at the section of the battlefield known as The Cornfield.

Anna and I walked around a bit, then drove a short distance to a parking lot near what is called the Sunken Road. Anna stayed in the car, having soon tired of looking at monuments and markers, thus ending her historical career. Walking over to the Sunken Road alone, I found myself the only visitor to this portion of the battlefield. Built into a stone wall was a piece of metal grillwork with a large button next to it with the word "Push." Much like Alice in Wonderland, my curiosity got the better of me and within a few seconds I was listening to a tape recording of what had transpired there during the battle. After listening to the tape, I walked down onto the road itself. I had only gone a few yards when something very strange happened, something the likes of which I hope will never happen again. A wave of grief, sadness and anger washed over me. Without warning, I was suddenly being consumed by sensations. Burning tears ran down my cheeks. It became difficult to breathe. I gasped for air, as I stood transfixed in the old roadbed. To this day I could not tell you how much time transpired, but as these feelings, this emotional overload passed, I found myself exhausted as if I had run a marathon. Crawling up the steep embankment to get out of the road, I turned and looked back. I was a bit shaken to say the least and wondered at what had just taken place. It was difficult getting back to the car because I felt so weak. I had regained most of my normal composure on the way back and said nothing to Anna about what had just happened. What could I say? How could I explain it to her? I did not have any answers, just questions. I would one day receive my answers, but not until more than a year later and then from a most unusual source.

On a day that is set aside for the unusual, I was soon to discover just how far from the commonplace a Halloween night could be. Life for me had become pretty routine, but that was all to change on All Hallows Eve 1992. Anna and I attended a birthday party for the husband of her friend who just happened to be born on Halloween. Anna's friend, Lourdis McBroom rented a ballroom at Roberto's restaurant in Monroe, Connecticut. I know what a few of you may be thinking. Halloween? McBroom? He's making it up. No, I am not. Lourdis's last name was McBroom. This name may conjure up visions of an old crone, but Lourdis was the farthest thing from it. She was petite and pretty, a firecracker of a redhead with a wonderful Spanish accent. Regretfully, I must use the past tense. Lourdis left us a short while back after a long illness. She is missed. Lourdis had decorated the place lavishly for her husband's party. On all the tables were bags full of masks, spiders, candy and the like. She had hired two people for the evening, one a cartoonist and the other a palm reader. Anna and I had walked around for a while, then waited to have a caricature done.

While we waited, I watched the people having their palms read. The woman doing the reading seemed sincere and was not repeating anything she had said to others. People who had waited in line would sit down one at a time in front of this woman. Taking their hands in hers, she used a small flashlight to look at the lines in their palms. She talked about things like their personalities, travel and so on. When we sat for the caricature, the artist asked our occupations and hobbies. When he finished, he handed us the completed picture. The cartoon showed me wearing my fire helmet and sitting at a desk while Anna stood nearby cooking up a storm with a frying pan in one hand and a rolling pin menacingly close to my head in the other. The young artist was quite clever and talented. Anna and I returned to our table to eat.

With dinner finished, I asked Anna if she was going to have her palm read. She said, "Yes," and I said, "Me too." I had never had my palm read before. I put Anna ahead of me in line so I could hear what the woman said to her first. Before it was Anna's turn to sit, I told her to watch when it was my turn. She said "why?" All I could reply was, "I don't know, I just have a feeling." The line moved on. Anna sat for her reading. The woman proceeded to hit her personality right on the head. I was laughing and Anna said, "You better stop laughing, you're next." There were some pink sheets of paper on the table near the palm reader so I picked one up and it read:

> Hi! My name is Barbara Camwell. I am a Clairvoyant, Clairsentient and Clairaudient. As far as I can remember, I have been this way all of my life. What this means is that I may be able to see, hear or feel (emotionally) past and present issues for you, as well as some trivial and not so trivial information. I use palmistry as a tool. I will need both hands for this. What helps me? For you to think positively. Think of something good that has happened to you recently or something that makes you feel happy. This tends to make the reading clearer. Nervousness and anxiety tend to blur the

reading. Don't be afraid! I won't say anything to scare you! Honest! I don't believe in negativity, unless I can help you avoid it. So enjoy, and importantly ... HAVE FUN!

Well, after a good dinner, a few drinks, and laughing at my wife with the palm reader, I guess I was having fun already. Barbara told Anna that she would come into money within the next five years. She felt something about a little boy. She said she saw Anna surrounded by ocean and that she loved it. Anna told me later that she thought Barbara had been way off on this one. At the time I thought so too, as I knew Anna had a great dislike for water. Years later Anna stood on a black sand beach in Hawaii, the water swirling about her calves and tickling her legs as she watched giant sea turtles bobbing up and down in the surf. She had to confess Barbara had been right. Now it was my turn. I sat down and smiled at Barbara, and she smiled back. Barbara took hold of my extended hands and held them for a short while. (She did not use the small flashlight she had used on all of the others). Suddenly she dropped my hands and sat back in her chair. She said, "That is only the second time I have seen that." She told me she has a friend who has a simian line that crosses their hand and runs down the side. She said that mine was almost as long.

I asked, "Simian like monkey?"

She replied, "Yes." Barbara took my hands in hers. She started looking at my left hand. She said, "You have some real nasty stuff here. You have one line that you only see on insane people."

I chuckled and said, "I've been there."

"Your right hand shows that you have it under control; you are right-handed, aren't you?" I nodded yes. (I think that at that point, if I had been a lefty, I would have switched!) She said, "You are going to come into money within the next five years. I see ocean. You're going to take a trip to Sweden? Switzerland?" (At that point I informed her that my wife had been born in Austria and that was most likely the area). Barbara continued, "I see an accident, nobody is killed or hurt bad, it's just going to be a pain in the butt, so be careful. Do you play an instrument?"

I replied, "No."

"Did you ever play an instrument?" I said I had tried to play the drums, but it hurt my legs to do the bass. Barbara said, "You should play one even if it's only a hobby." There was a long pause as she studied my hands. She said, "You are very intelligent, very, very intelligent."

She suddenly dropped my hands and sat back in her chair. "You know what I mean by intelligent—you know about things like time and doors opening and closing, things like that?" I nodded. (Who was I to argue with someone who just finished telling me how intelligent I am?) "Do you believe in past lives?" she asked.

I said, "Yeah?"

She said, "There is a question mark there. I just take past lives for granted." I explained that I have seen and felt a few strange things in my life. She asked "like what?"

I told Barbara about the unusual thing that happened to me on our visit to the Antietam Battlefield. Barbara sat across from me nodding her head. "That's because you died there," she said.

"Oh, that's nice," I replied.

Barbara seemed deep in thought for a short time. She said, "When you were hovering over your body looking down, you were very angry and yelled NO!"

There was a pause, and I told her for reasons unknown to me, "Not yet!"

She said, "Yes, like not yet, but you hung around for a long time." Well, that was the end of the session, for others were waiting in line for their turn. I went back to our table with Anna. I asked her if she had been watching. She said yes, but she could not hear much. She asked why I looked so serious while talking to Barbara. I told her what Barbara had said to me.

I sat thinking over what Barbara had said. After a while, I returned to the line to see Barbara again because I wanted to ask her two questions. I sat down in front of Barbara, she sat back in her chair and said, "I have taken you as far as I can."

I said, "Just let me ask you two questions. Number one, are you sure that I was dead? What about wounds?"

She said "Oh honey, you had holes shot all through you." Why the first question was important to me I did not know. Then I asked her about something that had happened to me when I was stationed in Florida during my hitch in the Air Force. I had returned to my barracks at Orlando Air Force base hospital after a long Labor Day weekend at Daytona Beach with some of the guys. I was lying on my bunk starting to drift off to sleep when I saw someone walk into the room. (The door was open and the light in the hallway was on.) He walked over and stood at the foot of my bed. I said, "Hey, what's happening." I wanted to get him to talk so I could figure out who it was. There was no reply. I boosted myself up on one elbow and leaned out so that the upper bunk was not blocking my view. I started to say something again when I noticed I could see the picture hanging on the wall directly behind whoever this was. The problem was I was looking right through him. I slowly brought my knees up to my chest, pushed my feet out from under the covers and down to the floor. I stood and moved rapidly to the door. The figure did not move; he remained in the same position. All I could make out was black hair combed back, dark sunken eyes and hollow sunken cheeks. I heard a television on in one of the rooms, so I went in and told them that I could not sleep. I watched television for a while not saying anything to the other guys about what had just happened. I sat in contemplation over what had been the most frightening experience of my life. Did I have a hallucination, or was it just that state that lies between asleep and awake? But why could I still see him as I exited the room? Maybe I had simply overdone it out at Daytona, or gotten too much sun on my head. After a while, I decided to return to my room. I walked down the hall, passed my door, turned around and made a beeline back to watch some more television, for standing just inside the doorway was the same man that I had seen earlier. I watched a lot of television that night. I was awake, alert and confused.

Who was this apparition in my room? This was the second question that I asked Barbara.

She asked, "Did he speak to you?"

I said, "No."

"Did you see a uniform?" she asked.

Again I answered, "No."

"Well maybe it was someone from your past," she said. I thanked her and went back to my table. Over the years I have told many people about the story of the man in my room, and the best way that I could describe his looks was to say he was "Abe Lincolnish," when Lincoln was young, with sunken eyes, hollow cheeks and black combed back hair. On the way home from the party, Anna asked me, "What were you at Antietam? Just a soldier?"

I said, "I guess so."

The next day Anna went to work. I sat alone in my living room wondering about what had happened at the party. Was there anything to this past life stuff? Some curious thoughts came into my head. Here I am, a man in his mid-forties, and the only picture on my dresser for a long time was of my Great Grandfather, Lewis Knapp, 1st. CT. Heavy Artillery United States Volunteers. In the picture, he is wearing his Civil War uniform. Something else struck me as strange. When Anna and I were leaving the Sharpsburg area during our trip, we stopped in a gift shop. Anna wanted to buy some wine called Lake Anna, a local brew. I was looking around and picked up a bullet from the Civil War that had been found in the area. A magazine on the counter caught my eye, the *Civil War Quarterly* [Special Edition ANTIETAM]. I picked it up and took both the bullet and the magazine to the checkout counter and told Anna, "I want these." We left and returned to our home in Connecticut. Now the strange part. That magazine was the first Civil War book or magazine I had ever purchased. The bullet had been placed on my dresser next to my Great Grandfather's picture. The magazine had been placed in with our phone books. Our trip was taken in May of 1991. Here it was a year and a half later, and I had never read the magazine. I had come across it many times, every time I had used the phone books, but had never read it. As Lewis Carroll would put it, "Curiouser and Curiouser." The picture and the bullet on my dresser, the magazine I never read.

I was then aware that I had treated that magazine like no other I had ever owned. I figured it was time to read it. I turned to the section on the Sunken Road. A picture at the top of the page showed the road near the spot where I had that unusual experience I had told Barbara about. My eyes scanned down the page and stopped at a two-word quote. The hair on the back of my neck stood up. "Not yet," it read. That is what I had said to Barbara. I read on. "Not yet," John B. Gordon had told anxious members of the Sixth Alabama who requested permission to fire. "Wait for orders." "Closer and closer the Federals tramped, coming at last to the crest of the low ridge that fronted the confederate position. There they appeared in brilliant outline against the eastern sky, perfect targets less than 100 yards from the defenders. Shouted orders to 'FIRE' from the sunken road must have been audible to many of the attackers an instant before a tremendous volley struck them. In a moment the drill-like precision of the attack dissolved into chaos." I read on. "A huge volume of musketry spewed out from the sunken road. My rifles flamed and roared in the Federal's faces like a blinding blaze of lightning," wrote Gordon. "The effect was appalling. The entire front line, with few exceptions, went down in the consuming blast." Tears welled up in my eyes. I continued reading, and later in the account of the battle, I came across the wounding of Gordon. "On Rodes end of the line, John B. Gordon of the Sixth Alabama was hit in the left arm, the right shoulder, and twice in the right leg before passing out from loss of blood after receiving a wound in the face."[1] From what Barbara Camwell had said I figured this fifth wound was the one that Gordon would have died from. I turned back to the page with the picture of the sunken road, and on the page across from it was another picture. This time a chill ran through me and the hair on the back of my neck stood up again. The picture was of Brigadier General John B. Gordon. The face was not unknown to me. I knew it well; I shave it every morning. In the story they referred to Colonel John B. Gordon? He must have lived through his wounding to become a general. Was I going crazy? I wondered if I was imagining the likeness of the photo.

I read more of the magazine; a story called "Lee's Lost Orders." The story was about Special Orders number 191, the most famous orders General Lee ever issued. To capsulate, Special Orders number 191 were written at Frederick, Maryland, some forty miles northwest of Washington D. C. They were phase two of the first invasion of the north by the Army of Northern Virginia. Nine copies were written. Their fame is derived from the fact that one copy was lost in transit. The lost copy was found by some Union soldiers and upon discovering their significance, the orders made their way to General George B. McClellan, then commander of the Union Army. Now the Union Army had the game plan, whereabouts and dispersion of the Army of Northern Virginia. The result of receiving this information was the battle of Antietam, or Sharpsburg as it is known to Southerners. Now here we go with the chills and the hair on the back of the neck again. The date the orders were written? September 9, 1862. The date was well known to me, I would celebrate it every year. My birthday is September 9th. Let's backtrack now and see what we have so far from the time of the party. In one day, I see a palm reader, the first one I had ever talked to. I tell her about things that happened to me on an old battlefield. She tells me I died there. I have the picture and the bullet on my dresser. I read a magazine I have kept for one and a half years without reading. I read a quote that I said to Barbara, "Not yet." I see a picture that looks like me. I read about the orders that cause the battle and find that they were written on my birthday. Put yourself in my place. What would you think? What would you do? Oh yes, and one other thing. The picture of Gordon shows him wearing a double-breasted uniform with three stars on the collar. I am presently an assistant chief on the Westport Fire Department in Westport, Connecticut. My dress uniform is double-breasted, the rank insignia on the collar is three trumpets.

I needed another person's opinion on the picture (of Gordon), and did not want to impose my feelings on them. I took the magazine to work with me that night. I went to the dispatcher's room to talk to my good friend, Maria Macauda, who was working the night shift. I told her about the party and the palm reader. She listened to me about what Barbara had said. I told her about my reply of "Not yet." I placed the book in front of her and showed her the picture of the Sunken Road. I said not a word about the picture of Gordon. I stood back and waited. She read the part with the quote "Not yet." She said, "That's what you said to the palm reader." I nodded and remained silent. She looked over and saw the picture of Gordon and said, "Who is this?"

I said, "That's Gordon; it appears he didn't die from the five wounds."

She looked at the picture and up at me again. Sort of a double take. She said, "He looks like you!"

I said, "Thank you, now I know I'm not nuts."

What should I do now? What could I do? It would be very hard to forget all of this. The next day I decided to go to the library. I figured that if he was a Confederate General, there might be some information about him. I went to the Trumbull (Connecticut) library and looked up John B. Gordon in the index file. I noted that he had died in 1904. I found a copy of *Who's Who* 1903–1905, it read:

> GORDON, JOHN BROWN (February 6, 1832 - Jan. 9, 1904), soldier, statesman, was born in Upson County, Ga., although shortly before his birth his parents, the Reverend Zachariah Herndon Gordon and Melinda (Cox) Gordon, were living in Wilkes County, N. C. His great-great-grandfather, Adam Gordon, emigrated from Aberdeenshire, Scotland, about 1760 and settled near Fredericksburg, VA. Adam's son, Charles Gordon, moved to North Carolina and became prominent in the civic affairs of that state; and Charles's son, Chapman Gordon, was a soldier in the American Revolution. John matriculated in the University of Georgia and was a member of the class of 1853, but did not graduate. Studying the law privately, he was admitted to the bar and practiced for a while in Atlanta. The outbreak of the Civil War found him engaged in developing coal mines in the mountains of extreme northwest Georgia where the state touches Alabama and Tennessee. He was only twenty-nine years of age and his life up to this time had been without noteworthy events. Though destined to become the most important military figure in the history of

> Georgia, Gordon was wholly without training and experience in martial affairs when he was elected captain of a company of mountaineers. This company, the "Raccoon Roughs," was accepted by the Governor of Alabama and was soon at the front in Virginia. Gordon in September 1854 had married Fanny Haralson, of Lagrange, Ga. She went to the war with her husband and was his companion throughout the struggle. Under fire, Gordon's personality and genius for war speedily asserted themselves. He was promoted rapidly and in less than two years became a brigadier-general (November 1, 1862). In May 1864 he was promoted to major-general and near the end of the war he became a lieutenant-general, being one of the three Georgians to reach that rank. He commanded the II Army Corps and one wing of Lee's army at Appomattox. He participated in the battles of Seven Pines, Malvern Hill, Chancellorsville, Gettysburg, Spotsylvania, and Petersburg. In an official report, D. H. Hill spoke of Gordon as the "Chevelier Bayard of the Confederate Army." Returning to Georgia on the conclusion of the war, Gordon resumed the practice of law in Atlanta. He was still a young man, thirty-three years of age, and, with the prestige of his military record and his outstanding ability as a popular leader, naturally entered politics. (The book went on to say that Gordon became a one-time governor and a three-time senator of Georgia.) More than any other Georgian, Gordon fired the imagination of his native state. For nearly forty years he was the idol of the people. In physique, bearing, and manner he was courtly and impressive. From the organization of the United Confederate Veterans in 1890 to his death he was commander- in-chief.... In 1903 he published his Reminiscences of the Civil War. This volume gives a detailed account of the major battles in which he participated, but it is more notable because of its entire lack of sectional rancor and its uniform generosity and fairness toward friend and foe alike. Gordon died on January 9, 1904, at Miami, Florida.[2]

He wrote a book called *Reminiscences of the Civil War.* What would you do if you were in my place? Would you seek out the book? In the words of Sherlock Holmes, "Come Watson, the game is afoot!" By using the library computer I found that there was a copy of his book at the Fairfield library. I drove to Fairfield. In the library I found the book and turned to the section on Antietam. Gordon described the battle: "The Union forces numbered about 60,000, the Confederates about 35,000.

This battle left its lasting impression on my body as well as upon my memory." Well, now I know he had a sense of humor. He describes that sunny morning in September 1862 and the rolling farmland that surrounded him. Then the artillery of both sides opened fire; the battle had begun. The fighting off to the left of his position came to be known as the Battle of the Cornfield. Gordon wrote: "Again and again, hour after hour, by charges and counter-charges this portion of the field was lost and recovered, until the green corn that grew upon it looked as if it had been struck by a storm of bloody hail." The fighting had not commenced in the Sunken Road, which was the center of Lee's line. General Lee and General D. H. Hill rode by. They urged the men to hold the line at any sacrifice. Gordon writes: "I called aloud to these officers as they rode away. These men are going to stay here, General, until the sun goes down or victory is won. Alas! Many of the brave fellows are there now." Gordon went on to describe the Union soldiers' movements at the start of the battle over the Sunken Road.

> Drums, music and precision steps like a "holiday parade." Every act and movement of the Union commander in my front clearly indicates his purpose to discard bullets and depend on bayonets. He essayed to break through Lee's center by the crushing weight and momentum of his solid column. It was my business to prevent this: And how to do this with my single line was the tremendous problem which had to be solved, and solved quickly; for the column was coming. As I saw this solid mass of men moving upon me with determined step and front of steel, every conceivable plan of meeting and repelling it was rapidly considered.

Gordon shared his thoughts, which ended in a plan to hold their fire until the Union soldiers were almost upon them.

Now we come full circle to the "Not Yet" portion of the story that I described earlier. We continue from where we left off. "The entire front line, with few exceptions, went down in the consuming blast. The gallant commander and his horse fell in a heap near where I stood, the horse dead and the rider unhurt." Gordon tells of four successive charges in an effort to break through his line with bayonets. Speaking of the Union Commander, Gordon writes: "Finally, his troops were ordered to load. He drew up in a close rank and easy ranges and opened a galling fire upon my line. I must turn aside from my story at this point to express that I have never been able to ascertain the name of this lionhearted Union officer. His indomitable will and great courage have been equaled on other fields in both armies: But I do not believe that they have been surpassed." (Please remember this unknown Union commander for he enters into my story later on.) Gordon tells of his wounds:

> My extraordinary escapes from wounds in all the previous battles had made a deep impression upon my comrades as well as upon my own mind. So many had fallen at my side, so often had balls and shells pierced and torn my clothing, grazing my body without drawing a drop of blood, that some sort of blind faith possessed my men that I was not to be killed in battle. This belief was evidenced by their constantly repeated expressions: "They can't hurt him." "He's as safe one place as another." "He's got a charmed life." If I had allowed these expressions of my men to have any affect upon my mind the impression was quickly dissipated when the Sharpsburg storm came and the whizzing minies one after another, began to pierce my body. The first volley from the Union lines in my front sent a ball through the brain of the chivalric Colonel Tew, of North Carolina, to whom I was talking, and another ball through the calf of my right leg. Both sides stood in the open at short range and without the semblance of breastworks, and the firing was doing a deadly work. Higher up in the same leg I was again shot; but still no bone was broken. I was able to walk along the line and give encouragement to my resolute riflemen, who were firing with the coolness and steadiness of peace soldiers in target practice. When later in the day the third ball pierced my left arm, tearing asunder the tendons and mangling the flesh, they caught sight of the blood running down my fingers, and these devoted and big- hearted men, while still loading their guns, pleaded with me to leave them and go to the rear, pledging me that they would stay there and fight to the last. I could not consent to leave them in such a crisis. A fourth ball ripped through my shoulder, leaving its base and a wad of clothing in its track. I could still stand and walk, although the shock and loss of blood had left but little of my normal strength. I remembered the pledge to the commander that we stay till the battle ended or night came. I looked at the sun. It moved very slowly; in fact, it seemed to stand still.

Gordon tells of his movement over to the right side of his line where he saw a problem:

> I was bloody and faint, my legs did not bear me steadily. I had gone but a short distance when I was shot down by a fifth ball, which struck me squarely in the face, and passed out, barely missing the jugular vein. I fell forward and lay unconscious with my face in my cap; and it would seem that I might have been smothered by the blood running into my cap from this wound but for the act of some Yankee, who, as if to save my life, had at a previous hour during the battle, shot a hole through the cap, which let the blood out. I was borne on a litter to the rear, and recall nothing more till revived by stimulants at the late hour of the night. My faithful surgeon, Dr. Weatherby, who was my devoted friend, was at my side, with his fingers on my pulse. As I revived, his face was so expressive of distress that I asked him: "What do you think of my case?" He made a manly effort to say that he was hopeful. I knew better, and said: "You are not honest with me. You think I am going to die; but I am going to get well." Long afterward, when the danger was past, he admitted that this assurance was his first and only basis of hope. General George B. Anderson of North Carolina, whose troops were on my right, was wounded in the foot, but it was thought, not severely. That superb man and soldier was dead in a few weeks, though his wound was supposed to be slight, while I was mercifully sustained through a long battle with wounds the combined effect of which was supposed to be fatal.[3]

As I thought of his wounds, a humorous parallel crossed my mind. It seems both he and I came close to departing this world under similar conditions. At the age of one, I spent a week in the Danbury Hospital in Danbury, Connecticut where I was born. I had a week of transfusions to save my life. The ailment?—lead poisoning. After reading this small portion of Gordon's book I believe what Barbara had seen when she said, "You were hovering over your body," then adding, "but you hung around for a long time," was not a death, but a near-death experience or N. D. E. as they are called today. Now I understood why I went back and talked to Barbara that second time. And why I asked her, "Are you sure I was dead? And what about wounds?" When she said there were holes shot all through the body, I think that would be a pretty good depiction of Gordon on the ground after the fifth round hit him. We see Gordon himself questioning why he was spared from death, given the severity of his wounds and the medical practices of the day, he surely should not have survived.

I had a strange dream many years ago, strange for a few reasons. Back then I very seldom remembered my dreams, but this one I remembered and it was vivid although blurred. I was lying on my back in the dream with my head tilted back slightly. Not far from my face was a man, who was muttering and seemed to me to be cursing. I could not make out his face very well, but I thought he looked like one of the assistant chiefs I work with, John Gottfried (AKA Jocko). This man seemed to be doing something to my neck; there was a spurt of blood from the right side of my neck and everything went black. In the morning I told the dream to some of the men I worked with. I wondered if this was an omen of something to come. Was there to be some injury to myself and the only thing that would save my life was a tracheotomy? Does Jocko attempt doing one and end up cutting my throat? We had a good laugh. The right side of Gordon's face and neck had been blown apart. Did his good friend Dr. Weatherby work over him in despair, trying to stop the massive bleeding, swearing as he worked hard to save his friend's life? I wondered if he resembles Jocko. Maybe the dream was not a dream after all; maybe it had been a flashback to another time.

As a young boy, I remember doing one of the Venus Paint by Numbers pictures of a Gettysburg scene, only it was the colored-pencil version. Once, when I was around seven or eight years old, I was playing at home using an old bench my grandfather had made out of logs. I turned it on its side, not realizing it greatly resembled breastworks I would see later in life. After a few rounds of pretend shooting at imaginary enemies, I was wounded. I remember crawling across the floor using only one arm and one leg. There is a little-known story about Gen. Gordon. I found it in an old interview where he tells of crawling and the strange feelings he went through after being wounded at Antietam.

I also built a fort with one of my friends—not an odd thing for children to do, but this fort was different. We dug a hole in the ground and then covered it with wooden planks. We then covered the planks with the dirt we had removed while digging the hole. Photos of Petersburg, Virginia, taken toward the end of the Civil War, show numerous forts such as the one built by myself and my companion, only they didn't call them forts; they called them "bombproofs" or "bunkers."

My friend, Dr. Ian Baillie (Ph.D.), called all this, "Spontaneous subconscious memory reenactment ... and at an early age before possible contamination from the media...." At the time I just called it playing.

One other thing: when my Uncle Joseph Knapp returned home from Korea, he gave my brother Jack and I some of his army helmets and army hats. One day I was wearing one of his old caps. I saw my brother playing near the road where we lived. I decided to sneak up on him and scare him. I crawled through the high grass, to a big tree where I could jump out and yell "Boo!" I jumped out from behind the tree and yelled, but I was the one who got the surprise. I was unaware that he was throwing rocks and one hit me square in the forehead. I ran home bleeding with the cap catching the blood. To this day my mother still remembers my coming in the house and handing her that army cap full of blood.

At the end of the chapter (about Antietam) in General Gordon's book, he reserves a spot for a very special person, Fanny Gordon.

> Mrs. Gordon was soon with me. When it was known that the battle was on, she had at once started for the front. The doctors were doubtful about the propriety of admitting her to my room; but I told them to let her come. I was more apprehensive of the effect of the meeting upon her nerves than upon mine. My face was black and shapeless - so swollen that one eye was entirely hidden and the other nearly so. My right leg and left arm and shoulder were bandaged and propped with pillows. I knew she would be greatly shocked. As she reached the door and looked, I saw at once that I must reassure her. Summoning all of my strength, I said "Here's

> your handsome (?) husband; been to an Irish wedding." Her answer was a suppressed scream, whether of anguish or relief at finding me able to speak, I do not know. Henceforward, for the period in which my life hung in the balance, she sat at my bedside, trying to supply concentrated nourishment to sustain me against the constant drainage. With my jaw immovably set, this was exceedingly difficult and discouraging. My own confidence in ultimate recovery, however, was never shaken until erysipelas, that deadly foe of the wounded, attacked my left arm. The doctors told Mrs. Gordon to paint my arm above the wound three or four times a day with iodine. She obeyed the doctors by painting it, I think, three or four hundred times a day. Under God's providence, I owe my life to her tender nursing through weary weeks and anxious months.[4]

The Sunken Road, from the time of the battle, was christened with a new name: Bloody Lane. The Battle of Antietam, to this day, holds the grim distinction of being the bloodiest single day in the history of the United States. Like Gordon, I too was to find what a lasting impression this battle was to leave on me.

CHAPTER TWO

A Helping Hand

ON THE PINK SHEET OF PAPER that I brought home from the Halloween party were some names and addresses of research and spiritual centers in the New England area. The papers were placed there just in case anyone wanted more information. After the events of the past few days, the party, the magazine, and the strange parallels from Gordon's story of Antietam, one word kept coming to mind—HELP! I called the nearest center in Branford, Connecticut and made an appointment for the afternoon of November 5, 1992.

Upon arrival, I met Jean Loomis, Director of the Aquarian Center in Branford. She's a professional psychic, astrologer and a certified clinical hypnotherapist. Jean is a lovely lady with dark hair, sparkling eyes and a sweet, soft style of speaking. Jean told me how she had gotten into her line of work. In 1975 she had a clinical death experience. The story was much like the near-death experiences we hear about more and more every year. She said it changed her life and the direction of her life.

Jean looked at my palms and told me I have a long lifeline. She informed me that she had done my astrological chart (I had given her my birthdate information over the phone). Jean said I was in a phase, and had been for a few years, where I probably was getting little bursts, sometimes big ones, memories from other lifetimes (bleedthroughs she called them) and *déjà vu* feelings. She said I was a Virgo with Mercury in Virgo, so part of my mind must question it like crazy (it did). Jean told me how she had spoken on a program with Edgar Mitchell, the astronaut. "Mr. Mitchell had said that, up until this generation (which began in 1980), scientists were able to predict the rate of changes which they judged by birth rate and population increase. Now, since 1980, the rate of population increase has kind of gone off the scale and their formulas don't work any more. They have gone back to the drawing board, questioning even the foundation of quantum physics. His point was that we are living in a time when the rate of change on planet earth is more rapid than at any other time in recorded history. There are more souls here, more energy and more information. The rules that our parents lived by, which they got from their parents and worked from generation to generation, no longer work."

Jean told me to trust my intuition. We talked about what had happened with Barbara Camwell at the party. Jean also explained that feelings and thoughts could carry over from past lives. She said I was in the profession I'm in as a result of some of those feelings I carried into this lifetime. We talked about the Civil War magazine quote, "Not Yet," and how Barbara said I was hovering over my body. Then she said, "It's not your only lifetime by any means; there's a whole past history here." Jean told me that, when these things start to come out, it's for a reason. They have some bearing on the present or the information wouldn't want to come up. It could be my career at the moment, or might be an expiation of killing people. She said afterward that, if there has been life in times of war, the soul says, "I don't want to kill any more, I want to save people." She felt there was a direct connection and probably more than one.

I had been a medic in the Air Force, worked in a local hospital and now I am with the Fire Department. Maybe there was something to what she said.

Jean believed that a past life regression would be beneficial for a release of any emotion that had been brought up from my visit to Antietam. I showed Jean the picture of General Gordon. She thought the resemblance was amazing. I told her of the dream about someone leaning over me doing something to my throat. I showed her some other pictures I had found of Gordon and again she was amazed at the likeness Gordon and I share. Jean even remarked on the set of the jaw (we will talk about the jaw later). Jean asked me if there was any other more recent time period that I felt an attraction to. At that time, the answer was "no." I said that maybe because of my recent trip to Antietam.

She said that this Civil War period was what she called "the trigger lifetime" for me—a lifetime that activates memories, ones that we are deeply associated with. Jean talked about hypnosis and meditation. She told me how the brain works:

5–10%	Conscious Reasoning Thinking
20%	Subconscious Storehouse of memories, past and present lives
70–75%	Unconscious Past life memories, psychic area

Jean recommended that we set up an appointment for the following week, for a hypnosis session. She gave me some pointers on how to remember my dreams better, spontaneous writing (if I lived before...), and meditation. During the coming week Jean wanted me to meditate in the morning and again at night, to quiet my mind and as a preparation for the next session. Jean walked me through a meditation exercise. I was reclining in a chair while Jean talked in a soft voice about things that were very relaxing—blue skies and a field filled with flowers. She said, "If you have a feeling or memory, it is okay, and if you don't, that's okay too. When the meditation session ended, Jean asked me if anything happened. I said, "Yes, a little." I told her I had felt as if I was on horseback. There were woods off to my left. I was wary of something in that direction.

The feeling of being on a horse brought back a memory of something that had happened when I was stationed with the Air Force in Florida, more than twenty-five years before. I told Jean the story. One night I was in my barrack room and I heard a bunch of the guys in the hallway. I popped my head out into the hall and asked them where they were going. They said, "Horse-back riding."

I said, "But it's 11:00 P.M." They said it was a midnight ride and asked if I would like to come along. I said "okay" and got dressed. When we arrived at the horse ranch, there were quite a few people there. The foreman looked worried, as if he was running out of horses. He came over to the group of us who were not yet mounted. He called out, "Are any of you experienced riders?"

I raised my hand and said, "I am!" I put my hand down and wondered to myself why I had said that.

The foreman came closer, cocked his head, squinted a little and asked, "Are you good?"

I replied without hesitation, "Yes, I'm good." He turned around and walked away in the direction of the barn. Now I was really confused by what I had said. I had been on a horse perhaps 3 or 4 times in my life. Once I had been in fear for my life. I was on my cousin's horse, "Blackie," when it decided to run at a high speed through a wooded area. We brushed trees; I dodged limbs, and yelled, "whoa," while pulling hard on the reins, but to no avail. My cousin Dave was on his mother's horse and when Blackie had caught up to them he slowed down his pace. My Uncle Harry had heard the noise and asked why I had been yelling. When I told him, he said, "Yelling won't help, the horse is deaf."

I said, "I pulled on the reins hard and he still wouldn't stop."

My Uncle said, "You probably made him mad doing that." He explained that the people who owned Blackie before had left a training bit on him too much and he had a split tongue. Great, I'm flying around in the woods screaming at a deaf horse, yanking on the reins and making him mad. Now you can see why my reply to the foreman seemed inappropriate. He had not asked if anyone had a horror-filled experience while on a horse.

The ranch foreman walked away from our group. As he did, he called to a man closer to the barn, "Bring out Rebel." My heart sank; what had I done? I had visions of a horse ten feet tall with smoke and flames coming out of his nostrils. A large grey horse was brought out to me. I carefully mounted. I patted the big horsey's neck saying in my mind, "Please don't hurt me." After a while I felt at home, as if I was with a friend. I pressed my knees into the horse slightly. He moved forward until I stopped.

When I turned my toe into his right side, he turned right in place until I stopped. We repeated a left turn the same way. I pulled back on the reins slightly and the horse backed up. The ride wasn't much; we rode in line to an old gravel pit where we stopped and drank warm soda that had been given to us by the foreman before we left the ranch. Once during the ride as we were passing through an orange grove, the automatic sprinklers came on, scaring the horses. We had to dismount and lead the horses the rest of the way out of the grove. At one point, Rebel's front hoof came down on my right foot. I thought I would hear bones crack any second but instead he just tapped the top of my shoe and raised his hoof. I can't say much for the midnight ride, but I guess the horse was memorable.

I asked Jean if she caught the name of the horse; she said, "I got it," with a chuckle. "No accident," she added. When I have told this story to other people, often their response is to say that maybe the horse was well trained. My reply to them is "HOW DID I KNOW WHAT TO DO TO MAKE THE HORSE ACT IN THAT WAY?"

Jean ended by telling me to use meditation and the other tips she had given me for the next week. She warned that I might get feelings of being alone, but the more I learned, the more centered I would be. The more centered I became, the better for myself, my life and the people around me. Jean said because my face looks so much like the face of that other lifetime, it tells her I'm holding in my body structure a lot of the thoughts from that lifetime. She said the body tends to conform itself to our thoughts, so the set of my jaw, my whole physique, tells her that I have carried over a lot from that life. She said that going through this regressive process can be a release of some negative emotions.

I left thinking about what Jean had said. It was up to me, whatever I wanted to do. I returned home with my head in a whirl. I had some answers but also more questions. More and more things tied me to Gordon. Jean said to trust myself and that I should be my own authority. Were all these strange things from a past life? How do you go about proving something like this? I decided the first thing I would do was to get a library card and check out Gordon's book, *Reminiscences of the Civil War,* and to follow Jean's tips. Little did I know that before a year was up, I would read more books than I had in all my life, travel thousands of miles, and visit many, many battlefields.

CHAPTER THREE

The Quest

I NOW HAD IN MY POSSESSION Gordon's book and the only portion I had read was Chapter VII, the one on the battle at Antietam. I decided not to read any more of the book for a while. I wanted to try meditation, spontaneous writing, and to see what my dreams would turn up first. I did not want to be influenced by the book. I've found that the periods just before sleep and just upon awakening are deep thought times. The day after seeing Jean Loomis, my thoughts lingered on what a complete turnabout the battle at the Sunken Road had been for Col. Gordon and his men. That day started bright and beautiful, even the approaching Union soldiers gave the appearance of being on parade. The Alabama 6th had repelled many charges without sustaining any casualties. By day's end the scene had changed dramatically. Gordon had been shot five times, the landscape was strewn with human wreckage, and the little roadbed now held many in a slumber that would carry them into history.

On the evening of November 6, 1992, I did my first solo meditation. It turned out to be very sad indeed. I remembered how Gordon had told of the mens' concern about him and how they wanted him to go to the rear to be attended. The last line of my meditation I wrote, "They are dying and they worry of me and my wounds, they cannot see the wound in my heart, it will never mend." I was too upset to continue. Upon awakening on

November 7, many thoughts came to me: a stone barn, lying on straw, being thirsty, having difficulty swallowing and then there were the men! What had become of them? I decided to get up. I went to the family room. It was clear to me that the process once begun would have to be played out to its conclusion (whatever that would be). It was 5 A.M. I got out a notepad to write down whatever came to mind. I played out the battle of the Sunken Road in my head. I would not fight the feelings nor end the meditation until it came to its own conclusion. It turned out to be one of the best things I have ever done for myself. It also turned out to be extremely draining. I had opened an emotional Pandora's Box. For over two hours I cried non-stop. Please bear in mind that I am 6 feet tall, close to 200 pounds. I have been a medic in the Air Force, worked in the operating room of a hospital, and have over 25 years experience doing fire rescue. I am not one who is prone to weeping at the drop of a hat.

Some of the things I wrote I will share with you, some I will not. They are mine alone. Since the first meditations I have discovered some strange facts:

> I had written of a stone barn. Gordon had told of being taken to a barn but said nothing of its construction. On one of my trips to Antietam I inquired about where this barn may have been. I was told it was probably the barn on the Piper Farm to the rear of his line that day. From a window in the visitor center the roof of the barn was pointed out to me. I asked if it was the same now as then and was told, "It had been added on to." I asked what the barn was made of before and was told it was *stone.*

> I had written of Gordon thinking: "We sure drew the short straw on this spot." Of all the places along the Sunken Road, the most shallow and least affording protection was the position of the 6th Alabama. Also, their right flank ended where the road made a 90-degree turn to the right. On a ridge on the Union side the men could shoot straight down the length of the Alabama 6th and did so with deadly effect.

> I wrote in my meditation about the Union officer that Gordon was never able to put a name to: "He holds his sword in his left hand, now there is a sign of the Devil." Not that many years ago the use

> of one's left hand was discouraged. Remember Gordon said he saw the officer and horse go down in the first volley of gunfire? "The horse dead, the rider unhurt." I found the name of that officer—it was General Max Weber. "On the receiving end the Federal Brigade of Brigadier General Max Weber, a 38 year old German trained officer. For five minutes, the Federals stood bravely. Then they fell back and took cover behind the crest. Weber was shot in the right arm. His brigade suffered an appalling 450 casualties." In the same book I found a picture of him with a caption that read, "he suffered a shattered right arm while leading the initial charge."[5] If Weber's right arm was shattered, he would have been forced to hold his sword in his *left* hand.

During my initial meditation with Jean Loomis I had that feeling of being on horseback. I decided to meditate and see if I could go back to that scene. Meditation of November 9, 1992—I was on horseback. I turned my head to the left and saw a rider approach from a wooded area. He saluted and held forward a piece of paper. I removed my gloves, took the paper and read it. I nodded to the rider and he rode off. The message said to bring the men to Gettysburg. I folded the paper and put it inside my shirt, something that I still do to this day. I don't mean put it in my shirt pocket; I mean unbutton my shirt and stick it inside. I called for an officer to pass the word to the other officers that we will stop to allow the men to cool off and talk over the orders I had just received.

When I came out of this meditation, I wondered if this was just my imagination. Ask anyone to name a battle of the Civil War, even someone who knew little about it (as I did at that time) and they would most likely reply "Gettysburg." What would Gordon be doing off by himself? As Jean Loomis said, "Trust yourself." I would later find a passage from a book on Gordon which read: "On June 30, Gordon marched his brigade from York to near Heidlerburg, where he received orders to move to Cashtown the following day. While on the march the next morning, new orders arrived; instead of turning west to Cashtown, Gordon was to continue south to a new destination—Gettysburg."[6]

Reading *Reminiscences of the Civil War,* I came across more areas where Gordon's life and mine touched. After helping to raise a group of men who were known as the Raccoon Roughs (because of their headgear and the Raccoon Mountain area from which they came), they headed off to war. They had wanted to go as cavalry, but cavalry was not needed at that time. Gordon writes: "We resolved to go at once to the front as infantry without waiting for orders, arms or uniforms." They were turned away.

After I had finished high school, I signed up for the Air Force. I was 17 years old. I passed the physical and was given a date to return for induction. The date was September 9, 1965. At the time I didn't think anything unusual about the date, but I do now. It was my 18th birthday. Why would I have consented to entering the service on my birthday? I volunteered, I was not drafted. Why didn't I stay home and party? I was sent home from the induction center that day to return at a later date. They took all the other men but not me. There was a war on and they sent me home! One hundred years after the end of the Civil War (1865) I spent my 18th birthday at the induction center and got sent away? I returned for induction at the end of September.

Gordon and the men went to Montgomery, Alabama and became part of the Alabama 6th. Some of the men, not having arms to fight with, were given "Joe Brown's pikes"—steel lances fastened to long handles (firefighters use these today on the hook-and-ladder trucks, the hooks are long handles with points on the end; they are also known as pike poles). The first part of my basic training was done at Lackland Air Force Base in Texas, the only place one could go after joining up. The second part of my training to become a medic took place at Gunter Air Force Base. Gunter at that time was located in *Montgomery, Alabama.* Now many people will say that all of this is coincidence, but at what point do things stop being coincidental? When you get a list of five things? Ten? Twenty?

Jean Loomis had picked up on the way my mind works. She knew I could be a hard nut to crack. She wanted to tell me some of what she had seen and felt about me, but did not want to lead me. It would be better to find out things for myself. Remember, Jean had remarked about the "set of my jaw." I have a pronounced jaw, something that has caused me some dental problems over the years. When I was in the service, I asked some dentists about my jaw. I was told it could be fixed, all that needed to be done was to remove a piece of bone from each side of my jaw and shove it back and wire my mouth shut until it healed. My face today remains in the same pristine condition in which God gave it to me. Gordon writes about his return to service: "It was nearly seven months after the battle of Antietam, or Sharpsburg before I was able to return to my duties at the front. Even then the wound through my face had not healed; but nature at last did her perfect work and thus deprived the Army surgeons of a proposed operation."[7] It seems military doctors like to play with people's faces.

One night many years ago, after a union meeting at Fire Headquarters, my brother Jack, a co-worker, and myself went to the local V.F.W. We had a few drinks and left shortly after midnight. In the parking lot I started getting a pain in the right side of my jaw down my neck and out to my shoulder. The pain grew steadily worse, so much so that I told my brother to drive me to the hospital. Having been a medic, I knew the pain might be a sign of a heart attack, even though I was not having chest pains. At the Norwalk Hospital emergency room they ran some tests, E.K.G. and such, and could find no cause. I remained there for an hour or so and the pain slowly subsided and then vanished altogether. I remember the date that this all happened ... at the stroke of midnight; it was September 9, 1977, my 30th birthday.

Gordon's fifth wound at Sharpsburg was the bullet that entered just below his left eye, traveling through his face exiting the right side almost severing the jugular vein. This is the same area where I had the pain. At the time Gordon was wounded at the Sunken Road, September 17, 1862, he was 30 years old.

During some of my meditations, things surfaced, things not connected with Gordon. Leather armor, a rifle with a scope and words like Tamerlane and Mara Poso. I telephoned Jean and told her I needed to see her, that it was a special day. On the afternoon of November 11, 1992, I drove to Branford, Connecticut once more. I told Jean what had happened and the parallels I had found during the past week. I told her about being hit so hard emotionally. She explained that the process I was going through was a cleansing of "body and mind, spirit and emotion." She said, "I needed to remind myself that I was an innocent child of God. It is the mind that makes us guilty. Whatever I had done in the past, I did the best I could at that moment. Guilt comes in retrospect; it is not in the moment of the doing."

I told Jean about asking Barbara Camwell if she could identify the man that entered my barrack room. Barbara couldn't, or I feel now, wouldn't answer my question. I had found the answer myself. I had obtained many pictures of Gordon and in one he didn't look quite himself; he looked rather haggard and worn. I covered up the portion from the nose down and bingo, he was the man in my barracks. I called a couple of my men at the firehouse into my office one at a time, as they happened by. I covered the lower portion of Gordon's picture and asked, "If you had to guess who this is, what would you answer?" They replied "Abe Lincoln." I had always described the man in my room as looking "Abraham Lincolnish." Now, around 25 years later I had an answer to my question of who it was ... John Brown Gordon. I told Jean that I was going to read the rest of Gordon's book and that I bet he worked to help the veterans after the war. She caught the significance of what I had referred to as a special day. She said, "It's Veterans Day, bless your heart." Instead of a regression session, Jean gave me another meditation for a "wider spiritual framework." I had asked her how I could protect myself, because many things that I came across during my meditations were nasty. I left Branford more at ease.

In my quest for information I became a sponge. I'm told that there are over 60,000 volumes written on the American Civil War. I was to find many that spoke of General Gordon. There are quite a few magazines for Civil War buffs. There are people known as Reenactors, who dress in authentic reproductions of uniforms and use weapons and accoutrements (some authentic) and recreate battles of the Civil War. In the movie *Gettysburg,* most of the soldiers used as infantry, artillery and cavalry were from re-creation organizations.

I wanted a photo of General Gordon, not a reproduction, but a real one. I saw an ad for photographs from the original plates. In the list of people available, I found John B. Gordon among them. Upon receiving the photo I was surprised how clear it was. I took it to a local camera store. I asked a salesman if I could have a copy made. We walked over to a machine that looked like an ordinary copier. This machine could take a photo of a photo and develop it in all different sizes. The salesman said he had just finished changing all the solutions in the machine and if I didn't mind waiting, he wanted to run through all the sizes. He said he would only charge me for the one copy. How could I refuse a deal like that? When I left the store I had eight copies of varying sizes.

When I arrived home I checked the photos out. Ever after from the time of being shot, Gordon was always photographed from the right side because of the deep scar under his left eye (the entry point of the bullet). Anyone who knows about bullet wounds knows that the damage becomes greater as a bullet travels through flesh, striking bone, expanding and fragmenting as it goes. The photo was a 3/4 view. One of the copies was an enlargement of Gordon's face. You could just make out the indentation under his left eye. You could see where the right side of his face had been blown out. There was an area from his right cheekbone down to his jaw and back to his ear that had seen better days. Then something caught my eye, a line that started at mid-ear and zigzagged across his cheek, almost like a lightning streak.

I walked into the bathroom and stood before the mirror, photo in hand. I remembered my friend Maria doing the double take; now it was my turn. On the right side of my face starting at mid-ear is a scar, light but discernible. It moves across my cheek in a zigzag pattern. Under my left eye there is an area about the size of a quarter, indented a little with a jagged line outlining most of it. I looked at the photo again and did a second double-take. The mark on the left side of my face was in the same place as the entry wound under Gordon's eye. I was not only receiving confirmation of a past life; I was being beaten over the head with it.

Thinking back over the years, I cannot for the life of me recall receiving any injuries that would explain these markings on my face. (Author note: I have a small cluster of spider veins on my right calf and a larger one higher up on the thigh of the same leg. Gordon said during the Battle of Antietam that he was shot through the calf of his right leg and later was shot "higher up in the same leg." My left forearm bears a scar at the point where I had a blood clot removed. When I asked the doctor how I got the blood clot, he said, "It just happens." I have been unable to find medical records that indicate the exact location of the wound to Gordon's left arm, but find it odd that the blood-clot scar *just happens* to be in the same general region. The spider veins on my right leg are the only place on my body where they occur.) I decided to continue reading Gordon's book. Gordon tells a story about a horse, one he had a problem with. He received the horse from the quartermaster in exchange for one of his own.

> He was an immense horse of unusually fine proportions and had behaved very well under the cannonading; but as we drew nearer to the blue line's front, and their musketry sent the bullets whistling around his ears, he wheeled and fled at such a rate of speed that I was powerless to check him until he had carried me more than a hundred yards to the rear. Fortunately, some of the artillerymen aided me in dismounting and promptly gave me a more reliable steed, on whose back I rapidly returned in time to redeem my reputation.[8]

Gordon describes the animal: "He was solid black in color and dangerously treacherous in disposition." I thought back to my ride of horror and to my cousin's horse Blackie.

About the battle of Malvern Hill Gordon writes:

> A great shell fell, buried itself in the ground, and exploded near where I stood. It heaved the dirt over me, filling my face and ears and eyes with sand. I was literally blinded. Not an inch before my face could I see; but I could think, and thoughts never ran more swiftly through a perplexed mortal brain. Blind! Blind in battle! Was this to be permanent? Suppose there should be an assault upon my command from the front? Such were the unspoken but agonizing questions which throbbed in my brain with terrible swiftness and intensity. The blindness, however, was of short duration. The delicate and perfect machinery of the eye soon did its work. At last came, also the darkness for which I longed, and under its thick veil this splendid brigade was safely withdrawn.[9]

Anyone who has lost their sight even for a short period knows how Gordon felt. I know because it happened to me. A motor vehicle accident, on South Compo Road in Westport, left a car hanging sideways on an embankment. The occupants were trapped in the car. The first thing that needed attention was stabilizing the car. Only then could work begin on removing the people. The Hurst Tool, AKA the Jaws of Life, was set up to force open the driver's door. It was at this point that I walked over behind the two firefighters using the tool. As I stood there, something hit me. It felt as if fine sand had been thrown in my face. My eyes started to burn and there was a taste on my lips. Hydraulic fluid! There was a pinhole leak in the hose line for the Hurst Tool and I had been sprayed in the face with a corrosive liquid. My vision started to blur. I went to the closest fire engine and opened one of the outlets. I used the water from the tank carried on the pumper to flush my eyes. The water was not very clean, but it helped to take away some of the burning sensation. Many of the thoughts that went through my mind were the same as Gordon's at Malvern Hill. Quickly I washed my eyes out as best I could with the rusty water. An ambulance took me to Norwalk hospital where they flushed my eyes out for forty- five minutes. Both of my eyes were covered with tiny scratches caused by the rust in the tank water. Thankfully, I fully recovered my sight.

In a book called *Lee's Dispatches,* I found this interesting letter to Jefferson Davis from Robert E. Lee:

> Head Qrs. Army No. VA. 26th May 1863
> His Excy Jeffn Davis President Confed. States.
>
> MR. PRESIDENT.
> Since my letter of the 20th inst. which I stated that I would assign General Gordon to the command of Rodes' old Brigade, I have received the enclosed petition of all the commissioned officers of Lawton's Brigade. I respectfully submit it to your better judgement, whether it will not be best, if General Lawton is still unfit for the field (as it would that he is from a late letter I have received from him) to keep General Gordon in his present position where he is so acceptable, and where he is entirely willing to remain, being a Georgian by birth. If you decide that this is best, then a brigade commander will be necessary for Rodes' Brigade. In reference to this I enclose Genl Rodes' letter upon that subject/ Col. Morgan is highly spoken of by General Rodes. He formerly commanded an Alabama Regiment of Infantry, but retired before the reorganization. Col. O'Neal is the Senior officer in the brigade, and commanded it in the late battles, and had been one of the three officers mentioned by General Rodes, but would recommend the appointment of Col. O'Neal as perhaps the most fit-as he has been identified with his regiment and the brigade by long service as lieut. Col. and Colonel.
>
> I am with great respect, Your obt. Servt. (Sgd.)
> R. E. Lee General[10]

The mention of a petition brought a memory of a similar incident. I did not get on the Fire Department on the first attempt, but on the third. The first test I had taken was good for two years. Two years and one month later, another test was given. Two men had been hired, leaving two people remaining on the first test list, myself being one of them. Instead of hiring us for two new openings, they had waited for the test to run out. I fared no better on a second attempt. A third test was completed and the marks were posted. Now they were required to pick from the top three. My brother Jack, a Firefighter at the time, was working as dispatcher the day the Chief posted the test results. Jack saw the list and called me. He told me "Come on down here, you won't believe this." I went to the firehouse and my brother showed me the posted results of the test, I was in 4th place, which put me out of the running. Truly though, I was tied for second place. What's the old saying? "I smell something rotten." My brother said he asked the Chief about the results and was told that the State of Connecticut had broken the tie. The Union President called the state office that administered the test. He was upset that they had broken the tie. They responded that the state had done no such thing and that they would send an amended copy to the town. To make a long story short, the results were changed to my being in a tie for second place. It was apparent that someone lurking in the background did not want me on the department. I went to the VFW and told my story about the tests and the tie-breaking. I told them my father was a retired firefighter and my brother was currently on the department. I was informed by a member of the Veteran's Council (made up of members of the VFW and the American Legion) that my grandfather was one of the first volunteer firefighters in town, a fact of which I was not aware. They told me they would see what they could do. So, thanks to these fine gentlemen and others, I became a member of the Fire Department. I feel that one of the biggest contributing factor for my getting the job was that all the firefighters had signed a *petition* saying they believed I should be the one to fill the vacancy.

The things that we do today in the fire departments are much like what is done in combat during wartime. Instead of rifles, we use nozzles or deluge guns. We use offensive and defensive modes, but instead of riding horses we ride in big red fire engines. Many of the same thoughts go through my mind during the course of my duties as those that must have been of concern to Gordon. At Wrightsville, Pennsylvania, Gordon had a taste of my job. Union troops had set fire to a bridge so that it could not be used by the advancing confederates. Gordon writes:

> With great energy my men labored to save the bridge. I called on the citizens of Wrightsville for buckets and pails, but none were to be found. There was, however, no lack of buckets and pails a little later, when the town was on fire. The bridge might burn, for that incommoded, at the time, only the impatient confederates, and these Pennsylvanians were not in sympathy with my expedition, nor anxious to facilitate the movement of such unwelcome visitors. But when the river's banks, and the burning lumber fired the town, buckets and tubs and pails and pans innumerable came from their hiding places, until it seemed that, had the whole of Lee's army been present, I could have armed them with these implements to fight the rapidly spreading flames. My men labored as earnestly and bravely to save the town as they did to save the bridge. In the absence of fire-engines or other appliances, the only chance to arrest the progress of the flames was to form my men around the burning district, with the flank resting on the river's edge, and pass rapidly from hand to hand the pails of water. Thus, and thus only, was the advancing, raging fire met, and at a late hour of the night checked and conquered.[11]

The following is a letter that I wrote to the Chief of the Westport Fire Department. It may give you an idea of what it is like to be in charge of an emergency scene and how I feel about my men:

> Incident #200-752 On Saturday, May 30, 1992 at 1451 hours a call was received by dispatch of a propane line severed and propane gas leaking at 87 Maple Avenue South. My vehicle was the first on the scene at 1455 hours. The owner of the house and her friend were waiting by the road. I was informed that there were two leaking gas cylinders at the rear of the building. All the other apparatus had been advised to stand off from the scene to avoid all possible ignition sources. After a short conference with my driver (an ex-fire inspector) we determined it was two 100-pound propane tanks leaking. Firefighter Eugene Maloney donned full gear and headed towards the rear of the building, while I gathered more information from the owner. While trying to place the apparatus, I lost use of my portable radio, which forced me to return to my

command vehicle. During that period Firefighter Maloney (with no portable radio because he had the presence of mind not to take a possible ignition source with him) with only the protection he was wearing, sized up the situation and reacted. At great risk to himself, he turned off the valves to both tanks, stopping the leak which reduced the problem. After finishing that task he reported his actions to me. With my radio restored, manpower and apparatus were brought in and put under the guidance of Acting Lieutenant Christopher Ackley. While setting up a plan of action, Lieutenant Ackley displayed good common sense, knowledge, training and a deep concern for the safety of the firefighters under his command. A large amount of gas had entered the structure by way of an open window. Though we tried to remove all possible sources of ignition, we were able to remove all but two. The owner informed us that the house contained an oil-fired furnace and a hot water heater. There was no way to shut them off from the inside or outside. I made Lieutenant Ackley aware of the situation (I need not explain the destructive force propane gas in a confined space represents). Using metering devices, a positive pressure fan and by opening and closing windows the hazard was removed. When reading fire reports, they don't tell the whole story; they list things like ladders raised, amount of hose used, etc. Recognition is usually reserved for the saving of a life and not often enough given the fire service personnel for placing their lives in jeopardy. It is my recommendation that a well deserved WELL DONE be given to all involved; paid, volunteer, and Dispatcher Maciver (Dispatcher Maciver re-routed Engine #4 to report to Headquarters after I had put them in service. This gave us a centrally located engine and someone to man Rescue #8 in the absence of the Truck #1 driver). It is my feeling that special attention should be paid to the actions of Firefighter Maloney and Lieutenant Ackley. Anyone passing that house five minutes after we left would not have known that anything had happened there. If I were given the chance to explain the situation to them they undoubtedly would not appreciate the courage and selflessness I saw displayed for that one-hour period.

Respectfully submitted,
Assistant Chief, Jeffrey Keene

The homeowner mentioned in the letter asked me a question as we stood in the roadway in front of her house. She said, "Is this a dangerous situation?"

I replied, "Did you see those men go into your house?" (She nodded) "I love those guys and they could be gone in a heartbeat."

She said, "You don't look nervous."

I said, "I'm not supposed to, but you can't see me on the inside, can you?" She looked at me a little puzzled. I returned to the job at hand.

In Gordon's book, one of the few moments he stops to give some insight into what it's like to be in command, is at the wounding of General Robert Emmett Rodes at the 3rd Battle of Winchester.

> As the last words between us were spoken, Rodes fell, mortally wounded, near my horse's feet, and was borne bleeding and almost lifeless to the rear. There are times in battle—and they came often—when the strain and the quick shifting of events compel the commander to stifle sensibilities and silence the natural prompting of his heart as cherished friends fall around him. This was one of those occasions. General Rodes was not only a comrade whom I greatly admired, but a friend whom I loved. To ride away without even expressing to him my deep grief was sorely trying to my feelings; but I had to go. His fall had left both divisions to my immediate control for the moment, and under the most perplexing and desperate conditions.[12]

What I had gone through during the first meditations, the ones that had drained me emotionally, were some of the feelings deep inside Gordon and myself—feelings that we do not have the luxury of purging at the moment they arise. The job comes first, the feelings must await a later time. The General and I share much more than a physical resemblance; we share a common heart. I had found Gordon, or I should say, he found me. We did not meet that day I opened that Civil War magazine, nor when I read his name or saw his picture. Long before the Halloween party, palm reader or library books, we knew one another. We were never strangers. We met again when our hearts touched, a reintroduction at a place called Bloody Lane.

CHAPTER FOUR

Back to the Front

I DISCOVERED A BOOK written about Gordon. It was on a list of books my mother had sent me. I called and ordered it right away. In a few days I had the book in my hands: *John Brown Gordon: Soldier, Southerner, American* by Ralph Lowell Eckert. In the first chapter he tells of John Gordon's early years:

> John was fourth of twelve children born to Zachariah and Malinda Cox Gordon. Although successful in Upson County, the reverend moved his family to Walker County in northwestern Georgia around 1840. He settled about ten miles from Lafayette, on property he dubbed Gordon Springs because of the great abundance of mineral water that flows from twelve main springs in the space of a quarter of an acre.

The author continues with,

> Ironically it was in the peaceful fields and valleys surrounding the Gordon homestead in northwestern Georgia, over which John roamed during his adolescence, that the Battle of Chickamauga—one of the Civil War's bloodiest struggles—would later rage.[13]

The book also told of Gordon's education:

> Gordon's early education differed little from what the sons of most small planters received at the time. He attended rural schools until his father became dissatisfied with the quality of instruction in Walker County. The reverend established a school on his own and

> assumed responsibility for securing and paying a good teacher. He also provided housing, at a nominal cost, for neighborhood boys who attended the institution.

The author tells of Gordon's entry into College.

> After finishing his father's school, Gordon ventured to Lafayette, where he entered Pleasant Green Academy, reputedly "one of the best schools in all northwest Georgia." The reputation was evidently well deserved, because when Gordon completed his studies there near the end of 1850, he enrolled at the University of Georgia in Athens as a second semester sophomore.[14]

I picked up the phone and called my mother, one of the sweetest souls ever put on earth. This is not just my opinion, but that of many others who know her. My mother had recently sold her home in Florida and bought a house with my sister Joy. The house was in the northwestern corner of Georgia, Walker County. The name of the town? *Lafayette*. While talking to my mother, I asked if she ever heard anything about John B. Gordon. She said there was a Gordon Mill and that in a local church there was a stool or table which had been used by a John Gordon. She asked, "Why do you ask?" I told her about the palm reader and so on and, when I finished, there was a short pause and she said, "You're nuts, Jeff." Now, is this any way for a mother to talk to her son? My mother was planning to come up north for the summer and my sister was getting married. I had never visited my mother and sister in Lafayette and barely remembered the name of the town. I decided to drive down and attend the wedding, then drive my mother back to Connecticut. It was a good opportunity to stop at some of the places I had read about. I planned my route and left a few days before the wedding, to give myself time to stop a while on the way. Civil War battlefields run the scale from large tracts of land with visitor centers and hundreds of monuments to tiny areas where you need a local inhabitant to point it out. Most saddening are the ones under tract housing and shopping centers, gone forever.

I drove on I-95 to just outside Washington D.C., then turned inland across Maryland to my first stop, Monocacy

National Battlefield. It is located just three miles south of Frederick, Maryland. The battle was fought on July 9, 1864 and is known as the battle that saved Washington, D.C. On the confederate side was Lt. General Jubal Early, and on the Union side was Major General Lew Wallace (who would later pen *Ben Hur*). Early and his men were en-route to Washington. Wallace wanted to stop them, or at least stall for time, so that reinforcements could reach the Washington area. Gordon's division was assigned to Major General John C. Breckinridge's command. (Breckinridge had been Vice President of the United States under Buchanan.) Gordon wrote, "The battle of Monocacy which ensued was short, decisive and bloody."[15] I have visited Monocacy twice. On the first visit, I stopped at the visitor center in the old Gambrill's Mill. The mill was used as a hospital during the battle. I asked some questions about a stream I had read about in Gordon's book. The park ranger said she was not sure which one was the one in question. She was surprised at my knowledge. She asked how long I had studied the Civil War. At that time it had been six months. The ranger looked puzzled and asked, "How did you get interested in it?" I walked over to a book on one of the shelves, removed it and skimmed through the pages, until I came to a picture of Gordon. I handed the book to her and pointed to the picture. She looked at the picture and then at me. I said nothing. She looked at the book again and said, "Just how closely related are you?"

"About as close as you can get," I replied. I thanked her for her help, walked to a container near the entrance and put in some money to help preserve the park. Through a little research, I received my answer about the stream.

On a return trip to Monocacy with my mother, we visited the visitor center and near the road in front of it runs the little stream I sought. Why the search for the stream? Gordon's men pushed back the first Union line to a second line. Gordon writes:

> The Union lines stood firmly in this second position, bravely defending the railroad and the highway to Washington. Between the two hostile lines there was a narrow ravine down which ran a small stream of limpid water. In this ravine the fighting was

> desperate and at close quarters. To and fro the battle swayed across the little stream, the dead and wounded of both sides mingling their blood in its water; and when the struggle was ended, a crimsoned current ran toward the river. Nearly one half of my men and large numbers of the Federals fell there.[16]

A local authority put this stream moving across the Thomas property, running down to Bush Creek and Gambrill's Mill. As my mother and I walked near the little stream, she found a small glass bottle with a metal top. She was talking about it to me, but my mind was elsewhere, back to when this pretty little creek ran red. An idea came to me. I asked my mother if I could have the bottle; she complied. I carefully climbed down the steep embankment to the water. The water was cool and clear. It trickled over stones and sticks, causing it to make little bubbly sounds. I dipped the bottle into the water, tilting it so it would fill. The bottle full, I capped it and we returned to the car. I put the bottle in a bag and we drove on through the rolling hills and green fields. At home I transferred the water to an old perfume bottle and glued the top on. I mounted the little bottle, along with other mementos and photos, in a large frame. There is a small brass plate under the bottle engraved with one word: MONOCACY.

In a book by John H. Worsham, a Confederate veteran, he tells of coming across General Gordon during the Battle at Monocacy. "There was Gordon—I shall recollect him to my dying day—not a man in sight—he was sitting on his horse as quietly as if nothing was going on, wearing his old red shirt, the sleeves pulled up a little, the only indication that he was ready for the fight."[17] I have seen a painting of the battle. In part of the picture Gordon is on horseback wearing a double-breasted red shirt. In a earlier phone call to my mother I asked, "Mom, do you remember that red shirt I had as a kid?"

"Red shirt?" she said.

"Yes, a double-breasted one," I said. It was one of my favorite shirts and I remembered it very well. Many years ago, a boy in the old neighborhood had thrown a match at me while I was wearing my double-breasted red flannel shirt. The match stuck to the front; a second later a flame started licking up toward my face. My brother Jack and the boy beat on my chest to put out the fire.

My mother replied "A flannel shirt? Vaguely, why?" I told her about the quote and painting. I do not recall any other kid having a red double-breasted flannel shirt, not then and not now.

At the visitor center at Monocacy, I had picked up a small map on the shortest route to Antietam Battlefield. The route went through Middletown and over South Mountain. On the directions it read, "at the top of South Mountain you will find several Civil War markers." These were markers for the Battle of South Mountain. Colonel Gordon and the 6th Alabama held the left flank at Turner's Gap. "Brigadier General Rodes reported that on South Mountain, September 14, Gordon had handled the Sixth Alabama 'in a manner I have never heard or seen equaled during the war.'"[18] Division Commander D.H. Hill, in his official report, styled Gordon "the Chevalier Bayard of the army."[19] I looked up Bayard in the encyclopedia. "Bayard, Pierre Terrail, Seigneur de (c1473-1524) French Commander famous for his bravery, who became the epitome of French chivalry. He first distinguished himself in French campaigns in Italy. Later at Mezieres in 1521, with only 1,000 men against 35,000 he held off an invasion of central France by the emperor Charles V."[20] This was high praise indeed.

Shortly after the battle of South Mountain was the battle of Antietam, which we spoke of earlier. I stopped at the Antietam visitor center. It was at this time that I had inquired about the barn to which Gordon had been taken after his wounding. I visited the Sunken Road once again. There were no strange feelings this time. I guessed I was finished with that aspect, and the deepest emotions had been purged. I walked the old road and stood where the Sixth Alabama was placed to defend Lee's center. Looking around, it appears much the same as during the fighting there. Following a tradition I had started for battlefield visits, I said a prayer for the souls who had given their lives. I returned to my car and drove away, catching myself glancing in the rear view mirror as the little hill on Bloody Lane became smaller and smaller.

I drove to Winchester, VA. Winchester changed hands more than seventy times during the Civil War. I followed signs for General Jackson's Headquarters, but found it closed. I headed east out of town on the Berryville Pike to find the site of the Third Battle of Winchester, fought on September 19, 1864. I continued for a while, but saw no markers or signs indicating where the battle had been. It seemed to me that I had driven too far, so I turned and headed back. Stopping at a small store, I asked about the Battlefield and was directed to a local woman who worked in the store. She told me about a marker across the street, but that was the only one she knew of in the area. Across the Pike, set way back off the road was a small marker. No wonder I had missed it on my first pass. Standing on a little rise and gazing north, I could see the fields where Gordon, Rodes and Ramseur formed their line of battle. It was there that Rodes fell with his mortal wound. Sweeping the field from right to left, my eyes followed the path of the battle as the Confederates were pushed back into Winchester. In Winchester at that time was Mrs. Gordon. She had come close to being captured that morning by Federal Cavalry; only with the help of General Rodes and his men did she escape such a fate. Gordon writes about finding Mrs. Gordon in Winchester:

> To my horror, as I rode among my disorganized troops through Winchester I found Mrs. Gordon on the street, where shells from Sheridan's batteries were falling and Minie balls flying around her. She was apparently unconscious of the danger. I had supposed that, in accordance with instructions, she had gone to the rear at the opening of the battle, and was many miles away. But she was stopping at the house of her friend, Mrs. Hugh Lee, and as the first Confederates began to pass to the rear, she stood upon the veranda, appealing to them to return to the front. Many yielded to her entreaties and turned back—one waggish fellow shouting aloud to his comrades: "Come, boys, let's go back. We might not obey the general, but we can't resist Mrs. Gordon." The fact is, it was the first time in all her army experience that she had ever seen the Confederate lines broken. As the different squads passed, she

> inquired to what command they belonged. When, finally, to her question the answer came, "We are Gordon's men," she lost her self-control and rushed into the street, urging them to go back and meet the enemy. She was thus engaged when I found her. I insisted that she go immediately into the house where she would be at least partially protected. She obeyed; but she did not for a moment accept my statement that there was nothing left for her except capture by Sheridan's army. I learned afterward that her negro driver had been frightened by the shells bursting about the stable, and had not brought out her carriage and horses. She acquainted some of my men with these facts. With the assurance, "We'll get it for you, Mrs. Gordon," they broke down the fences and brought the carriage to her a few moments after I had passed on. She sprang into it, and, taking her six-year-old son Frank and one or two wounded officers with her, she was driven rapidly away amidst the flying missiles from Sheridan's advancing troops and with the prayers of my brave men for her safety.[21]

I drove back to Winchester and headed south to a route that would take me to my next destination, Fredericksburg, VA. It was late afternoon when I arrived. I drove around to familiarize myself with the area, then checked into a motel and had dinner. I went to my room to plan for the next morning. There are four battlefields all within a short distance and in some cases they even overlap one another: Fredericksburg, Chancellorville, The Wilderness and Spotsylvania Court House. I was tired from the long drive of the day and fell asleep before I knew it. I awoke early—too early. It was still dark outside. Unable to return to sleep, I showered, packed my bag and checked out. Soon I was on Marye's Heights, overlooking the city of Fredericksburg. Marye's Heights is now a National Cemetery. During the Civil War, the Heights played an important part in many battles. In April 1863, less than seven months after being wounded at Antietam, Gordon took command of one of the largest brigades in the Confederate Army. Gordon's first task, as commander of this unit, was to retake Marye's Heights during the battle of Chancellorville. It was during this fighting that Gordon came into possession of his favorite battle horse. The horse Gordon was riding had become partially disabled. At this time, a Union officer had been shot from his mount's back. The horse galloped into the Confederate line and Gordon was quickly upon her. He named her Marye after the hill. "Her courage was equal to her other high qualities. She was afraid of nothing. Neither the shouting of troops, nor the rattle of rifles, nor the roar of artillery, nor their bursting shells, intimidated her in the slightest degree. In addition to all of this, she seemed to have a charmed life, for she bore me through the hottest fires and was never wounded."[22]

As I stood on the heights overlooking Fredericksburg, the blacks and grays of night slowly turned to the blues and greens of dawn. The sun peeking over the horizon transformed the stone markers of the cemetery to a light warm pink. The flow of sunlight moved slowly down the hillside coming to rest on the wall near its base. This was the infamous wall of Fredericksburg. It was here during the Battle of Fredericksburg (December 11–13, 1862) that General Burnside, in an attempt to take Marye's Heights, sent brigade after brigade across four hundred yards of open ground, all the while under well-placed artillery fire. After running the gauntlet of shellfire, the Union soldiers came up against the riflemen behind the stone wall. Tongues of flame licked out at them from behind it. Wave after wave of the blueclad fell. From midday until dark they kept up their assault. Not a man finished the journey. Approximately eight thousand men lay in front of that wall. Many remained there for days before help would reach them. Some of the wounded froze to death in the cold December air. Burnside's decision to attack this area became one of the biggest blunders of the Civil War. What a scene it must have been as the cannons and muskets fell silent, the smoky curtain rising to reveal the brave men who followed their orders and now covered the scarred earth with their twisted forms. It must have seemed as if they had been scorched by dragon's breath. The Union men were not soon to forget the wall, and in many battles afterward the men would go into the fight with remembrances of Fredericksburg on their lips.

I drove on to Chancellorsville. Near the visitor center is a monument marking the spot where Stonewall Jackson was mortally wounded. The Confederacy would never recover from the loss of Jackson. His tactics are taught to this day in the military schools. Some said his name alone was worth a division in battle.

Not far from the Chancellorsville visitor center is the Wilderness Battlefield. It is well named, for there are few open areas. Tall trees and a thick growth of smaller trees, tangled bushes and other assorted flora cover most of the land. In much of the area it is difficult to see ten yards ahead. Many units on both sides became lost or disoriented, often resulting in heavy casualties or capture. On May 5, 1864, two divisions of Ewells II Corps came under attack. The division commanded by General Rodes was to the South of the Orange Turnpike. They had been hit so hard that the center units were falling back. At this time, General Ewell rode to the rear where he found Gordon. With a yell, Gordon's men counter-attacked with such force that what happened next even caught Gordon by surprise. The Union soldiers in his front had been pushed back so fast as to cause Gordon's men to come into line with the Union troops on the left and right. If Gordon's men moved forward, there was a good chance of them becoming surrounded. Gordon halted the men, and while some of the men held the front, the others were divided and turned to face to the right and left. Gordon writes:

> This done, both these wings were ordered forward, and, with another piercing yell, they rushed in opposite directions upon the right and left flanks of the astounded Federals, shattering them as any troops that were ever marshalled would have been shattered, capturing large numbers and checking any further effort by General Grant on that portion of the field.[23]

I found a marker that showed the area where this maneuver took place. I marveled that it was done in a place with such thick growth. I drove back to the Orange Turnpike and found a visitor shelter. There were maps of the battlefield and a walking trail. A box had been placed at the beginning of the trail; big letters spelled out "Gordon Flank Attack Trail" on a pamphlet. On May 5, Gordon's men were shifted to the far-left flank. Scouts returned and told Gordon that the Confederate line overlapped the Union flank. More scouts were sent out, and then Gordon went himself. He could not believe their good fortune in placement. On the morning of May 6th, Gordon approached Generals Ewell and Early with a plan for a flank attack on the Union right. He awaited orders, but none were forthcoming. Many attempts were made by Gordon that day to get the Generals to act on his plan. Shortly before sundown on the 6th he was given the go ahead.

> He struck the enemy's flank fairly and squarely. The surprise was complete, and the panic very great. The Federal officers endeavored to draw out brigade after brigade, division after division and form at right angles to the breastworks, so as to check the impetuous attack. But Gordon's men were upon them before they could be properly placed in the new position. He met with no check until sometime after dark, when in the confusion attending all night attacks, one or two of his regiments on the right faltered and gave way. But the other troops pressed on until the enemy's lines had been captured by Gordon's one brigade for more than a mile, nearly 1,000 prisoners taken, including Brig. Gens. Seymour and Shaler, and a complete disorganization effected in a large portion of the Sixth Corps of Grant's army.[24]

I walked the trail to where the flanking movement had occurred. Even though the sun was out, the canopy of trees above filtered the light, giving the surroundings a dusk-like appearance. Rills in the ground showed where entrenchments had been placed. The thick underbrush hindered sight, limiting it to a few yards in some places. The area had changed little; the confusion of the terrain nearly cost Gordon his life. On the night of May 6th, General Gordon rode with a courier by the name of William Beasley to check on pickets that had been sent out.

> There was no moonlight, but the night was cloudless and the stars furnished enough light for us to ride without serious difficulty through the woods. It was, however, too dark for us readily to distinguish the color of uniforms. Before we had proceeded far we rode into a body of men supposed to be the troops whom I had sent out on picket. There was no sort of deployment or alignment, and I was considerably annoyed by this appearance of carelessness on

the part of the officer, to whom I had given special instructions. But before I had time to ascertain what this indifference to orders meant, my trusted courier, whose sight was clearer than mine at night, said to me in a whisper "General, these are not our men; they are Yankees." I replied, "Nonsense, Beasley," and rode on, still hoping to ascertain the reason for this inexcusable huddling of my pickets. Beasley, however, was persistent, and taking hold of my arm, asserted in the most emphatic manner, "I tell you General, these men are Yankees, and we had better get away from here." His earnestness impressed me, especially as he strengthened his assertion by calling my attention to the fact that even in the dim starlight the dark blue of the uniforms around us presented a contrast with those we were wearing. I cautioned him to be quiet and keep close to me as I began to turn my horse in the opposite direction. Meantime, and at the moment we discovered our alarming position, we heard the startling calls from Union officers close by us, who were endeavoring to disentangle the confused mass of men: "Rally here, New York." "Let all the men of the ___ Regiment of Pennsylvania form here." Up to this moment not the slightest suspicion seemed to have been contained by these men that Beasley and I were Confederates; and, apparently for the sole purpose of ascertaining to what Union command we belonged, an officer with his sword in hand asked in the most courteous manner to what brigade we were attached, evidently hoping to aid us in finding it. Both Beasley and I were, of course, deaf to his inquiry, and continued to move on without any reply, turning our horses' heads toward the gray lines in which we would feel more at home. Either our strange silence or our poorly concealed purpose to get away from that portion of the Wilderness aroused his suspicions, and the officer called to his comrades as we rode away from him. "Halt those men!" His orders were scarcely uttered when the "boys in blue" rushed around us, shouting, "Halt, halt!" But the company in which we found ourselves was not congenial and the locality was not at that moment a good place for us to halt. We had to go, and go instantly, back to our own lines or to a Northern prison. I instantly resolved to take the risk of escape, though we might be shot into mincemeat by the hundreds of rifles around us. Beasley was well mounted, and I was riding a thoroughbred stallion, the horse General Shaler rode when he was made prisoner a few hours previous. Both Beasley and I were fairly good riders. Instantly throwing my body as far down on my horse's side as possible, my right foot firmly fixed in the stirrup, my left leg gripping the saddle like an iron elbow, I seized the bridle-rein under my hoses's neck,

> planted my spur in his flank, and called, "Follow me, Beasley!" This courier had intuitively followed the motion of my body, and was clinging like an experienced cowboy to the side of his horse. As the superb animal which I rode felt the keen barb of the spur, he sprang with a tremendous bound through the dense underbrush and the mass of startled soldiers. It seems probable that the Union men were in almost as much danger from the hoofs of our horses as we were from the Union rifles.[25]

Beasley and Gordon were lucky that night, while the luck of others had run its course. Fires caused by the fighting erupted in the dry woods. Whipped by brisk winds they moved across the battlefield, consuming the dead and wounded who were unable to move out of the path of the flames.

I continued along the trail and emerged back into the sunlight near the visitor's shelters. Returning to my car, I headed to my next destination, Spotsylvania Court House. I drove the winding country roads, following the signs for the Spotsylvania battlefield. Turning into the Battlefield Park, I did not bother to stop at the information signs. A short while later, I looked to my left and my mind said, "Mule Shoe, I'm at the Mule Shoe."

> At dawn on May 12, Grant sent Hancock's men storming out of the fog and misty rain in a massive surprise attack on the so-called Mule Shoe Salient at the center of Lee's lines. They overran the defenders, as a Southerner recalled, "like a swollen torrent through a broken mill-dam."
>
> The Yankees swept up twenty guns and thousands of prisoners, including two general officers and most of the famed Stonewall Brigade, but success so disorganized the Federals that a slashing counterattack by John B. Gordon's division knocked them back to the first line of captured trenches. They held there, and what followed was the most vicious struggle of the Civil War.[26]
>
> No printed page, no cold type can convey to the mind the realities of that terrible conflict. The results were appalling. The whole engagement was practically a hand-to-hand contest. The dead lay beneath the feet of the living, three and four layers deep. This hitherto quiet spot of earth was devastated and covered with the slain, weltering in their own blood, mangled and shattered into scarcely a semblance of human form. Dying men were crushed by horses and many, buried beneath the mire and mud, still lived.

> Some artillery was posted on high ground not far from the apex of the salient, and an incessant fire was poured into the Confederate works over the Union lines, while other guns kept up an enfilade of canister along the west of the salient. Until three o'clock the next morning the slaughter continued, when the Confederates sank back into their second line of entrenchments.[27]

Driving around a corner, my eye caught a street sign. It read "Gordon Drive." This road runs along the remains of the second line that the Confederates fell back to after the long battle of the 12th of May. Between this road and the apex of the Mule Shoe, there is a marker alongside what remains of the foundation of the McCool House. Gordon tells what happened here on the morning of the 12th:

> I was at the centre of that line when General Lee rode to it. With uncovered head, he turned his face toward Hancock's advancing column. Instantly I spurred my horse across Old Traveller's front, and grasping his bridle in my hand, I checked him. Then, in a voice which I hoped might reach the ears of my men and command their attention, I called out, "General Lee, you shall not lead my men in a charge. No man can do that, sir. Another is here for that purpose. These men behind you are Georgians, Virginians, and Carolinians. They have never failed you on any field. They will not fail you here. Will you, boys?" The response came like a mighty anthem that must have stirred his emotions as no other music could have done. Although the answer to those three words, "Will you, boys?" came in the monosyllables, "No, no, no; we'll not fail him," yet they were doubtless to him more eloquent because of their simplicity and momentous meaning. But his great heart was destined to be quickly cheered by a still sublimer testimony of their deathless devotion. As this first thrilling response died away, I uttered the words for which they were now fully prepared. I shouted to General Lee, "You must go to rear." The echo, "General Lee to the rear, General Lee to the rear!" rolled back with tremendous emphasis from the throats of my men; and they gathered around him, turned his horse in the opposite direction, some clutching his bridle, some his stirrups, while others pressed close to Old Traveller's hips, ready to shove him by main force to the rear. I verily believe that, had it been necessary or possible, they would have carried on their shoulders both horse and rider to a place of safety.[28]

While walking the Mule Shoe, my thoughts returned to those days of the struggle between the blue and the gray. It was hard to conceive that at this spot so many had fallen. It is such a beautiful landscape of rolling fields with tiny streams zigzagging across them, trees standing as silent sentinels keeping watch over the tall grass gently waving in the wind. It is hard to believe that this gift to the eyes had seen so much horror. My heart felt heavy. The sky, now filled with birds, was then clouded with iron and steel—tempered in brave men's blood and mothers' tears. All those men, gone, but were they gone? The ground had been soaked with their blood; it had seeped into the earth, around the base of the trees and the roots of the grasses. Suddenly, I realized those brave men were still there. The mingling of their blood with the soil had made them part of it and therefore a part of everything else. They are in the grass, trees and in the animals that live off the land. No, they are not gone, but live on in a different form. My eyes searched the ground for a sign of something, anything from that time so long ago. It had recently rained and there were tiny rivulets of water running everywhere. Walking on, a flash caught my eye, off to the right near the edge of the woods. It happened again, just about eye level. It came from a medium sized tree about five inches in diameter. As I approached it, it happened once more, a bright sparkle from the area of a knothole. A knothole—could there be something stuck in the tree? A bullet? I wondered. No, the tree is too small; it wasn't even here one hundred and thirty years ago. Could it have picked up something in the ground as it grew? It deserved a closer look. I walked to the tree and examined the knothole. My finger probed inside. Moss, just moss, but why had it sparkled? I guess it was just wishful thinking that I would find anything. Disheartened, I lowered my head and my eyes focused on the ground an inch in front of my left foot. I blinked my eyes and focused again. I was looking down on a pile of old wood. It might have been a log or a stump, but time and weather had turned it to the consistency of sawdust. A dark brown spot stood out in the top of the pile, washed into view by the recent rain. I stooped and took hold of the brown object; it yielded itself willingly. Convex on one side, concave on the other, made of heavy metal—a cannonball, it was part of a cannonball! I cleaned it off a little more. Never had it even crossed my mind that I would make such a find. I realized that at this place, on this day, under these conditions an unseen hand had guided me. I had been manipulated, but in a pleasant way, to be at that spot at that time.

I drove to Spotsylvania Court House and visited a museum there. I asked for directions to my next destination, Petersburg, 25 miles below Richmond. Following the directions I had been given, I soon found Interstate 95 and was on my way south. It was not a very long ride. Just outside Petersburg, signs appeared for the National Battlefield. I took the exit for the Battlefield and drove to the Visitor Center, parked, and went inside. The gift shop and information desk area of the center was filled with shelves of books and souvenirs. The pretty girl behind the counter said, "The movie on Petersburg will be starting soon." I said "thanks, but I'm in a hurry." She said, "It's a short film." I told her I was pressed for time but could use a battlefield map. My request was granted with a smile. Upon reading the map, my eyes came across the words I sought, Fort Stedman. I will give you a bit of information, so you will understand my interest in Fort Stedman. Fort Stedman was named after Col. Giffin Stedman of the 11th Conn. Vol. Regiment, who was killed August 5, 1864 on Hares Hill, where the fort still stands. Petersburg was the longest siege in American warfare; it lasted nearly ten months. Approximately 2 A.M., on a bitterly cold February night in 1865, General Lee sent for General Gordon. Gordon rode to the commanding general's headquarters in a house on the outskirts of Petersburg.

> As I entered, General Lee, who was entirely alone, was standing at the fireplace, his arm on the mantel and his head resting on his arm as he gazed into the coal fire burning on the grate. He had evidently been up all the previous part of the night. For the first time in all my intercourse with him, I saw a look of painful depression on his face. Of course he had experienced many hours of depression, but

> he had concealed from those around him all evidence of discouragement. He opened the conference by directing me to read the reports from the different commands as he should hand them to me and to carefully note every important fact contained in them. The revelation was startling. Each report was bad enough, and all the distressing facts combined were sufficient, it seemed to me to destroy all cohesive power and lead to the inevitable disintegration of any other army that was ever marshalled. I was not prepared for the picture presented by these reports of extreme destitution—of the lack of shoes, of hats, of overcoats, and of blankets, as well as of food. Some officers had gone outside of the formal official statement as to numbers of the sick, to tell in plain, terse, and forceful words of depleted strength, emaciation, and decreased power of endurance among those who appeared on the rolls as fit for duty.[29]

In the reports the number of Confederates fit for duty was put at 35,000, around and nearby Petersburg. Grant had approximately 150,000 well-fed and well-equipped troops. General Lee sat down across the table from Gordon, and posed a question to him. He asked his opinion on what he though best to do under the conditions stated in the reports. Gordon answered:

> "General, it seems to me there are but three courses and I name them in the order in which I think they should be tried: First, make terms with the enemy, the best we can get. Second, if that is not practicable, the best thing to do is to retreat—abandon Richmond and Petersburg, unite by rapid marches with General Johnston in North Carolina, and strike Sherman before Grant can join him; or, lastly, we must fight, and without delay."[30]

Gordon asked Lee for his feelings on the matter. Lee replied "Certainly, General, you have the right to ask my opinion. I agree with you fully." Lee returned from the conferences in Richmond and informed Gordon that peace talks or abandonment of the capital were not viable issues at that time. There was but one option left, fight. Gordon writes: "This was the prelude to my assault upon Fort Stedman on March 25, 1865—the last confederate attack on Grant's lines at Petersburg."[31]

> As the solitary signal shot rang out in the stillness of the early morning, the Confederate pickets, who had crept close to the Union sentinels, silently sprang upon them and killed or captured them without the discharge of a single Federal alarm. Simultaneously, the fifty axe-men sprang over the parapets and with swift blows, slashed down the Federal obstructions. Close behind followed the selected three hundred men and after them the main body of the infantry.

The battle escalates:

> Up to this point success had exceeded Gordon's fondest expectations. The Confederates had succeeded in cutting through the heavy Federal obstructions and had taken Fort Stedman and several works on either side, besides capturing nine heavy cannons, eleven mortars, and nearly 1,000 prisoners, including General McLaughlin, who commanded Stedman.

Things seemed to be going well:

> Select officers and men in Stribling's battalion had charged the enemy's breastworks and turned the four light 12's of Fort Stedman upon the Federals. The guns of Battery No. 10 were brought into action against them. According to Freeman, Gordon had "anticipated in miniature by fifty years and more the tactics of the breakthrough."

Gordon makes a report to Lee:

> From the Fort, Gordon sent word to General Lee, who was on a hill in the rear, that the Confederates were in the works and the 300 select men were on their way to positions behind the Federal lines. Anxiously Gordon received a message from General Lewis that he had passed the Federal lines with no difficulty, but had lost his guide and could not find the fort.

Thing start to turn bad for the Confederates.

> Presently similar reports came from the other two advance columns. Daylight was coming, and faintly Gordon could see the gathering preponderance of Grant's overwhelming forces. He could make no further advance and found it necessary to draw in

> his forces toward Fort Stedman, where they could presently be subjected to a heavy fire of artillery from both flanks.

Without reinforcements there is no chance of success:

> There was no hope of reinforcements, as Lee had already warned him that the arrival of Pickett's division was doubtful. Accordingly, Gordon notified Lee that his men could not reach the rear forts and that the advance had been halted. Gordon was not long in realizing that tenure of Stedman was impossible.

The fight disintegrates:

> His men had not been able to capture Battery 9, though they had come within 500 yards of it only to be fired upon so hotly that they had to seek shelter in a depression of the ground. Here they were held under fire of canister until most of them surrendered. As soon as the haze of the morning cleared away, thirty pieces of artillery opened a concentrated fire upon and around Fort Stedman.

The end draws near:

> By 7:30 a.m. Federal forces had regained Batteries 11 and 12 and had drawn a cordon of troops around the Fort and Battery 10. Most of Gordon's men were driven back into these works, where they suffered heavy casualties from the artillery on both flanks as well as from the reserve batteries in the rear.

Hope disappears.

> By 8 AM. confusion increased and became general throughout the Confederate ranks. At about this time General Lee sent orders to evacuate the captured works.[32]

I left the visitor's center and slowly drove the short distance down the twisting little road through the battlefield. Parking near Fort Stedman, I found only one other vehicle occupying a space. Two gentleman walked nearby. [Let me pause here and explain a few things to the reader. It does not come easy to me, this book writing. I know from my own readings that you are most likely waiting to see what I find or feel of a tangible nature on my visits to these historic places. I, too, approach them with anticipation. I understand your anticipation and hope I do not disappoint you. But, be forewarned, not all of my stops were as rewarding as the Mule Shoe. Be aware also, that I refuse to fabricate anything purely for your enjoyment or just to make a good story. Maybe at these places there were no psychic events or deja-vu feelings, but I never left empty-handed. Just being there has an effect on anyone who has knowledge of what transpired on these hallowed grounds. Point made, we return to the parking lot at Fort Stedman.] Exiting my car, I walked the path through the remains of the fort. Now not much more than dirt breastworks remain, covered with grass and a few cannons placed here and there, its passive facade belying the fact of its violent birth. The two men walking on the sidewalk returned to their car and drove off. I was now alone on this portion of the battlefield, something I prefer, but which rarely happens. Near the fort is a monument to the 1st Maine commemorating the greatest regimental loss in a single action of the Civil War. I walked across the open field to Colquitt's Salient from where the Confederate attack had originated. It was here during the retreat that, once again, General Gordon was wounded, in his leg, but it was not serious. Strolling unimpeded and unencumbered on the short cut grass to the salient, it was an enjoyable trip this time. Blue sky, birds chirping and squirrels scampering to and fro. I stood for a while, looking over the field to Fort Steadman and then made the short return trip. I realized, upon my arrival at the fort, that by transecting the field as I had, I had traveled exactly opposite to the trek of March 25, 1865. I thought back to a picture I had seen in a book. It was of a 14-year-old boy, a Confederate, lying dead in the bottom of a trench in Petersburg. He was ragged and barefoot. A small mark on his chest indicated where a bayonet had penetrated. Petersburg is another case of a pretty place with sad memories.

The battle of Fort Stedman was one more example of things that could have gone one way or the other, but swung in favor of the Union. Gordon was involved in a few such conflicts: the Wilderness and Petersburg, as I have mentioned, and Gettysburg and Cedar Creek, which we will cover later. Here is something to ponder—remember the picture of my Great Grandfather, Lewis Knapp, that sits on my dresser? As a Union soldier, he was at the siege and fall of Petersburg, with the 1st Connecticut Heavy Artillery. Day after day, they lobbed shells into the city and surrounding fortifications. Could it be that I came under fire from my own Great Grandfather?

The sun moved lower in the sky. I headed to the west in the direction of Appomattox Court House. It was approximately 90 miles away and I wanted to get there before the park closed for the evening. I traveled west on Rt. 460, pretty much paralleling the course taken by the Army of Northern Virginia. Gordon's last official report written on April 11, 1865 gives some insights into the condition of the Confederate Army. Gordon's men acted as rear guard during the retreat—moving, fighting, and moving again. Men already pushed to the edge were now being pushed over it. Lack of food, physical exhaustion and sleep deprivation continued to take its toll. Unable to reach supplies, and continually harassed by Federal Troops and Cavalry, the men in grey kept moving on by not much more than willpower alone. There was an added woe for Gordon on the night they left Petersburg. He had given the order to fire the bridges after the last troops had crossed. He did this with the knowledge that Fanny and his newborn son, John Brown Gordon, Jr., must remain behind. I spotted a sign that read Sayler's Creek Battlefield 6 Miles. Not having time to turn off, I would have to return another day.

Arriving at Appomattox Court House, I had about 45 minutes before they closed the visitor's center. I hurried up the walkway from the parking lot. I was struck by the charm of the little village. Buildings of many different construction types, wood frame, brick and log were scattered around the central feature, which was the courthouse itself. Fences of all descriptions, split rail, zigzag and picket among them ran along the country lanes and around some of the structures. The Old Richmond-Lynchburg Stage Road bisects the settlement leading up to and circling the Court House where the visitor center is located. I entered the courthouse and took a pamphlet, and then promptly headed for the McLean House (both the McLean House and the Court House are reconstructions). The McLean house has two outbuildings and is surrounded by a white picket fence. I walked through the gateway, passed the well-house and walked up the porch stairs to the front door. Just inside to the left is a parlor, with its furnishings set up as closely as possible to how it looked on April 9, 1865. A park guide stood near the front door and answered questions as they arose from the visitors. I hurried through the house and back to the Visitor Center. Heading to the second floor, I climbed two or three risers at a time (I would do this more often in my youth, but less after hitting the big 40). The upstairs contains a small theater that shows a slide program (closed because of the late hour). A small gallery of artifacts and pictures surround a small theater enclosure. One item in particular caught my attention—a wooden tabletop. To work out the details of the formal surrender, a commission of three officers from each army was formed. The names of the men picked by Grant and Lee were carved into the tabletop that stood before me. For the North, Grant sent Generals Griffin, Merritt and Gibbon. For the Army of Northern Virginia, Lee appointed Generals Longstreet, Gordon and Pendleton. I moved on and returned to the staircase. Over the landing hung some flags, one was all white except for the canton, which was the well known St. Andrew's Cross design of the Confederate battle flags. Gazing at the flag while descending, my mind said, "That's the flag that was used at the time of the surrender." Near the base of the stairs hung a print called the Last Salute depicting the formal surrender of the Army of Northern Virginia. Generals Joshua Chamberlain and John Gordon were in the center, sitting astride their horses, facing each other. Gordon's mount's head bowed, his sword pointed to the toe of his boot. Behind Gordon were the remnants of the Army of Northern Virginia, with one man holding a flag almost furled. Something caught my eye; this flag was the same as the one in the stairwell with one exception. A red bar ran across the end he held in his hand. It just did not look right to me. Looking back over my shoulder, I saw a park ranger standing near the information desk. I asked him if he could answer a question for me. "If I can," he replied.

Pointing to the flag in the stairwell I asked him, "Wasn't that the flag that was used in the surrender ceremony?" Then motioning to the print, I said, "The one in this print has a red bar across it?"

He stood there in his immaculate brown uniform, with a surprised look in his eyes. "You're right," he said. "The flag in the print is the third National Confederate flag. That was the official flag at the time of the surrender, but it had not been issued to the troops in the field yet." Turning toward the stairs he continued, "The flag over the stairs is the Stainless Banner. That's the one used at the surrender." I had surprised myself. How did I know about the flag? In a book I was to read long after my stop at Appomattox, there was another confirmation about the flag that was used. The book was written by Joshua Chamberlain. The title of the book: The Passing of the Armies. Major General Joshua Lawrence Chamberlain, Hero of Little Round Top and Congressional Medal of Honor winner, Chamberlain survived being wounded many times during the war. Later in life, he became Governor of Maine and President of Bowdoin College (of which he was a graduate and professor). Chamberlain is the protagonist in the Pulitzer Prize winning novel, *Killer Angels,* by Michael Sharra. General Grant picked Chamberlain for the honor of receiving the formal surrender of the Army of Northern Virginia, though many other generals outranked him. His counterpart on the Confederate side was John Gordon. I left the Courthouse and walked down the road to the Peers House. The House sits on the summit of a hill overlooking the Appomattox River. The Richmond-Lynchburg Road runs down the hill past the House and across the nearby river. Two small lanes run into the Richmond-Lynchburg road to form a large triangle in front of the Peers House. This area is known as the surrender triangle. I moved down the road near the Peers House and took a few pictures. More than one person has said to me, "I bet if you could go back in time, you'd like to go back to the

Civil War." Or "Why don't you become a re-enactor?" To the latter, my standard reply is, "I was there the first time." Followed by a grin. To the former I explain that I do not think anyone who knows what the Civil War was like would choose to return to it. As an example, in the three-day period during the battle of Gettysburg, North and South suffered more than 50,000 casualties, killed, wounded and missing. Approximately 5,000 horses lay dead on the fields in the summer heat and the wagon train carrying the Confederate wounded southward stretched almost 17 miles. Not exactly a stroll in the park. I have changed my mind though; I would go back, but to one day only—April 12, 1865, in front of the Peers House at Appomattox Court House. The reason I would return to that day is based on what transpired there. Chamberlain would do something that morning for which he would be criticized for the rest of his life. His actions have stood the test of time to become one of the most eloquent events in our Nation's history. I hope his critics lived long enough to read his book, *Passing of the Armies,* and his account of that day. General Chamberlain writes of a dejected Gordon riding at the head of the surrender column and tells of his response to a most gracious salute by the Union soldiers.

> At the sound of the machine-like snap of arms, General Gordon started, caught in a moment of significance, and instantly assumed the finest attitude of a soldier. He wheeled his horse, facing me, touching him gently with the spur, so the animal reared, and as he wheeled, horse and rider made one motion, the horse's head swung down with a graceful bow and General Gordon dropped his sword-point down to his toe in salutation. By word of mouth the general sent back orders to the rear that his own troops take the same position of the manual in the march past as did our line. That was done, and a truly imposing sight was the mutual salutation and farewell. Bayonets were affixed to the muskets, arms stacked, and cartridge-boxes unslung and hung upon the stacks. Then, slowly and with a reluctance that was appealingly pathetic, the torn and tattered battle-flags were either leaned against the stacks or laid upon the ground. The emotion of the conquered soldiery was really sad to witness. Some of the men who had carried and followed those ragged standards through the four long years of strife rushed,

> regardless of all discipline, from the ranks, bent about their old flags, and pressed them to their lips. And it can well be imagined, too, that there was no lack of emotion on our side, but the Union men were held steady in their lines, without the least show of demonstration by word or by motion. There was, though, a twitching of the muscles of their faces, and be it said, their battle-bronzed cheeks were not altogether dry. Our men felt the import of the occasion, and realized fully how they would have been affected if defeat and surrender had been their lot after such a fearful struggle.[33]

In my opinion, Chamberlain's clear vision, wisdom and heart were much greater than that allotted to most men. I was later to find that Gordon and Chamberlain had much in common. Both men were civilians before the war, both attained the rank of Major General and both would become Governor of their home states. Even stranger was the fact that each had received wounds that were believed to be fatal but survived, and both Generals' wives shared the name "Fanny."

I walked back past the Court House and turned down the road leading to the parking lot. When I arrived at my car, there was a man leaning against his car staring at the village. I struck up a conversation with him. He told me he had felt drawn to Appomattox. His wife and kids were off in a nearby city, but he had been compelled to drive to the battlefield. He asked me if I had ever been there before. I laughed and said, "Yes, but that was almost 130 years ago." He didn't run away, so I gave him a capsulized version of my story and showed him a picture of Gordon. He stood there and listened intently. He told me he was not sure about reincarnation but knew strange things happen, like his attraction to this place. We shook hands, I got in my car and drove off to Rt. 460 once more. No more battlefields for a while, there was a wedding to get to and many miles between Georgia and me.

CHAPTER FIVE

You Can't Go Home Again, Can You?

OVER THE BLUE RIDGE MOUNTAINS and into the Shenandoah Valley I went. Stopping at Roanoke for the night, I got an early start the next morning. The drive from Roanoke to the Tennessee line on Route 81 was nearly 100 miles. I had not eaten anything before I left the motel and now my tummy was craving a good old-fashioned southern breakfast. Just over the line near Bristol, Tennessee, my eye caught a sign. I can't remember exactly what the name of the place was, something like Mama's Country Kitchen. Exiting the highway and driving up a hill, I parked near the front door. Inside, the motif was sort of country cutesy, but I wasn't there for the scenery; I was there to eat. A hostess showed me to a table and gave me a menu. Upon perusing the bill of fare, I could see that I had made a good choice in restaurants. I ordered four eggs over easy, Virginia ham, grits, toast, sausage gravy with buttermilk biscuits, coffee and orange juice. The waitress asked if someone was joining me. "Nope, it's all for me," I replied. Entertaining myself with a game that had been placed on the table for just such a purpose, time passed quickly and the food soon arrived.

My breakfast was placed on the table in front of me. I quickly devised a plan. The egg yolks stared up at me like a couple of frightened Siamese twins, who knew they would go first. I ate two with the ham. Then, the grits were poured on the plate and the remaining eggs put in a place of honor on top. They too would succumb to my hunger, but not nearly as fast as the others had. I cut the eggs in a crisscross manner and blended them together with the grits. This mixture was soon consumed along with the intermittent pieces of toast, a little O.J., and then it was time for the sausage gravy and biscuits. When finished I sat back and sipped my coffee. The waitress approached the table, her eyes scanning the empty plates. "I can't get you anything else, can I?" she asked. "Not unless you want to pick up the pieces!" was my answer. I paid the bill and waddled out the door, southbound once again.

I followed Interstate 81 to Knoxville, where I caught Rt. 75 South. The undulating hills rolled by and before I knew it, I was in Chattanooga. As Rt. 75 turned due South, I could see Lookout Mountain to my right. It loomed above the city, dwarfing its surroundings. A few miles later, a sign announcing the Georgia State line came into view. Following my mother's directions, I transferred to Route 27 for the last leg of my journey. Route 27 takes you straight through the middle of the Chickamauga Battlefield. Georgia had been hit with record snowfalls that previous winter and many trees bore the scars of the heavy snows. Branches and whole trees lay scattered along the roadway. The scene looked much like what the artillery damage must have been after the battles fought there. There are wooded areas broken by open fields all through the park. It is not uncommon to see deer feeding at the edge of the woods. I had never seen a battlefield park with so many monuments—every size and shape, from small tablets to towering sculptures, from the plain to the ornate. They are well placed and the spacing does not intrude on the scenic beauty, but enhances it by reminding the viewer of the deeper meaning of their surroundings. Shortly after exiting the park, a few miles down the road, something strange happened. A feeling, one I had learned to pay attention to, a subtle, dull pressure at the bridge of my nose and up to my forehead, much like being struck on the nose but without the pain. I looked around, and as I gazed out of the car to the right, I was struck by a most beautiful sight: a large expanse of fields stretched from the roadside to the base of a distant mountain ridge. Sunlight shone through the clouds, illuminating the grasses with its golden light. A stream snaked its way across the landscape. All this was framed by the contrasting colors of the blue mountains in the distance and the green trees along the roadway. It was not just the beauty that hit me, but a familiarity, like meeting a friend after a long absence.

I continued my drive until I found myself on Main Street in Lafayette, pop. 6,313. Finding my mother's and sister's house, I pulled into the driveway. After a round of hugs and kisses, I settled in, tired from my long drive. The next day was my sister's wedding, at a lodge in Tennessee. With that behind me, I could rest, visit with family and explore the area.

My youngest brother, Joel was up from Florida. It was especially good to see him, because our meetings are usually many years apart. Joel directed me to John B. Gordon Hall, a few blocks north of my mother's house. It is reported to be the oldest standing brick schoolhouse in Georgia. Set back from the roadway and surrounded by mature trees and plantings, it can easily escape detection in the casual drive down Main Street. The schoolhouse was built in 1836 from bricks made from the local Georgia clay. The two-story structure is a simple Georgian style, with one large room on each floor. At the Lafayette library I came across Allen P. Tankersly's book, *John Brown Gordon, A Study in Gallantry*, written in 1955. In the beginning of the book, he tells of John and his brother Chapman attending this school and boarding at the Marsh House just North of Gordon Hall. They would stay in town for the week and return to Gordon Springs on Friday evenings. In front of the school is a walkway lined with tablets marking this historic spot. A large pyramid of cannonballs was centered in the walk and a tall, slender stone monument crowned with a Confederate soldier, standing guard near the edge of the road. What tales this red brick schoolhouse could tell if it was given the power of speech, for it had stood as a witness to the comings and goings of generations of local children.

In 1863, Confederate General Braxton Bragg used the hall as headquarters and mapped out the battle plans for the conflict with Union Troops at Chicamauga. The great oak tree, under which Bragg and his staff devised their strategy and tactics, stood until struck by lightning in the early 1920s. In 1864, the Hall once again became an Army headquarters, only this time under Union control during the Battle of Lafayette. What a strange mixture of echoes the walls of this school must retain, the rattle of muskets and the moans of wounded men intertwined with the laughter of school children.

I walked around snapping pictures, then paused a while to ponder an inscription at the base of the stone monument. "It is a duty we owe to posterity, to see that our children shall know the virtues and become worthy of their sires."

I feel it would be beneficial for all generations to study the lives of their forefathers (and mothers): to know the struggles and trials they endured, to give one a sense of whence they came and a deeper foundation on which to base their own identity. Walking around the school, I tried to get a look inside. The only windows not blocked by bushes were five feet or more off the ground, so there I stood or should I say hopped, up and down like a kangaroo. My attempts to see what the interior looked like were futile. I would have to settle for the view outside. At that time, the Hall was not open to the public.

The Marsh House is a private residence so I could only admire it from afar. Like the schoolhouse, the Marsh House was built in 1836 and the structure is of the style known as "Plantation Plain." The house shares much of the same history as the school. After the battle of Lafayette, stories were told of soldiers on horseback riding in the north door, down the central hallway and out the south door, leaving the walls smeared with blood and the flooring imbedded with their horse's hoofprints.

I took a few more pictures and then was on my way. Doing more research at the library, I came up with a map of Walker County from 1893. The map showed Gordon Springs, near Taylor's Ridge, not too many miles away. I was off again. I set the odometer on my car to zero. From Tankersly's book and other sources, I knew I needed to travel about ten miles. Driving along the base of the ridge, I watched the odometer snap to the ten-mile mark and at almost the same time I spotted a marker set back in the woods.

I parked the car as best I could, because this country road did not have much of a shoulder; it was more like a ditch. I walked with camera in hand to the marker. "Gordon Springs Gap," the tablet announced with a brief history after. This was the beginning of the old road east through a gap in Taylor's Ridge to Gordon Springs. The road was used by many in the Army of the Cumberland; "General Hooker in person" stated the sign. The road was no more; it had returned to nature.

Now the hillside was covered with dense woods. I felt much like a prisoner looking through bars. I had found Gordon Springs but I was on the wrong side of the ridge. Night was approaching and I would have to wait until the following day to visit Gordon Springs. I headed back to the main road to return to Lafayette. Upon approaching the main road, I was greeted with the same view that had struck me so hauntingly on my way into town. I wondered how many times a young John Gordon was blessed with this lovely panorama after emerging from Gordon Springs Gap? I turned left and drove to Main Street with a warm feeling in my chest.

The next morning, along with my mother, we embarked once more on the quest to find Gordon Springs. Over the ridge we went, following the twisting roads until we reached an area near Taylor's Ridge at around the ten-mile mark. Stopping at a store, I asked the owner where Gordon Springs was. He gave me directions to a small country road. When I say small, I mean one of those roads that you worry what you will do if you were to meet another car coming from the opposite direction. We scanned the area for any remnants of Gordon Springs; none were found. A few houses and structures of modern construction dotted the countryside. I was forced to be content with the stories John Gordon told of this area. It was here that Gordon became an able horseman. In a boyhood sketch he wrote for "Youth's Companion" magazine, he tells of "fox chase with packs of carefully bred hounds and in the exhilarating pursuit of wolves when these ravenous beasts would steal from their hiding places into the sheep fold at night. There were few Southern boys who did not become, through these experiences, expert riders before they were fifteen years old."[34] With a hint of sadness, Gordon tells of days gone by, of "Fourth 'o July barbecues," "Christmas times" and "corn shucking." He told of events shared by whites and blacks; good times enjoyed by all. John Gordon laments in his post Civil War writing that, "only picturesque memories remain." It was in his youth while attending the school set up by his father, that John would develop his ability as a orator, a seemingly natural gift that would serve him well both in war and peacetime politics. Leaving Gordon Springs behind, we traveled back to Lafayette ("LaFet" as it is pronounced by the local inhabitants.)

Back at my sister's house, I was talking to Joy in the kitchen. Her best friend was on the telephone in one of the bedrooms, chatting with her ex-husband, Trey. She called me to the phone to speak with him. It turned out that Trey is very much into the Civil War and relic hunting. I talked with him, telling him that I was interested in John Gordon. Trey really caught my attention when he spoke about a friend of his who had been using a metal detector around a house once owned by Gordon. This treasure hunter had found an old watchback with the letters J.G. stamped in it. Trey gave me the relic hunter's name and phone number. I called him and asked him about the watchback. He didn't seem interested in parting with it so I gave him my name and number, just in case he ever wanted to sell it. I hung up and sat there, a little discouraged. I had always hoped to come across something that had belonged to Gordon and what could be better than a personal item that he carried with him? I filed away the man's name and phone number with the hope that some day I might receive a phone call from him.

I mapped out a route that would take my mother and myself back up north. I planned to stop at some places I did not have time to visit on my way down. It was a beautiful day for driving when we left. We drove over the mountains of the Chattahoochee National Forest and caught Interstate 75 South. In Atlanta, we stopped at a used bookstore. When we were ready to leave, I asked for directions to the Capitol Building, for there was something I very much wanted to see. We found the Capitol Building with little effort. There, on the corner, stood a statue of Gordon on horseback, a sight that neither Gordon nor I had seen before. The Gordon Monument had been unveiled May 25, 1907, years after his passing. The artist that sculpted Gordon astride his horse Marye was Solon H. Borglum. I was later to find some interesting facts about Borglum. Solon was born in 1868 in Ogden, Utah. His brother Gutzon sculpted Mount Rushmore. He studied under his brother (John) Gutzon de la Mothe Borglum and Rebisso. He was a member of the Cincinnati Art Academy, National Academy of Design (1911), and The Silvermine Group. He also created the Sailors and Soldiers monument in Danbury, Connecticut. He is the Founder of the School of American Sculpture in New York City and served as YMCA Secretary in World War I were he was awarded the Croix de Guerre for courage under fire. He died in Stamford, CT, in 1922 from war injuries. Two things stood out when I read this. I had once taken an oil painting class at Silvermine School of Art and many times admired the Sailors and Soldiers Monument (not being aware of the creator's name) in the city of my birth Danbury, Connecticut.

I rounded a corner adjacent to the statue and parked the car. I told my mother to stay with the car in case it needed to be moved. I looped the camera strap around my wrist and bounded across the street to the base of the statue. It was gorgeous and surrounded by beautiful trees and plants. I am told, although I don't know if it is a fact, that it is the only equestrian statue in Atlanta. Click, click went the camera and back I went to the car before I got a ticket. Not far away we found Oakland Cemetery, the last resting-place of John B. Gordon. I asked some workmen if they knew where he was buried and they directed me to the visitor's center. At the center I picked up some pamphlets. Margaret Mitchell, who wrote *Gone with the Wind,* rests here along with 2500 Confederate soldiers and five General Officers: Gordon, Evans, Iverson, Gartrell and Walker. They all rest in the shade of old oaks, magnolias and dogwood trees. I received directions to John Gordon's grave and then asked where the family plot was. I was told there was no family plot. I had a strange feeling that there was a family plot so I posed the question again. "Just Fanny buried with John," the woman at the desk replied with a stern voice and cold stare. I dropped the subject. My mother and I walked to Gordon's grave, a modest stone monument about three feet high, six feet wide and about two and a half feet thick. One side simply read GORDON, the other

John B. Gordon
Feb. 6, 1832–Jan. 9, 1904
Fanny Haralson
Wife of John B. Gordon
Sept. 18, 1837–Apr. 28, 1931

"Wife of" somehow did not seem fitting. It should read "The other half of John B. Gordon"—sweet Fanny, who followed John all over the countryside through most of the major battle campaigns of the Army of Northern Virginia. Her presence and tender nursing had saved John's life at Sharpsburg. Gordon writes:

> General Early was a bachelor, with a pungent style of commenting on things he did not like; but he had a kind heart and was always courteous to women. As might be expected, however, of a man who had passed the meridian of life without marrying, he had little or no patience with wives who insisted on following the army in order to be near their husbands. There were numbers of women—wives and mothers—who would gladly have accompanied their husbands and sons had it been possible for them to do so. Mrs. Gordon was one of the few who were able to consult their wishes in this regard. General Early, hearing of her constant presence, is said to have exclaimed, "I wish the Yankees would capture Mrs. Gordon and hold her until the war is over!" Near Winchester, as the wagon trains were being parked at night, he discovered a conveyance unlike any of the others that were going into camp. He immediately called out to his quartermaster in excited tones: "What's that?" "That is Mrs. Gordon's carriage, sir," replied the officer.

> "Well, I'll be ——! If my men would keep up as she does, I'd never issue another order against straggling."

Mrs. Gordon was fully aware of the general's sentiments, and had heard of his wishing for her capture; and during a camp dinner given in honor of General Ewell, she sat near General Early and good-naturedly rallied him about it. He was momentarily embarrassed, but rose to the occasion and replied: "Mrs. Gordon, General Gordon is a better soldier when you are close by him than when you are away, so hereafter, when I issue orders that officer's wives must go to the rear, you may know that you are excepted." This gallant reply called forth a round of applause from the officers at table."[35] In wartime and peace, she was always by his side.

> After Gordon entered politics in 1868, she was of great assistance to him in his campaigns and in his study of current questions. She generally accompanied him on speaking tours, and when he could not remember the name of an old veteran who came up to greet him, she whispered it to him. The veteran, flattered at being recognized by his old commander willingly gave his political support.

Fanny Gordon helped her husband stay up to date.

> When the duties of public office did not afford him time to read the newspapers, she read for him and marked or clipped items that she thought he ought to see. She discussed the news with him and advised him in his political decisions. But Mrs. Gordon spent most of her time being a good wife and mother. Had her husband lived ten months longer, they would have celebrated their golden wedding anniversary.

Their love affair was called legendary by many.

> As long as he lived, he was romantically in love with the woman whom he had married on her seventeenth birthday and he was never too busy to think tenderly and sentimentally of her.[36]

She is by his side still and always will be.

A small tablet rests in the ground nearby, placed by the Alfred Holt Colquilt Chapter of the United Daughters of the Confederacy. It tells a condensed story of Gordon's life:

JOHN BROWN GORDON
1832–1904

> A native of Upson County, Georgia, and a Major General, Confederate States Army, was one of General Lee's most trusted officers. He brilliantly led his devoted men in every engagement in which the Army of Northern Virginia participated and was severely wounded at the Battle of Sharpsburg. He led the war's last charge and following the Appomattox surrender, returned to Georgia.
>
> Idolized by the populace, he served his state three times as U.S. Senator and as Governor 1886-1890. He was Commander-in-Chief of the united Confederate Veterans from its inception until his death—a fitting tribute to a gallant gentleman.

I stood there a while, just looking at the gravesite. I asked my mother to take some pictures of me by the stone. The camera was a Polaroid, so in a few minutes the pictures had developed. I looked them over and started laughing inside. I said, "Hey Mom! You know that old expression—He was beside himself?"

She said, "Yes."

I smiled at her, while holding up the pictures that she had just taken, saying "Now I have a picture of it." She gave me one of those patented mother looks, as if trying to remember how many times she dropped me on my head.

A short stroll downhill from Gordon's plot, I found the grave of General Clement Evans, a good friend of John's and the General that replaced Gordon in brigade command when Gordon advanced to a Major General position. Down the hill a little farther, stands a stone obelisk. When this monument to the Confederate dead was unveiled in 1874, its 65-foot height made it the tallest structure in Atlanta. We walked back to the car. Oakland cemetery has a large grid-work of roads; I drove a little, turned right, drove a little more and then turned right again. As we started up a small incline, my mother said "Hugh Haralson Gordon." I hit the brakes and brought the car to a sudden stop. "Where did you see that?" I asked. "Right back there, on your side. Why? Who is he?" she asked. "Gordon's son," I replied as I shifted the car into reverse and backed down the hill. The woman at the visitor's center had been wrong, there was a family plot. Of all the roads we could have taken, we took the right one. If my eagle-eyed mother had not been with me, I would have driven right by, my mind still on Fanny and John. We got out of the car and walked to the small cluster of headstones. The three nearest the road were John's son Hugh, his wife, Caroline and their daughter, Mary. I walked over towards two headstones that were at the rear left of the small enclosure, one small but with ornate scrollwork, the other tiny and plain. The larger one of the two read:

John B. Gordon, Jr.
Son of John B & Fanny H. Gordon
1865-1884

This was the boy who had been born to the sound of guns at Petersburg. He died from typhoid fever at the age of 19. My eyes moved right to the tiny marker. My heart sank to the ground like an express elevator. A thought flashed through my mind—"My little girl, my poor little girl." My eyes started to well up, but I fought back the tears. My mother didn't need a 200-pound sniveling idiot on her hands. The tiny marker read:

INFANT DAUGHTER
OF
John B. Gordon and Fanny Haralson Gordon

No dates, for none were needed, as the baby had not survived long enough to even receive a name. It had not dawned on me at the moment it occurred, but now as I stood there it hit me. The word "MY," not "poor little," but "MY poor little girl." It had flowed so naturally and the effect had been swift and immediate. Had I not been with my mother, I might have had a replay of what happened at the sunken road in Sharpsburg. I busied myself with taking photos of the headstones and then told my mother it was time to leave. My mother said, "Are you going back to tell that woman she was wrong about the family plot?"

"Not me," I said. "Besides, who else would ask the whereabouts of the Gordon's family plot?" We left the cemetery and worked our way through traffic to the interstate. Next stop—Richmond, Virginia.

Just south of Richmond, we turned off the Interstate onto Route 156, a road that would take us to an area south and east of the old Confederate capital. In 1862, Union General George B. McClellan's peninsular campaign was launched in an attempt to capture Richmond. We followed the twisting roadway to our first stop, a large clearing of sloping farmland. I drove the car into a small parking area and walked over to an information shelter near a row of cannons. "Malvern Hill" read a sign. The battle here had been fought on July 1, 1862. I was standing at the position where the Army of the Potomac had rimmed the crest of the hill with more than 100 pieces of artillery to hold back the Confederates and allow McClellan's men to withdraw from the peninsula. It was here, on the slope of Malvern Hill, that Gordon was blinded for a short time by dirt thrown into his eyes by an exploding shell.

Looking downhill across the green fields to the woods beyond, it was sad to think that when the southern troops fell back, they left behind over 5,000 casualties lining the slopes.

> Colonel Gordon had the butt of his pistol carried away by a Federal bullet, and his canteen was pierced by another, while his coat was torn open by a third. Hill had promised Gordon reinforcements, but they came too late. Finding his brigade isolated from the rest of the army, Gordon halted his men and ordered them to lie down and fire upon McClellan's flank.[37]

After darkness fell, Gordon and his men were then able to make a safe return to their lines.

We drove off following Route 156, passing the White Oak Swamp and through Seven Pines. Tankersley's book on Gordon tells of the fighting in the area:

> The Confederate losses were appalling. More than sixty per cent of Gordon's entire command were killed or wounded. His lieutenant colonel, major, and adjutant were all shot down. As he rode at the head of his regiment, he saw his own brother, Captain Augustus M. Gordon lying wounded and bleeding profusely, but he could not stop to help him.

Somehow Gordon escaped being wounded.

> The Colonel's clothes were pierced by three bullets, and his horse wounded but still able to carry him. He was then the only mounted officer left, but he rode so close to the Federal lines that his men distinctly heard Union officers command: "Shoot that damned Colonel!" Finally his horse was shot from under him, and he was forced to command afoot for the rest of the battle.

The terrain was not much help to the men fighting in it.

> Fighting in water several feet deep, the Confederates formed a detail to prop the wounded against trees and stumps to prevent their drowning. Of the 600 in Gordon's command, more than 300 were killed or wounded; yet the Colonel stood at his post till the end of the action, unhurt and unshaken. For his conspicuous gallantry, he was put in command of Rode's brigade while the latter recovered from wounds received in the battle.

Gordon was a bit uneasy about his elevation.

> Because of his inexperience and youth, Gordon found his new position "unwelcome and extremely embarrassing," but, as he later wrote, his brother officers "did everything in their power to lessen my embarrassment and uphold my hands."[38] Gordon's part in the battles around Richmond had not been inconspicuous. Before the battle of Seven Pines he was hardly known outside of his regiment.

That was all to change.

> One month and two days later his valor had secured the attention of the whole brigade and even Division Commander D.H. Hill. He

> was now the veteran of three hotly contested engagements, and was acting commander of a brigade. If he could maintain his fine record, he might reasonably expect a brigade of his own.[39]

Entering Richmond, I drove to 1201 East Clay Street, the home of The Museum of the Confederacy. I enjoyed the museum, with all its beautiful galleries filled with paintings, prints and photographs. Relics from the Infantry, Cavalry and Artillery fill the building's displays: tattered Southern battle flags, weapons of all types, including revolvers belonging to General Beauregard and Jackson, now lying silent in their showcases. I stood for a long time in front of one display in particular; it was filled with items that had belonged to General Lee. The display was a tent set up as if it were sitting on the edge of a battlefield. On the left side was a small metal camp bed with a blanket. Placed on the bed were the General's frock coat, leather gauntlets and sword belt. Next to the bed stood a tall pair of black riding boots. At the rear of the tent was a wooden camp chest with assorted utensils on top. To the right, was a small table with a square top. On the table rested a gray hat, field glasses and a model 1851 Colt revolver. One other item on the table caught my eye. It is the smallest thing on display but without question, the most powerful, the pen used to sign the surrender at Appomattox Court House.

We left Richmond heading North until we reached Fredericksburg, Virginia. I gave my mother a quick tour of Marye's Heights, the stone wall and Visitor's Center. Once more I followed Route 3 to Chancellorsville. The roadway became narrower and started to undulate like a small rollercoaster. Houses and stores became fewer and farther apart, strip malls gave way to fertile farm land and patches of aged trees. We paused briefly at the small Visitor's Center and viewed the monument where Stonewall Jackson fell. A short drive later and we were at the Wilderness. Driving here and there, I explained to my mother about the battles that had transpired on this splendid landscape of small fields and thick woods. We returned to Route 3 and headed back toward Fredericksburg, but there was one more place I wanted to stop. On my first pass through this area, I spotted a store called Stars and Bars Military Antiques. I had been on the road so early that it was not yet open. I had made a mental note to stop on the way back. The lady who runs the store greeted us as we entered. The place was filled with a wide range of items from World War I, II and Vietnam and of course, the Civil War. My mother talked to the woman as I scampered about the store looking for anything to do with the battle of the Wilderness. Inside a glass case I spotted some small items and asked if any had been found on the Wilderness battlefield. The woman went through the cases turning over each piece to read the description on the sticker on the back. Very few had been recovered from the area that I had requested. But there was one I really liked, a round Union breastplate with an eagle on it. I asked to see it. It was in pretty good shape and still had a small amount of brass coloring in some of the little nooks. I turned it over and read the sticker: "Found Wilderness Battlefield." Under that was the price. I handed it back to her and asked if she had anything less expensive that was from the Wilderness. She checked a little more, but came up empty handed. "Why do you want something from the Wilderness? Did you have a relative there?" she asked.

I looked at my mother and then back to the woman. "Yes, I guess you could say that," I replied.

"What regiment was he with?" she asked.

"He was with General Gordon," I replied.

"What regiment?" she asked a second time.

I looked back at my mother again. My mother said, "Go get the picture." The woman looked puzzled as I walked out the door to my car. I returned with a picture of Gordon and placed it on the counter in front of her. She looked at it and said "I know who that is, it's General Gordon. He was a gentleman." I told her the story of what had happened to me at Antietam, about the cannonball, Halloween party and the story in the magazine. She listened to me intently. She told me some of her thoughts on the subject of reincarnation. She didn't put much store in it; she felt that there might be some sort of a genetic remembrance passed down, like you might retain some of your relative's memories. I told her that as far as I can tell I am no blood relation to Gordon, so, in my case, her theory didn't apply. We talked more and she said reincarnation went against her religion, so that is where we left it. I thanked her for her help and started for the door. I stopped and turned to face her once more. "Let me leave you with this thought" I said. "I heard you tell my mother that you were born in Chattanooga, Tennessee on the anniversary of the Battle of Chattanooga and look at where you are now." I left her standing there with a strange look on her face as she gazed around the store. I would return to this store while on another trip South, and when I did, it would be her turn to tell me a story.

It was not a very long ride back to Connecticut, but it gave me time to think about my first trip to Lafayette, Georgia, about the battlefields I had stopped at along the way, and the strange and unexpected things that had happened to me. This was my first quest into the past. It would not be my last.

CHAPTER SIX

Insights and Wonderments

I WANTED A COPY OF GORDON'S BOOK, *Reminiscences of the Civil War,* so before leaving Lafayette, I had called a book dealer and ordered one. A few days after my arrival home, the book arrived. It was not the same as the 1903 edition I had borrowed from the library; it was the 1904 Memorial Edition published after John Gordon's death. An introduction by General Stephen D. Lee (Gordon's replacement as Commander-in-Chief of The United Confederate Veterans) and a memorial account by Frances Gordon Smith had been added. There, in the center of this book, I came across a drawing of Gordon. It was done from a daguerreotype taken when he was twenty-two. This was the first time I had seen Gordon's face without his mustache, only a close cropped beard covered his chin. I looked at his mouth and was reminded of something that I was told years ago. Sitting across the kitchen table from my then mother-in-law Bette Brennan, she remarked that I have a cupid bow mouth. I said, "I have a what?"

She said, "Your mouth is shaped like Cupid's bow." I had never heard this description used for anyone's lips before and just filed it away in my memory bank. Now, while looking at Gordon's youthful face, I turned the book sideways and sure enough, there was a cupid bow mouth if ever I saw one.

It took several attempts to read the memorial sketch by Gordon's daughter, Frances. So moving was this tale of a nation's grief, I found myself halting every paragraph or so to wipe my eyes and swallow the lump in my throat. Words like "beloved" and "loved" were used unsparingly. It was not the outpouring of love for him that impressed me, so much as the realization of how much he must have loved, for I'm a big believer in you get back what you give out.

It seems Gordon and I share not only physical features, but also mannerisms. I have a habit of standing with my arms crossed. When people ask me to sit, I usually decline the offer and explain that I prefer to stand, and when I stand, I almost always have my arms crossed in front of me. In a book called *Their Tattered Flags,* I found a quote that brought home to me something that I had overlooked. It was a description of General Gordon that read "John Brown Gordon, he of the hitched shirt-sleeves and fiery eye."[40] Well, I don't know about the fiery eye part, but I realized that in three or four of the pictures I had seen of General Gordon, he has his arms crossed. This pose carried over to civilian photos taken after the war. I guess you could say even our bearings have a bearing.

Ever since the time of the Halloween party, I had alternated between reading about reincarnation and books on the Civil War, sometimes reading one of each at the same time. I would walk through bookstores, stopping in the History and New Age sections. I felt guided to certain books; they would stand out from the others, sometimes lying alone on the top of a counter. The books seemed to come to me in the order that I should read them. Not just books, but people too. I have learned not to fight these occurrences and to go along with the flow of things. One of the first books to come my way was titled *Many Lives Many Masters,* written by Dr. Brian L. Weiss, a graduate of Columbia University and Yale Medical School.

I had made a perfect choice in picking this book, if indeed it had been my choice. The first few lines sum up my feeling exactly. "I know that there is a reason for everything. Perhaps at the moment that an event occurs, we have neither the insight nor the foresight to comprehend the reason, but with time and patience, it will come to light."[41] Dr. Weiss had been skeptical when it came to past lives. All that was to change during his treatment sessions with a young woman. While under hypnosis, past life memories surfaced and times between lives emerged. The woman gave information to Dr. Weiss about his family—information, which she could have had no way of knowing. Later on in the book, Dr. Weiss expressed something that he was going through.

> Doubts would surface. It was as if my mind, when not focused, tended to drift back into the old patterns, belief and skepticism. But then I would remind myself—this actually happened! I appreciated how difficult it is to believe these concepts without having personal experience. The experience is necessary to add emotional belief to intellectual understanding. But the impact of experience always fades to some degree.[42]

Well said. I know the feelings. A few times I had started to doubt the conclusions being drawn by the events in my life, much like a dazed prizefighter rising from the canvas in disbelief after being floored. I have had my conclusion reinforced, many times, by the equivalent of a jarring right to the head. Things can be strange or frightening to us, especially if we are unfamiliar with them. The key lies in knowledge. Words like "occult" or "psychic" for some, conjure up visions of things supernatural or satanic. Occult means "hidden or secret" and psychic simply means "of the soul." There are more than a few people who may have just cause to fear having a soul. One of the universal laws I have read about, and have seen in action, goes like this: "You reap what you sow." Albert Einstein once stated, "God does not play dice with the universe." I believe he is right; I believe that there is lawfulness at work around us. Einstein also was of the view that a man was not capable of knowing the full results of his actions. We can see the truth in this in our lives today. If, within the family unit, we teach hatred or violence to our children, that pattern may continue for generation after generation. The same would apply to children taught love and respect for others.

I attended a week-long school for Fire Officers, held just outside Boston, Massachusetts. One day the instructor set up a problem for us on the blackboard. There was a fire that involved a large tank of propane gas next to an apartment house. We were told the backgrounds of all the occupants. One was a Nobel Prize winner, another a wino, a child, a pregnant junkie and so on until we knew the history of all the occupants in the building. The instructor said, "The gas tank will explode in exactly five minutes. You can only save one person. Who do you save?" I raised my hand and was called upon. "You are asking us to make a value judgment on the people in the building and that cannot be done. They are all humans and their value is intrinsic." He stood there with a look on his face as if I had caused a cloudburst over his parade. Maybe he was looking forward to spending the whole class in chatter about the fictional residence. I could feel the predicament he was in. I added, "I know who the firefighter would go for—the kid." The loss of a child in a fire has a devastating effect on firefighters. They take it personally. Once, before I was on the department, I walked into Westport Fire Headquarters to inquire how a fire had gone. "We lost two kids," was the reply. This normally raucous group became hushed and milled about doing their tasks in silence, but the tracks of the tears down their soot stained cheeks spoke for them. By my adding that they would try to save the child, the room came to life with banter and a smile returned to the instructor's face. As far as I was concerned, class was dismissed. There is another law, "Judge not." We are all here for a purpose although we may not be aware of what it is. There could be many reasons; to learn lessons, pay back debts to other souls or to serve as an example for others. The list has no end. I believe I am performing one of my requirements at this very moment by writing this book. If we are not aware of our own purpose, how can we presume to judge others? What yardstick do we use to measure the deeds of our fellow humans? It can become difficult and subjective. You may say something is for the greater good. Whose greater good? Yours, your family, your town, your country or maybe even the world? You can see the dilemma, much like someone asking you which is more beautiful, a painting by Monet or a child's smile? Our time would be better spent on learning about ourselves rather than judging others.

What have I found out about myself? Many things. I am an ordinary man, no better or worse than anyone else. I find many of my favorite things are in-betweens. I love sunrises and sunsets, those times just between night and daylight. I enjoy the songs of the birds as they greet a new day or bid the old farewell. I was once treated to a beautiful in-between, as I traveled across the Piedmont area of Virginia. The sun was setting in the West, causing half the sky to turn an azure blue, while long finger-like clouds took on a bright pink color. The other half of the sky to the East, from horizon to midpoint directly overhead, was filled with dark clouds. Right in the middle of these clouds was an opening, with a large full moon shining very brightly against the dark background. If you were to stand facing North, on your left was day and on your right was night sharing the same sky, perfectly divided. I find I am never more aware than during that period just before falling into a complete slumber or just before becoming fully awake. I have found many answers in those lands of transitions, answers to problems, sometimes insights, sometimes messages and gifts. Past, present and future collide to form one continuous stream, a confluence that forms the river of life, a river that defies all laws of our world and flows back to its source. I have found that I have lived many, many times before. One life in particular, Gordon's, proved that to me, and if one past life, why not more than one? I had wondered why this past life person had turned out to be a historical figure, but how else would there be information enough for me to find all the photos and parallels of our lives. Edgar Cayce claimed that most souls make their greatest advancement while living obscure, normal, everyday lives. He also stated that it didn't matter how famous or important you once were in one lifetime, but it was very important that you live a decent life in the present one.

There is a store called the Tabergerie, which my good friend Tony Esposito and his wife Sandy own. Tony is the local tobacconist, and upon entering the store, one is greeted with the aromas of the pipe tobaccos. Exotic odors of perique and latakia waft through the air mixing with sweet Cavendishes to become a smorgasbord for the senses. The clientele is mostly male and the store has become a gathering place, much like the general stores of old. Stools line the front of the tobacco bar and behind it sits Tony, ready to hold court. One never knows what the topics of discussion will be at any given time; it could run the gambit from cabbages to kings. Many of the world's problems have been solved in less than a day at that little counter. It was here that I met Jim Lomuscio, a reporter/correspondent for the Connecticut Post newspaper. We shook hands and he told me that Tony had mentioned I was writing a book. I was having some difficulty with my novice attempt, so I asked him about ghostwriters and possible places to get technical help. As we talked, the smoke from our cigars rose to a point just below the ceiling, then flared out across the room. Jim seemed to be only mildly interested in my tale of reincarnation.

Months went by before our paths would cross again. When we saw each other again, not much more was said about my book. But then, one day, all that changed. I strolled into Tony's store on a warm June morning to find Jim sitting at the tobacco bar. I selected a Macanudo cigar[43] from the humidor and took up my customary spot at the left-hand side of the bar. Jim seemed deep in thought and was gazing out the window. Suddenly, he swung around on his stool to face me and said in a louder than necessary voice, "Hey! How would you like me to interview you for a newspaper article?" I jumped a little, biting down on my cigar, thankful it wasn't my tongue. This was a big change, from no interest to being all over me, like a mudslide. Jim was talking about calling his editor and getting a photographer. I thought for a moment and figured that the timing must be right, based on Jim's enthusiasm. I agreed to do the interview. Jim disappeared out the front door. A short time later, he returned. He said he had called his editor and that he liked the story. We set up a meeting time for the interview. The day of the interview, I gathered up some things that I would need to show Jim, including the rough draft of the first two chapters of my book and some photos.

On the way to meet with Jim, I kept in mind the fact that he was a reporter. I had dealt with reporters many times at emergency scenes. More than once, I had read articles written about incidents where I was present, only to wonder if the reporter telling the story had been at the same location. I entered Tony's store to wait for Jim. I resolved to think twice and speak once, while answering his questions. When Jim showed up, we took our normal positions at the tobacco bar. I showed Jim some photos and gave him the first two chapters of the book. I asked him to read it while we waited for the photographer. By reading the chapters it would save me rehashing the story and allow him to ask questions as he read. He had not read far when he raised his head and through slightly squinted eyes asked, "What proof do you have of reincarnation?" I love this question. My reply had the same effect on him as it has on most people; it stopped him cold, as if he were teetering on the edge of a cliff. "What would be proof to you?" I said. There was a long silence and then he said, "I don't know." He returned to his reading.

Enter Patrick Whittemore, the photographer. He was not the man Jim was expecting. Pat was filled in on the storyline. He roamed around the store a little shaking his head and muttering "No, no, too dark." Pat and I talked a short distance from where Jim sat reading. Pat asked me if I had a Civil War uniform.

I said, "No."

"How about a sword?" he said.

My answer again was "No."

"How about a Musket?" he said.

"Sorry," I said, "but I don't play dress-up."

Jim piped in and said "He's an Assistant Chief on the Fire Department." Jim went on to explain the similarities of my dress uniform to Gordon's.

Pat's eyes lit up. "That's great! You can wear that for the shot!" he said.

"No," I said. "I want to play down the Fire Department aspect of the story." Back and forth went this discussion. Pat wanted me to wear my uniform. I told him I didn't want to bring the spotlight onto the Fire Department.

He said, “That’s okay.” Jim took my side in the debate.

Pat turned to me and said, “Don’t listen to him, all he needs is paper and pencil.” I tried once more to explain my feelings about the department and not wanting to wear the uniform for the picture. “That’s okay,” Pat said. “The uniform will be great in the photo.” I could see I needed a different approach to this seesaw battle.

I said, “I’ll tell you what, I will talk to the Deputy Chief and the Chief and ask them if they think I should wear my dress uniform or not.”

Pat’s face took on a dejected look. He said, “They’ll both say no.”

I said, “Well, I guess the vote is three to one in favor of the nos.” Pat finally gave in. He told me there was an old cemetery in Westport with some headstones from the Civil War.

Jim said, “Jeff’s great grandfather was in the Civil War and he’s buried in Branchville.”

Jim looked at me and asked, “Is there a chance that your great grandfather and Gordon were at any of the same battles?”

“Yes, Petersburg.” I said. Pat’s face brightened a little. I gave him directions to the cemetery. He took my phone number and was off to check things out. Jim said he needed the photo to go along with the story, so we would wait to do the interview. I left the rough drafts with Jim to read at his leisure. As I was leaving, I asked Jim if he caught the crack that Pat had made about all he needed was a piece of paper and a pencil.” He had. “It seems he is an artist and you’re shit,” I said. We laughed at what appeared to be Pat’s high opinion of himself or his low opinion of Jim.

Later, I would receive a dose of Pat’s medicine, the only difference being I would refuse to swallow it in silence. I drove home and had hardly been in the house ten minutes when Pat called. He said he had found the grave and the light was good “Right now.” Could I be there in twenty minutes? I said that at that time of day, with commuter traffic, it would take me at least thirty minutes. He told me what colors to wear and to bring some of the photos I had of Gordon. I dressed, grabbed three different colored sports jackets and was out the door. Thirty minutes later I found Pat at the gravesite. He had set up his camera on a tripod facing the headstone. I emerged from my car and held up the three coats for his approval. "The blue one," he said. I put on the jacket. Pat picked out a photo and we walked over to the grave. He had me lie down in front of the stone marker, placing a photo of Gordon in my hands. Back to his camera he went. "Raise the photo up." "Bring your left knee up more." "Tilt your head more to your left." On and on he went, until I was in a very uncomfortable position. I told him I was having trouble holding the pose because it was not natural. I should have saved my breath. "That's okay," he said, without even looking up from his camera. Click, click went the camera. Pat walked over and told me we had to mark the spots on the ground where my elbow and knee had rested so I could get back in the same position. Up and down I went, first with me in the picture then out. Once, while lying in front of the tombstone, Pat kept telling me to move back. I was back as far as I could go, because there was the stump of a rosebush sticking into my back. I told Pat about my predicament, to which he replied, "That's okay." When would I learn to keep my mouth shut?

A short time later, while I stood nearby, I saw a large St. Bernard lumbering up the road behind Pat. "There is a big dog coming up behind you," I called to Pat.

"That's okay," he said.

I said, "No, we're talking big, like Cujo," referring to the monster dog from the Stephen King thriller.

"That's okay," was again Pat's reply. The big dog just waddled past Pat and headed in my direction, frothing and drooling as he came. He stopped right next to me and started swinging his big, fat head so that slobber flew everywhere. I moved away to avoid being covered. Then the fuzzy oaf walked over to my great grandfather's tombstone and started lifting his hind leg. I chased him off before he could complete what he had started. I knew what Pat's reply would be if I protested about reclining in dog urine. It was quite warm, and the hairy beast was puffing like a freight train as he wandered off. I got down into position once more, making sure I was on my marks. I heard the huffing and puffing growing louder and louder somewhere behind me. Pat looked up from his camera. "The dog laid down right behind the headstone," he said.

I saw an opening and took it.

"That's okay," I said.

"No, it's not," he said, with anger creeping into his voice.

I said, "If he looks good in the picture, take it."

Pat said, "No, he doesn't look good in it." Pat commenced yelling at the dog to go away. Dummy dog arose and headed over to Pat, thinking that he was calling him. Around and around the camera they went. Finally, Pat was successful in his attempt to drive off the beast. I was glad that the camera's position had not been upset. I did not really want to go through a whole session of ups and downs and ups and downs again. We continued with the photo shoot.

A while later, I heard a woman yelling. Scanning the cemetery, I saw a woman with a small dog under her right arm, walking backwards over the cemetery plots. Her left arm was extended in front of her and in it she held a lit cigarette. A short distance from the cigarette the St. Bernard was plodding along after the woman. I yelled to her, "He's big and stupid and you're not going to stop him." She put her tiny dog in her car and closed the door. She yelled some more at the furry mountain that stood nearby. She turned in my direction and yelled, "You're right, he is stupid." I said, "Yes, but he's big too, so he thinks he can do whatever he wants."

We finished with the picture taking and Pat was loading his equipment into his car while I put my things away. Pat started to get into his car, but instead turned and walked over to where I stood. He said "For what it's worth, I believe that you believe in this story you're telling." I said, "Let me get this straight. You believe that I believe in this story I am telling?" He nodded his head in affirmation. I looked him straight in the eyes and said "For what it's worth, I don't give a shit what you believe!" I went on to give him a short lesson in history. How many people had died because others tried to force their beliefs on them? I explained that in my book all I ask is that the reader keeps an open mind, and comes to his or her own conclusions. When I was finished, Pat said, "That's a good attitude to take." Pat walked back to his car. He must have thought about the remark he had made to me and tried to recover a little by telling me he would call me later, and when he did, I should ask about the strange thing that happened at his mother's house. It's all right if people don't believe my story. It's fine if they say they don't know or are not sure. But I refuse to stand silent, while being patronized and patted on the head like the village idiot. As we drove along the small road through the cemetery leading to the main road, a large hairy mass stood defiantly in the center of the roadway. It was old fuzzy nuts making one last attempt at being a total pain in the butt. No amount of horn blowing or revving the engine could make him move. Pat carefully drove around him and I followed. As I passed around the St. Bernard, a thought crossed my mind that some day that dog would try something like this with a tractor-trailer with bad brakes. Then he will be in for one big surprise. After we had passed around him, he wandered off the road and disappeared into the cemetery.

Over the next few days, I talked to Jim on the phone. He had what there was of my book, so it was not necessary for us to meet for him to write the story. I received one last call from Jim. He asked a few questions and then told me the story would run on the front page. I asked, "What section?" He said "Front page, front page, there is only one front page, Jeff." Jim said the story was all set for Friday, in all editions and would run statewide. On the way home from Thursday's nightshift, I stopped at a store to get a copy of the *Connecticut Post.* There I was on the front page. The photo was a double exposure of me in repose, a ghostly image holding a picture of Gordon. You could see the headstone right through my body. I have to admit Pat did a great job. My wife said it was the best photo of me she had ever seen.

I read the article. The story flowed along pretty well. Jim told how I had held a picture to show him the likeness. He wrote, "Except for the Southerner's beard, the resemblance was striking." I read on and was pleased to see pretty much the same storyline as in the two chapters I had given Jim. Three quarters of the way through, I came to a paragraph that started "Over the past couple of years Keene has been undergoing regression with Jean Loomis, a certified hypnotherapist." I could not believe it. I had made a point of telling Jim that I had never been hypnotized and my reasons for declining hypnosis. It's not that I don't believe in it, it's just that in all my reading of past life studies the first questions they ask potential subjects was, "Have you ever been hypnotized?" If the answer was yes, they were dropped from the study. "Many people believe that a hypnotist can lead a person or plant things in their minds, such as a thought or suggestion. I did not want this stigma placed on me. I made all this very clear to Jim. I had two sessions with Jean Loomis, one week apart in November of 1992 and had never been hypnotized. I was amazed at one other thing in the article. Jim had talked to Anna on the phone, but she would not tell me what she said to him. She said, "You can read it in the paper." What the paper said was that because of my research, she now believes in reincarnation. I asked Anna about this and she confirmed it. This was the first time she had expressed her belief in the subject and I had to find it out from the newspaper. I was pleasantly surprised by the feedback I received from the article—pleased by the fact that most of it was positive.

I caught up to Jim at Tony's store a week or more after the story came out. He entered the store and scurried over to the humidor. "How did you like the article, Jeff?" he asked.

I said, "Jim, can I talk to you a minute?" He walked over to where I stood. I said, "Jim, didn't I make a point of telling you that I had never been hypnotized? Now I read that I've been going for hypnotic regressions for two years."

He just looked at me a while and then asked, "Aside from that, how did you like the article?" What could I say?

During my daily meditations, many amazing things would come to me. Fragments like faces, symbols or just eyes. At other times, short scenes of a minute or less in duration would unfold. These tantalizing tidbits beckoned me to press on in my search for my true identity, or should I say my other selves—the many pieces that make up the whole. It is very important to stay in the present and not fall prey to the problems of the past life personage. Each life carries with it its own set of problems and lessons to learn. If one gets too involved with past lives, one runs the risk of being incapacitated in the present and is likely to fall short in this life's lessons and goals. I do not put a large amount of stock into what I receive during my meditations, unless they are reinforced or validated in some way. One recurring image was that of a soldier. The first time I came across him, he was crawling through leaves that were covering the ground. He carried a rifle with a very long tube on top. I took it to be a scope. It occurred to me that the leaves could be friend or foe—friend in the fact that they could conceal and foe because of the noise they make as one makes his way through them.

I have only had one auditory episode. It happened as I was parking my car at the grocery store. While waiting for someone to back out of a parking space, I noticed a car behind me waiting to park also. A short distance up the line another car was backing out of a space. I figured I would take the farthest one and let the car behind me have the space in which I originally intended to park. (This gives you an idea of where my mind was.) I pulled into the space and shut off the motor. Just then I heard one word—"Fusilier." It was a strong voice, emanating from behind me, over my left shoulder. I looked around but saw nothing. I surveyed the area around the car and found no one in the immediate vicinity of my car. The windows of the car were closed because of the weather. The voice had been loud and very clear, as if someone were calling to me. I rested my head on the steering wheel. What was going on? What was the meaning of this strange word? Later that day, I stopped at the Trumbull Library. In the Oxford Dictionary I found the word "fusilier." "Originally, a soldier armed with a fusil. (A light weight musket or fire-lock.) In the British Army, the designation of "Fusiliers" is still retained by certain regiments which are distinguished from the other regiments of the line only by wearing a kind of busby and by some small peculiarities of costume." Further down, it read: "All officers belonging to fusilier corps have two epaulets." Now the voice started to make sense. If someone had knowledge of British uniforms, upon approaching a fusilier from behind and seeing the two epaulets on his shoulders, all they had to do was call out "Fusilier!" If the person did not know the soldier's name or rank, but saw the double epaulets, he may do just that to get his attention.

Now I had a name for the crawling soldier of my meditation—not a proper name, but a regimental designation, Fusilier.

The Fusilier has played a prominent role in my meditations. His episodes were the longest in duration. I have kept a log and will recount them for you as they occurred.

First came short bursts, like flash cards, a diamond shape on an epaulet, brown uniform and the word "tam." Symbols and insignia like a small crown, torch and wings with a dark border around them, popped in and out of view (I would make drawings of these images). Other times, names like Gwendy (Gwendolyn?) Daily and Becky McCall would come to mind. Once, I found myself in the company of another man. We were on a hill, looking down on a city street through field glasses. The man I was with said a three-word phrase in French. I wrote the words down phonetically (I do not speak or write French). The man then handed me the glasses and through them, I could see two men walking down the street. I repeated this phrase to a local storekeeper, who was born in France. I asked, "What does it mean?" He said, "It sounds like you are saying 'the two passing,' as if you were talking about two people passing in the street." I was surprised for this went along with my vision perfectly.

There was a view of a large city, with a fire raging at its center, a huge column of smoke rising into the sky. All these were a prelude to small vignettes. It was remarkable how abruptly most of these started. As I lay on the couch one day, a very loud noise to my right caused me to jump. It was the sound of a very powerful airplane engine, popping and sputtering to life. The sound was then repeated to my left. I was standing in the middle of the fuselage of a plane, facing toward the front. Above me, I could see the head and shoulders of the pilot and copilot. Directly ahead of me, on the same level I could see the transparent nosecone, metal bracing running through it.

A short time later, there were bright flashes, possibly from bombs, because of the low level we were flying at, or maybe from flack exploding near the plane. It may even have been from both sources. I remember thinking, "I'm not part of the crew, they don't even know who I am or what I am. All they know is they are dropping me over Germany. I am going to France by way of Germany. I get the impression that the crew had been warned not to talk about me or the drop zone, even among themselves. To do so may cause them to spend the remainder of the war in a cell."

One day in a bookstore, I saw a book on WWII airplanes sitting on top of the bargain book pile. I skimmed through it. There, in a short section on bombers, was the plane I had seen in my meditation. The nose was just as I had drawn it after my meditation. It was a "Martin Marauder," a fighter-bomber. There was one large engine on each wing. The American forces primarily used them but I was to soon find that some were also used by the British.

Beautiful photos accompanied the story. The pictures were of the only flying Martin Marauder now in existence. I had to laugh when I read who owned it—The Confederate Air Force. The name on the plane also stood out to me—"Carolyn." One of John Gordon's daughters was named Caroline. The daughter that died in infancy, had she survived, was to be named Carolina.

The next in the Fusilier series of meditations brought forth a scene of two women. It was a lovely day, blue sky and no clouds. The woman nearest in my vision was wearing a large hat with a brim that curved down front and back. It had a domed top with a wide band encircling it. She wore a suit-type jacket with wide lapels and squared off shoulders, and carried a dark clutch purse under her right arm. Her outfit was finished off with a mid-calf length skirt and clunky looking high-heeled shoes. She had dark hair and was very pretty. The second woman had long blond hair, slightly curled. She had a nice figure and was wearing a light colored floral print dress. I couldn't make out her face because she was holding one hand over her eyes to shield them from the sun. Both appeared to be looking at something, an airplane. They were at an airfield. I get the impression they came to see me off, then the scene fades to black. I lay there on the couch quietly for a few minutes. All of a sudden, there is a pop, a loud rustling noise and a sudden jolt, all in rapid secession. I find myself looking up into a fully deployed parachute. It is night, but I can tell the chute is dark gray in color. I understand that it is this color so it won't be easily seen. Everything fades to black again.

The next thing I know, I am on the ground. I feel that the chute has been hidden or buried and there has been a change of clothes. I have a compass in my hand, it is open and there is a slit in the top. Using the slit, I sight in on a church steeple in the distance to get my bearings, the meditation ends.

Before starting my next meditation, I asked to know more about the Fusilier. Instead of a meditative state, I fell asleep. This is a risk you run when you put yourself into a relaxed state. Upon awakening, I heard the words, "He clung tenaciously to life." I took this to mean he did not survive the war. This would make sense because the Fusilier's lifetime was between Gordon's and my own, which leaves a period of only 43 years.

The Fusilier was not to reappear again for two months, but his reappearance was sudden and dramatic. I grabbed at the couch on either side of me to steady myself. I was now standing on the bow of a fast moving ship. The ship was cutting through the water like a knife. I was facing the stern. There was a gun turret at my level and above it, a bridge. I think "battleship?" The word "Korvette" pops into my head followed by a large, red letter "E." Something is very menacing and ominous about the "E." Walking to the side of this ship I gaze up and see some numbers painted on the side. Only seeing the top two thirds, it seems to be the number 113. When the meditation was over, I drew a picture of the ship, as I viewed it from the bow. The gun turret I saw had very dark areas on each side of the barrels where they move up and down. I talked to a firefighter who had been in the Navy. I asked him about Korvettes and he said that they are a type of destroyer escort used by the British Navy. He later produced a photo of a Canadian Korvette and it was just as I had drawn, dark lines on the gun turret and all. I then queried him about the menacing letter "E." He said, "Maybe you mean a E-boat." I asked, "What's that?" I was told it was the German equivalent of a PT boat. It seems that E-boats were given the duty of patrolling river and coastlines. I talked to my driver, Gene Maloney, who is well-versed on WWII subjects. From the things that I told him on the Fusilier's exploits, he said, "It sounds like he was SAS." SAS stands for Special Air Service, an elite commando unit of the British Army. All the meditations now made sense in light of what I had learned from the two firefighters.

What better way to carry a commando behind enemy lines than in a fast fighter-bomber under cover of a bombing run. Once the mission was complete, though, he needed some way to be extricated. The most logical scenario would be to make his way to the coast and meet a submarine or maybe a fast ship, like a destroyer escort. If leaving on board a Korvette, I doubt very much that they would enjoy running into a German E-boat. I know for a fact that such a run-in would prove unpleasant for the Fusilier. The last vision I had of him was short and intense. I was sitting next to another man on a narrow metal bench attached to the metal side of a ship (I took to be a Korvette.) Large rivets held the pieces of metal together. We were drinking coffee as the ship moved quickly through the water. There came the sound of bullets striking the side of the ship followed closely by reports of rapid gunfire. The pattern of bullets moved across the ship from my right where the other man sat and continued toward the bow of the ship. It all happened so fast that neither of us had a chance to move. My companion was struck and a millisecond later, I was hit. Both my hands went up and grabbed my left chest area as I was slammed back against the bulkhead. I turned my head to the right and saw the man next to me had been caught mid-swallow as a bullet struck him. I remember thinking that he shouldn't even bother to swallow as I watched his jaw slacken and the coffee run out of his mouth and down the front of his brown uniform. He slumped over dead. Our ship was making a sharp left hand turn as some of the crew members ran over to me and asked something to the effect of how badly was I hit. One man took my hands away from my chest. As I looked down, I saw a large hole in my left breast and heard a horrible sucking sound. All went black after that.

Many things have come to me during meditations, names of places like Glen Kerry, Cork and the University of Edinburgh. Strange things like leather helmets, breastplates and unusual saddles and stirrups. Once, I saw a beautiful black horse with a white diamond shaped blaze on its forehead. Another time, a shield of red with a white band at a forty-five degree angle across it. Inside the band there were three red Bottony Crosses (I later found out that this band is know as a "Bend Sinister.") Other visions brought forth a large black dog, a panther and a bird of prey landing right on my arm.

Once there was a very deep sounding horn that would send chills up my spine. Another time a very beautiful oriental woman with emerald green eyes and jet black hair (I call her the pearl because she was holding a large pearl between her thumb and forefinger.)

One meditation was very short; I could see date palms and sandy, rocky hills. Two words came to mind, "Dark Remembrance." That was the extent of it, I didn't press this one, the message had been clear.

Many of these experiences from my meditations would fall neatly into place. Sometimes, their arrangement (or alignment) would be supplied from books, at other times by people. I never knew where nor when it would happen, but I did know it was just a matter of time.

CHAPTER SEVEN

Psychic Insights

On a bright, sunny September morning, I picked up my daughter Samantha. We were spending the day together and I was not sure what we would do. While driving, Samantha spotted a sign for a psychic fair being held that very day. I asked if she would like to go and she said "sure." She had never attended a psychic fair before. The fair was held at the Westport Inn in a conference room on the lower level. After paying the admission, we read the schedule we had been given. There were lecturers on Astrology, Numerology, Dreams and so on. Under a heading "Today's Readers" was a list of names broken down into categories such as Clairvoyants, Tarot Cards, Past Lives and Palms. What you do is pick a name under the desired topic and then pay for a session with that person. The cost varies with the time one wishes to spend. I asked Samantha, "Who do you want to see?" She wasn't sure. I said, "Did you ever have your palm read?" She said, "No." So I paid for thirty minutes with a palm reader named Alberta.

A flier on one of the tables caught my eye. I had seen this ad before at a local bookstore. I had meant to write down the telephone number before leaving the store, but had forgotten. The ad was for a woman name Yvonne Smith. Yvonne is a clinical hypnotherapist, hypnologist, regression therapist and master hypnotist. Yvonne is also a member of the International Association of Counselors and Therapists and The National

Guild of Hypnotists. One of her areas of expertise is past lives. She lectures on the subject and does past life regressions. I was informed by the gentleman taking the money that Yvonne was booked up. While this attested to her popularity, it also ended my hopes of seeing her that day. I paid for a session with another psychic. This turned out to be uneventful for me. Psychics are like any other profession; some are good and some are not so good. Psychics can have bad days just like the rest of us, or they may not be able to tune in on the person sitting before them. Some deal with generalities while others can be frighteningly specific. Samantha had fared better on her maiden voyage into the world of the paranormal. As we walked across the parking lot, she was looking at her palm. "How do they do that, dad?" she asked. I said, "Do what?" She said, "How do they read the lines in your palm; who teaches them to do that?" I said, "I guess it may be a gift they have. What did she tell you?" Samantha explained how Alberta looked at her hands and said, "Your parents divorced about five years ago, when you were eleven years old." She also told her, "You broke up with your boy friend about three weeks ago and you have been together recently, but just as a friend." All this was right on the money. We drove through the beautiful autumn scenery. Every once in a while, I would catch Samantha glancing at the lines in her palms, a quizzical look furrowing her brow. I knew the feeling well.

A week later, there was another psychic fair in Danbury, Connecticut. I asked Samantha if she would like to go. She said yes and asked if she could bring her friend Lara. I was anxious to go because Yvonne Smith was to be there. Maybe this time I would get to talk to her. The three of us left early in the morning for the twenty-mile drive. I wanted to arrive, as close to starting time as possible so I would have a better chance for a sitting with Yvonne. We zipped along the winding country roads and arrived in time for me to make a triple appointment (three fifteen-minute slots running consecutively, for a total of forty-five minutes). I waited for my turn while the girls were off doing their own thing. The appointed time came and I walked over to Yvonne's table. I said, "I've finally caught up with you." She gave me a strange look. I explained how I had seen her advertisement and how I was unable to see her at the last fair. I said "You're all mine for the next 45 minutes" as I handed her the three tickets.

Yvonne sat with her hands on the table in front of her. She reminded me of one of Raphael's cherubs only with a large shock of blond hair and pendant earrings. I will tell you one thing, whether Yvonne was right on or not with what she told me, the time spent with her was well worth the money for the sheer entertainment value. Yvonne had a marvelous sense of humor. She asked me, "What would you like to know?" "Past lives, just past lives," I said. For the next 45 minutes that is exactly what I got. I told her a little about John Gordon, but that I was interested in other lives. She reached her hands across the table palms up. I placed my hands on top of hers. Yvonne closed her eyes and sat up straight in her chair. I asked, "Just how far back do I go?" There was only silence for a few seconds after my query, then she spoke one word, "Tribes." Again, there was silence. What followed next was a cast of characters that spanned years, centuries, and even millenniums. I did not have a tape recorder with me and it was impossible to take notes because Yvonne was holding my hands. Upon my return home, I wrote everything down. The following is, to the best of my recollection, the conversation that transpired between the two of us. When a long period of silence was finally broken, Yvonne spoke. "You're a strange one, you have been following family lines. You have been reincarnating very quickly, I see the longest period between the lines as one time of 100 years." One hundred years may seem like a long time here on earth, but in the big scheme of things it's less than a nanosecond. Yvonne said, "You had a powerful influence over people." Then she asked me if I studied history and I said, "Just recently, the Civil War period because of John Gordon." She said, "You might want to ask yourself why you're in Connecticut."

Yvonne said she saw an "oriental monk, a round little guy with a bald head." Another monk showed up only this time a "Franciscan" who lived in a "cloistered order." "He had not taken a vow of silence," she said. "He was tall and thin and enjoyed working in flower gardens." This, she said, was a "happy lifetime." (As I sat writing this last sentence, Anna walked over and put three flowers in front of me, one purple, one pink and another a pretty salmon color. I guess the monk lives on still.) Yvonne picked up something about Manchuria. "Many battles, many killed." I asked, "Was he Samurai?" She said, "Yes, a very ugly man with a big hair knot on top of his head." She went on to say, "He was close to the Emperor and the Emperor found him entertaining. When he was young, he was very cocky until some elders put him in his place." She told how he would put on tournaments and taught martial arts. From my meditations and other events in my life I was well aware of the Samurai. I was also aware of a woman from that time period that seemed to be out of his reach (a different class or something to that effect). I asked Yvonne "Do you see any women?" She said, "There were many women. There was one in particular but she was *forbidden."*

Yvonne picked up an Irish lifetime; A pert redheaded girl named Margaret (Peggy). A lifetime as a girl, it struck me odd until I thought about it a while. If we are here to learn lessons and grow, why would we be restricted to one gender? How could we possibly understand things like motherhood or childbirth unless we went through it ourselves? She said, "There was a lifetime in Atlantis; you were with a pretty woman with black hair." She told me that we were very devoted to each other. Yvonne sat quietly across from me. I started to ask her a question until she shushed me saying, "Quiet!" "I'm into some X-rated stuff and I don't get out to the movies often." She was smiling a big smile as she sat with closed eyelids. Well, I was glad she was enjoying herself, but I was starting to get the feeling that maybe she should be paying me.

The next person to show himself was from the 1700s, a barrister. This barrister, she said, was friends with George Washington and Benjamin Franklin. "He had pushed Washington towards the presidency. He knew Franklin very well, all his affairs and projects." She said, "He's mentioned in one of

Franklin's diaries." I asked her if she got the name of any town or city and she replied "Jamestown." Yvonne went on to tell of his death. " He was murdered on the docks. It was not a planned killing but rather like a robbery. He was stabbed in the back." I said, "Where exactly in the back was he stabbed?" As Yvonne replied, I mouthed the exact same words, "Right between the shoulder blades." Now when someone links you in history with two heavyweights like Washington and Franklin, you should take it with more than a grain of salt. I did, but curiously, some things struck home. (1.) Several times, for no apparent reason, a sharp pain between my shoulder blades has taken my breath away. (2.) I have in my possession a large copper button with the inscription, "MEMORABLE ERA MARCH THE FOURTH 1789." The button is from Washington's inauguration in New York City in 1789. (3.) The button had belonged to my Grandmother, Grace Keene. It was given to my mother after my grandmother's death. My mother gave the button to me after my father passed on. My grandmother, Grace, was my grandfather's second wife and they married in their later years. Her maiden name was Burr, one of her relatives being Aaron Burr who killed Alexander Hamilton in the famous duel. For all I know, this button could have belonged to him.

I asked Yvonne if she could tell me anything about my most recent past life. I was surprised by her answer, although I should not have been. She said, "He's a British soldier." Then Yvonne talked as if to herself. "They're in Egypt, what are they doing in Egypt? It's a training camp of some sort." At this point, I asked if he was possibly a sniper. She said, "No, he is more like a spy; he's young, intelligent and very good with things like codes."

Yvonne sat for over half an hour and never opened her eyes. She said, "You have been mourned by many presidents." Something I had read came to mind; it was a telegram of condolence sent to the Gordon family. It read:

"I was greatly shocked and grieved at the report of General Gordon's death. I had the honor to number him among my personal friends and to have entertained him at my house. A more gallant, generous and fearless gentleman and soldier has not been seen by our country."[44] The telegram was signed: Theodore Roosevelt.

Of all the stories of past lives told to me that day, the next one hit me the hardest. Yvonne started with, "You were a Druid, a Druid priest; there was a forest fire." She had no sooner gotten the words "forest fire" out than tears started to fill my eyes. We were still holding hands, so there was no way to wipe them away. The story went on. "The Romans had set the fire to drive the Druids out from a sacred forest that they lived in." She said, "I can see you standing there crying. You know magic but are powerless to stop the fire. You lose many of your family and friends. You make a vow to pay back the enemy; but there aren't any Romans around any more." I said, "There's still fire around; do you know where I work?" She said, "No." I said, "The fire department." Yvonne laughed and said, "Well, maybe that has something to do with it." Our time together was over, but before leaving, I put five or six photos of friends and family on the table in front of her. Yvonne picked up a picture of Anna and started laughing and pointing to it. She said, "This is her, this is the woman from the Atlantis lifetime!" I smiled and said, "Well some things never change." I thought it really strange, the way the Druid story had affected me so emotionally. A couple of days later, I was sitting on the couch watching television, when a picture popped into my head. I went to the closet and dug through a bunch of old photos. I was looking for a black and white Polaroid of an oil painting I had done more than twenty-five years before.

When I was stationed in Florida in the 1960s, my mother sent my oil paints to me. Most of my paintings were landscapes, seascapes or still life. However there was one that did not fall into any of these categories. I developed the painting out of my head. I did not know where I got the idea or why I painted it. I did not like it after I finished it, and for some strange reason it bothered me to look at it. I don't know what ultimately happened to the painting; I left it behind hanging on the barracks wall when I shipped out to Orlando Air Force Base in Florida. I knew I had a Polaroid photo of it, but I was unable to find it.

Because of Yvonne, I now believe I know why I painted it and from where the idea sprang. It was a large painting, about 24 inches by 30 inches. The background was just a mass of flames. Suspended in the middle of the painting was a skull with the mouth wide open as if screaming (I guess you could say it was not a pretty picture). The most amazing thing was what the skull was wearing a helmet—a *Roman* helmet.

At work a short time later, Gene Maloney brought in a book for me to look at. It was the Lancer Militaria Winter Catalog, which was full of patches and insignias of armed forces from around the world. On a page dedicated to Britain, I came across a pair of wings with a parachute in the center. This emblem had a very thick, dark border around it, almost identical to the one I had drawn from meditation. These were British Paratrooper wings. At the back of the catalog was a section on books. A book titled *The Special Air Service* had a small write up that told of the book's contents. It's a story of "The world's most elite special unit." A concise history of the SAS starting from "Egypt in 1941." I flashed back to my visit with Yvonne and another puzzle piece fell into place. THE SAS TRAINED IN *EGYPT!*

I like having at least three different sources for validation or verification on things dealing with past lives. I had received many impressions from the Fusilier's lifetime; Yvonne had also picked up on it. The third verification came from psychic Reverend Michelle Wojcik. I posed the same question to Michelle that I had to Yvonne. "Can you tell me about the most recent past life?" Keep in mind that Michelle had no prior knowledge of my Fusilier. Michelle sat quietly with her eyes closed. She said, "I see brown all around. You are dressed in brown." Then she said, "There are all different colors." As she said this, she moved her right hand back and forth across her blouse just below her left shoulder. I asked, "Are you talking about ribbons on a uniform?" She said, "Yes, he's a soldier, a *British* soldier." My third confirmation on the Samurai was to come from an extraordinary source and in a most astonishing way.

The place was a Border's bookstore in Stamford, Connecticut. My wife and I went to the store to wait for a friend. Anna roamed the cookbook section while I hovered around the history books. A man and woman with a young boy of around five or six talked near by. It seemed that the man wanted the woman to keep the boy occupied so he could browse in leisure. The lady found a big book on airplanes and placed it on the floor for the boy to view. They sat on the floor turning pages while the lad made airplane sounds. I watched the boy as he sat crossed-legged on the carpet. He was a cute little guy. Suddenly he snapped his head up from the book. He was about five feet away and facing me. He was looking at me as if he were seeing through me. Silently he sat; his face set with an expression of deep thought. A few moments passed and then he spoke, one word, clearly, "Samurai." The woman asked him, "What did you say?" "Samurai," he replied with the same unblinking, thoughtful look.

A tingling sensation scampered up my spine. He had pronounced the word correctly, which I found odd for a child of his age. The woman asked, "Where do you see that?" He said "Nowhere. What is it?" The woman told him, "It's a sword." I could not hold myself back; I piped in and explained to them that a Samurai was a person and that they carried swords.

They returned to the airplane book. I looked around and could not see anything in the boy's line of vision that pertained to a Samurai; even if it had been spelled out in big block letters, I don't believe he could have read or pronounced it. The boy sat making gun noises while looking at the airplane books. I asked if they would like to hear a story. They said yes. I told them about finding the piece of cannonball at Spotsylvania. In a book I was holding there was a map of the Spotsylvania Battlefield, and I showed it to them.

I explained about the fierce fighting that took place there and the many lives that were lost. The boy's face grew sad. I wanted to show him the flip side of the story. I hope when it comes to things like war, he will look at it from more than one angle. They thanked me and returned to their book. As I stood there gazing at this small child, I smiled inwardly, for I knew what had just happened. When that boy looked up from his book, this young soul, yet untarnished and unencumbered by life, had been alerted to another soul nearby. Much like an animal sniffing in the air, he had honed in on me and picked up something from my past—a past that had been spent on a beautiful island called Japan.

At this time in my writing, I have tapered off on meditating for the purpose of obtaining information on past lives. There are several reasons for this. I would prefer to find hard facts and information of Gordon from books, photographs and assorted libraries. Another reason for the slowdown was that strange things started to happen once I opened myself up to my inner (or higher) self. It can become a case of getting too much of what is asked for. I was starting to have more psychic experiences.

It seems that I would, on occasion, pick up songs from others around me. One morning, in the kitchen at the Fire Headquarters, I stood buttering a bagel. It does not take much brainpower to butter a bagel, so my mind wandered off. Lieutenant Christopher Ackley was a few feet away washing some breakfast dishes. As I worked on my bagel, I was singing. The song was "Santa Claus is Coming to Town," a well-known tune but these unusual factors enter here:

It was the middle of summer.

I was imitating Leon Redbone (who has a very distinct voice and singing style).

I was not fully conscious of what I was doing.

Lieutenant Ackley said, "Do you like that song? I said "What song?" He said, "The one you were just singing, 'Santa Claus is Coming to Town' by Leon Redbone." I looked at him and said, "There is such a song?" He said, "Yeah! I was playing it on my tape player in my truck on the way to work this morning!" I hadn't been aware of this song until that morning. I found this strange but didn't give it much more thought until I had similar experiences.

On a trip to Vermont, Anna and I stopped at the King Arthur Flour Company store in Norwich, Vermont. Anna is a bread-baking nut—square, round, big, little, potato, and banana; she loves making them all. It was only natural then, while traveling through Vermont, we stop at one of her favorite suppliers. There were enough baking items there to give the Pillsbury Doughboy an apoplexy. I leaned against the cash register as Anna scooted back and forth, piling things on the counter like a supermarket sweepstakes winner. As I stood there, my brain drifted off and I started humming a song from Pinocchio called, "Got No Strings on Me." I heard someone say, "Thanks a lot." I looked at the girl behind the counter and said, "Excuse me?" She repeated what she had said and then elaborated. "Thanks a lot. I've been trying to get that song out of my head for three days and you stand there humming it." I said, "Well, I must have gotten it from you, so don't blame me."

Probably the strangest incident of this unasked for ability to pick up other's songs was one that transpired between firefighter Lisa Ruot and myself. Lisa is the only female firefighter on the department and is assigned to my platoon. Lisa is a diminutive brunette with a broad smile and an impish twinkle in her eyes. She is affectionately referred to as The Babayaga. She brought this nickname upon herself by using the phrase one-day. When asked what it meant, she explained it's a Russian witch and that they ride on houses instead of broomsticks.

Every once in a while, I would sing an old song called Pony Boy and do it with a Jewish accent, as I travel through Fire Headquarters. On one of these occasions, Lisa stopped me and asked, "How come whenever I'm thinking of my Grandfather you sing that song?" I asked, "Did he like that song?" She said, "Yes, he would sing it to me when I was a little girl." I asked her if he was Jewish and deceased. The reply was "Yes" to both. I asked her if she liked him, and she said she adored him. I said, "Well, I guess he's still around you." I walked away, leaving Lisa to muse.

These occurrences proved to me that I was receiving these songs externally. There could be no other explanation. The songs are not top forty hits. With the imitation of Leon Redbone in one case and a Jewish accent in another, what other conclusion could I come to? My favorite story of the three is the one about Lisa, because at that time I had been allowed to share a *true* love song from the past.

CHAPTER EIGHT

On the Road Again

My mother had returned to Connecticut to attend the funeral of her sister, Florence. I was glad to see her again, but not under these circumstances. When it came time for her to return home, I made arrangements to drive down and meet my sister, Joy, at Roanoke, Virginia, where I would transfer my mother to her care for the remainder of her trip to Georgia. Whenever possible, I timed my trips South so that I would reach Winchester, Virginia, at the end of the first day of driving. I stop here because I love to watch the sunrises in the Shenandoah Valley. In the predawn darkness of the mornings, I slip off and get a cup of coffee. With coffee in hand, I sit and watch the night gently fade away as the sun comes up over the Blue Ridge Mountains. The light gray fog rises like a large velvet blanket from the bed of the valley. If you sit there for a while at that time of day, it is not hard to imagine the sound of wagon wheels and horse hooves plodding along the old macadamized Valley Pike. If you have the ears for it, you may also hear a faint sound, a sound much like the low rumbling of distant thunder. Strain your ears a little more, and you could possibly pick up the rhythmic footfalls of thousands of men marching to war.

Just south of Winchester, we made a quick stop at the Opequon Church. During the second battle of Kernstown, July 24, 1864, Gordon's troops pushed the Union soldiers back past this church and through the small cemetery. Many of his men had fought on the same ground two years earlier under Thomas "Stonewall" Jackson. The small stone church, with its white steeple, invites picture taking, so I obliged. Confederate General Jubal Early pressed his army northward driving the Union army out of the valley. General Ulysses S. Grant, after taking charge, replaced many of the Union commanders and returned the Sixth and Nineteenth Corps to the valley. All operations in the valley were put under the command of Major General Philip Sheridan. This marked the beginning of the end for the Shenandoah as a travel route north for the Confederates and as a granary for their people.

Traveling a little farther south, Belle Grove came into view. Belle Grove is a beautiful mansion that was used as General Sheridan's headquarters before and after the battle of Cedar Creek. The area around the house was the scene of some of the heaviest fighting. The battle of Cedar Creek was one of the biggest turnabouts in military history.

The Confederates had come to a point where a decision had to be made either to attack Sheridan or leave the valley. General Early sent General Gordon, Major Jed Hotchkiss, Brigadier General Clement Evans and Major Robert Hunter to Signal Knob, a signal station on top of Massanutten Mountain. From 2,000 feet above Cedar Creek, they had an excellent view of Sheridan's army. Breastworks, cannon positions and even the color of the piping on the soldier's uniforms could be clearly seen (the color of piping is an indication of what type of unit, infantry, artillery or cavalry the men belong to). Hotchkiss made a map, and he and Gordon formed a plan of attack that they would present to General Early.

The plan consisted of night marches to get into position for an early morning attack by four converging columns. Hotchkiss and Gordon scouted a path that would take them around the base of Massanutten Mountain. This route would bring Gordon's men to a point where the assault could be launched on Sheridan's weakly protected eastern flank. The trail, at some points, would have to be traversed in single file, but they felt it could be done. Early approved the plan, and on the night of

October 18, 1864, the men started for their positions of attack. All nonessential items would be left behind to avoid making any noise that might alert the enemy. Surprise was a key ingredient of the plan. The officers synchronized their watches and made ready for the attack that would start at 5:00 am, October 19, 1864. At the appointed hour, the Confederates splashed across the north fork of the Shenandoah River and Cedar Creek. Rising up out of the morning fog, they caught the Federals completely off guard. The fortifications were taken and the Union soldiers were pushed back toward the town of Middletown. Just a month earlier, the Confederates had been chased up the valley after the third battle of Winchester; now it was their turn to push back.

Back the Federals went, past Belle Grove and through Middletown. Only a portion of the Sixth Corps held its ground, just north of Middletown. Gordon ordered his men to strike the Sixth Corps in front and both flanks simultaneously. He then called upon Colonel Thomas H. Carter to use all the batteries available and bring them to bear on this stubborn pocket of resistance, while his men made their assault. Carter, after surveying the position of Sheridan's men, made this reply to Gordon, "General, you will need no infantry. With enfilade fire from my batteries, I will destroy that corps in twenty minutes." It was at this time that General Early rode to Gordon and exclaimed, "Well, Gordon, this is glory enough for one day. This is the 19th. Precisely, one month ago today, we were going in the opposite direction." Gordon said, "It is very well so far, General, but we have one more blow to strike, and then there will not be left an organized company of infantry in Sheridan's army."

Gordon explained to General Early the plan that was being put into effect and the likely outcome of the attack. Early said, "No use in that; they will all go directly." Gordon then replied "That is the Sixth Corps, General. It will not go unless we drive it from the field." Early said, "Yes, it will go too, directly." Gordon writes, "My heart went into my boots. Visions of the fatal halt on the first day at Gettysburg, and the whole day's hesitation to permit an assault on Grant's exposed flank on the 6th of May in the Wilderness, rose before me. And so it came to pass that the fatal halting, the hesitation, the spasmodic firing, and the isolated movements in the face of the sullen, slow, and orderly retreat of this superb Federal corps, lost us the great opportunity, and converted the brilliant victory of the morning into disastrous defeat in the evening."[45]

Gordon's planned attack did not take place and what followed was what Gordon called the "fatal halting." Hours passed and with that passage of time, the absent commander, Gen. Sheridan returned. Sheridan had been in Washington for a meeting, and while returning, stopped at Winchester for the night. On the morning of October 19, he rode back toward Belle Grove, only to meet his army retreating along the valley pike. He gave orders to his officers to halt the men and turn them about. He galloped on his now famous ride back towards Cedar Creek. Shouting encouragement to his men, he arrived in time to turn his corps, once more, into the fighting force they had been. A smashing counter attack by Sheridan drove the Confederates back over the ground they had won that morning.

Gone was the ground the Confederates had fought for; gone also were the supplies and artillery they had captured. Worst of all, gone were many irreplaceable southern soldiers, either killed, wounded or captured. Major General Ramseur, mortally wounded, was taken to Belle Grove where Union classmates from West Point sat with him and gave him comfort until the end came. Gordon writes of his own narrow escape.

> In the dim starlight, after crossing the creek, I gathered around me a small force representing nearly every command in Early's army, intending to check, if possible, to enable the shattered and rapidly retreating fragments to escape. The brave fellows responded to my call and formed a line across the pike. The effort was utterly fruitless, however, and resulted only in hair-breadth escapes and unexampled experiences. It has never been settled whether, in escaping from the British dragoons under Tryon, General Israel Putnam rode or rolled or slid down the precipice at Horse Neck in 1779; but whichever method of escape he adopted, I can "go him two better," as the sportsmen say, for I did all three at Cedar Creek, eighty-five years later, in escaping from American dragoons under Philip Sheridan. At the point where I attempted to make a stand at

> night, the pike ran immediately on the edge of one of those abrupt and rugged limestone cliffs down which it was supposed not even a rabbit could plunge without breaking his neck; and I proved it to be nearly true. One end of my short line of gray-jackets rested on the pike at this forbidding precipice. I had scarcely gotten my men in position when I discovered that Sheridan's dragoons had crossed the creek higher up, and that I was surrounded by them on three sides, while on the other was this breakneck escarpment. These enterprising horsemen in search of their game had located my little band, and at the sound of the bugle they came in headlong charge. Only one volley from my men and the Federal cavalry were upon them. Realizing that our capture was imminent, I shouted to my men to escape if possible, into the darkness. One minute more and I should have had a Yankee carbine at my head, inviting my surrender. The alternatives were the precipice or Yankee prison. There was no time to debate the question, not a moment. Wheeling my horse to the dismal brink, I drove my spurs into his flanks, and he plunged downward and tumbled headlong in one direction, sending me in another. How I reached the bottom of the abyss I shall never know; for I was rendered temporarily unconscious. Strangely enough, I was only stunned and in no way seriously hurt. My horse too, though bruised, was not disabled. For a moment, I thought he was dead, for he lay motionless and prone at full length. However, he promptly responded to my call and rose to his feet; and although the bare places on his head and hips showed that he had been hurt, he was ready without a groan to bear me again in any direction I might wish to go. The question was, which way to go. I was alone in the dark wooded glen—that is, my faithful horse was the only comrade and friend near enough to aid me.[46]

Gordon worked his way back to Fisher's Hill to meet up with the remnants of the Southern forces; the long day of fighting was over. If the Confederate victory had been sustained, it may have caused a different result at the polls for Lincoln. A loss for Lincoln to one of his past Commanders, George B. McClellan (who was running on a peace platform), would have most likely brought both North and South together for an end to the hostilities and an equitable settlement. This did not occur and Cedar Creek stands as another case of what might have been.

I found it odd that Gordon should mention General Putnam. A little over twelve miles from my home in Connecticut is Israel Putnam Memorial State Park. This park commemorates the winter encampment of 1778-1779 of Major General Israel Putnam's Continental army troops. I took a ride to the park. At the main entrance stands a statue of Putnam on horseback. The horse is at a severe downward angle, Putnam leaning backward with left arm raised, as if shaking his fist in defiance at his pursuers. The metal tablet on the base reads:

ISRAEL PUTNAM

> Senior Major General in the Continental army when at Greenwich, Connecticut, in February of 1779, made good a dramatic mounted escape from pursuing British Dragoons down the perilous 100 Stone steps carved into the precipice at Horse Neck.

I have visited what is left of the "100 Steps" in Greenwich, Connecticut. The majority of them were covered over by the construction of Rt. #1. They are not much to look at now, but at the time of Putnam's ride they must have been a daunting obstacle.

Continuing our drive south, we stopped at New Market, for a visit to the New Market Battlefield Museum. The museum is located on part of the old battlefield. This museum houses the best collection of military artifacts I have ever seen. It covers items dating from the Revolutionary War through Operation Desert Storm. Further south, we stopped at Lexington, Virginia, home of Washington and Lee College. General Lee became president of the school after the war and the small chapel on campus is his final resting-place. Inside the chapel is a life-size recumbent statue of Gen. Lee created by Edward Valentine, a noted Richmond sculptor. Lee is portrayed in full uniform at rest on a cot in his headquarters tent. In each corner of the room hangs a Confederate battleflag that had been returned to the South long after its surrender at Appomattox Courthouse. Downstairs under this statue are the burial vaults and Gen. Lee's studies. Just outside the chapel are buried the remains of the General's famous horse "Traveler."

Upon meeting up with my sister Joy at Roanoke, Virginia, we checked into our hotel rooms. While unpacking, Joy reached into her suitcase and handed me something with the comment, "Happy Birthday." Looking down at the object, now in my right hand, it took me a moment to realize what it was. Metal, green with age and an engraved pattern covering the surface. The watchback! She had stopped on the way up and bought the watchback from the man who had found it. I got my magnifying glass and checked the inside and sure enough there were the two letters, J.G. I also checked and found the manufacturer's markings. I thought over why J.G. would be stamped into the watchback when most watches are engraved on the front inside cover. Then it hit me. When watch repairmen work on watches, they need to remove the back to get at the inner-workings. It made sense that in that era, when many pocket-watches were in fashion, the repairmen would need some system of identification for all the loose watchbacks lying around. Why not mark the back with the owner's initials? The main body of a watch could be easily tagged, but not so with the back. By checking the initials in an errant watchback, it could be simply matched with the owner's name on the tag affixed to the watch. I cleaned the watchback ever so slightly and placed it in my suitcase.

Before their return South and my return North, we all paid a visit to Appomattox Court House. I separated from them in order to be alone. Once again, I stood at the surrender triangle near the Peers House. My thoughts drifted back to that day in April 1865. It was an ending, but at the same time a beginning—a new nation that would stand as a model to others. I strolled back through the village to the other side of the town, up a gradual rise to the top of a small hill. Under the shade of some trees was a small cemetery, in it, the graves of eighteen Confederates and one Union soldier. The small gray stones showed signs of age. Weather-beaten, with cracks marring their surface, they stood as a monument to the last battle of the Army of Northern Virginia. Did these men, now interred here, know that they would be some of the last to die for their cause?

It was to this area that General Lee sent Colonel Charles S. Venable to find General Gordon and ascertain from him what progress was being made on this front. Gordon's reply to Col.

Venable was, "Tell General Lee that my command has been fought to a frazzle, and unless Longstreet can unite in the movement, or prevent these forces from coming upon my rear, I cannot long go forward."[47] General Lee, upon receiving this message is reported to have said, "There is nothing left me but to go and see General Grant, and I had rather die a thousand deaths." For The Army of Northern Virginia, the end had come; their struggle was over.

Back in the village, I caught up with my family members. We went to the second floor of the courthouse to take in the slide show that I had missed on my first visit to Appomattox. It was an emotionally moving presentation and I had all I could do to remain through the entire program. Sometimes, I am hit with what amounts to a combination of pride and sorrow for the men of both armies. In my case, it is literally heartfelt.

We all walked to the parking lot, and after hugs and kisses all around, we headed in opposite directions.

I backtracked over Lee's retreat route and shortly found myself standing in front of the Hillman House overlooking Sayler's Creek. On April 6, 1865, Union battle lines were formed around this house and artillery was set up in the yard to fire upon the retreating Confederates under General Ewell. A fierce battle ensued and when it was over, General Lee had lost a large portion of his already depleted army. Hillman House was used as hospital to aid the many wounded and remains today much as it was during the battle.

I have been told by a member of a rescue company in nearby Farmville, that mysterious lights have been seen inside Hillman House. These occurrences happen late at night, after the house has been locked up for the day. To add to the mystery, the house has never had electricity added. The same young man told me that more than once the rescue squad has responded to cars running off the road in the area of Hillman House, the drivers blaming the accident on a Confederate soldier standing in the middle of the road.

I drove off to find Double Bridge. I passed the Lockett House, pausing only long enough to take a picture, then continued down the hill to Double Bridge. The crossing gets its name from the fact that it is at this point that Sayler's Creek and Little Sayler's Creek merge. The wagon train that Gordon's men had been protecting bogged down in this swampy area. Gordon's men formed near the Lockett House to fight back the approaching Union army. After twice repulsing attacks, the men were forced to abandon the wagons and scatter across Sayler's Creek.

Driving on, I passed a sign for High Bridge. There were two bridges used by the Confederates to cross the Appomattox River at this point. One a tall railroad trestle, the other a small wagon bridge. Failure to completely destroy these two structures after crossing allowed Federal troops to forge the river and attack Lee's army from the rear. As I headed to my next destination, Spotsylvania Court House, I thought about all the back roads I had covered along Lee's retreat route. Some of these roads are yet unpaved. It is hard to imagine walking, let alone fighting, all the way from Richmond and Petersburg. This woeful trek stands as a reminder of the fortitude and courage displayed by the southern soldiers.

As I entered Spotsylvania Court House Battlefield the sun was edging down over the western horizon. I parked my car in the center of the Mule Shoe near the remains of the McCool House. As I grabbed my camera and exited the car, two deer popped up out of the tall grass nearby. My back was to the West, and as we gazed at each other, the setting sun illuminated their forms. The deer stood in the spot from which they had arisen, ears twitching, big brown eyes casting a questioning look in my direction. We remained motionless, time slowed, and what seemed like an hour was in reality only minutes. The deer, satisfied that I posed no threat, slowly walked off into the woods. I have a special affection for this battlefield. It always seems to know when I'm there and never fails to give me a gift of one sort or another. I had one last shot left in my camera and took a picture of the sunset. I now wish I had taken a picture of the deer, for I found that photos shot directly into the sun do not turn out so well. Seeing the deer reminded me of a most charming story I had read. It was written by John H. Worsham, a Confederate soldier who, at this very spot near the McCool House, had been an eyewitness to the "Lee to the Rear" episode. The story he tells happened a few days after the terrible battle of May 12th and stands in stark contrast to that battle.

> We remained in the rear until the morning of the 15th. We found in the middle of our camp, in the open field, an old hare's bed containing four little ones, the old mammy having run away on our approach! I do not know that I ever saw men more solicitous for the welfare of anything than were those grizzly warriors for those little bunnies. It was raining, and some wanted to make a house over them, others wanted to hold their oilcloths over them, no one was allowed to touch them, one might look as much as one chose, but hands off! When we left it was a sad parting.[48]

I drove to Fredericksburg where I spent the night. I had a leisurely breakfast and passed some time wandering around the area. I stopped at Marye's Heights, Salem Church and The Wilderness. I was waiting for Stars and Bars Military Antiques to open. This was the store I had visited on the earlier trip with my mother. As I entered the store, a familiar face looked up from behind the counter. The woman recognized me because she said "I remember you, you're the one who told me about the cannonball!" She continued, "Now I have a story to tell you!" She proceeded to tell of her walk down a road at a famous battlefield. "All of a sudden, for some unknown reason, I stopped and looked down, and there, right on top of the road was a mini ball." I laughed and said, "See, that mini ball was just laying there waiting for you." We talked a while and this time when I left, the Federal breastplate I couldn't afford on my first visit was now heading north with me. Upon arriving home, the breastplate and watchback took their places in my ever-growing trays of cherished mementos.

CHAPTER NINE

Gettysburg and Beyond

STRANGE AND WONDERFUL THINGS HAPPEN when I travel. I am forever making new discoveries. Gettysburg has been a treasure-trove of information and revelations. I have traveled there many times with family and alone. My oldest daughter, Shannon, attended Dickinson College in Carlisle, Pennsylvania with a desire to become a lawyer. Dickinson College is just thirty miles north of Gettysburg. I came across an interesting bit of history on General Gordon's family.

> After his father's death, Zachariah Herndon Gordon, the father of John B. Gordon worked so his brothers could finish college. Wiley and Charles P. were away studying at Dickinson College at Carlisle, Pennsylvania. Charles P. Gordon became not only a prominent lawyer, but a leader in civic and political affairs of the state of Georgia.[49]

It was sibling weekend at Dickinson College and I said I would bring my other daughter, Samantha, down to stay with her sister. I planned on dropping her off and then driving to Gettysburg to do some more research. Upon arrival at the school, I found that it was my two daughters' plan to have Dad entertain them for the entire weekend. The next morning, the three of us headed south to Gettysburg. We stopped to see the Electric Map program at the Gettysburg Battlefield Visitor

Center. The Electric Map gives a presentation of the famous three-day battle by using lights installed in a huge topographical map of the Gettysburg area. During the narration, they told a story about General Gordon asking Lieutenant Colonel H.P. Jones to bring some artillery to bear on an officer on horseback on Barlows Knoll. The officer was 19-year-old Lt. Bayard Wilkeson and his union cannons were wreaking havoc among the Confederates. A cannonball struck Wilkeson killing his horse and almost severing his right leg. The story went on to explain that young Wilkeson completed the amputation with a pocketknife but later died from loss of blood.

Almost in unison, my daughters turned to me and said, "Daaaadd!" What could I say; I just shrugged my shoulders and put on the face of a child with his hand caught in the cookie jar.

We visited a wonderful store called The Horse Soldier. It was filled with books, maps, photos and all sorts of Civil War memorabilia. To give myself some time alone, I sent Shannon and Samantha on a mission to find a magazine, an issue of the Civil War Time from May 1985. There was an article on Gordon in this particular issue and I had searched for almost two years, without success in finding it. Thirty seconds later, there was a tap on my shoulder. I turned to see two Cheshire Cat grins and the magazine that I had looked for so long. An old saying came to mind, "The best laid plans of mice and men...."

That evening, we drove east to Wrightsville. This was where Gordon and his men had been stopped from crossing the Susquehanna River by the burning of the bridge. Two markers, one in town and the other at the edge of the river simply stated that this was the farthest east the Army of Northern Virginia ever traveled. After viewing these signposts of history, I was surprised there was no mention of Gordon's men saving the town from flames. It would not be until many years later that I would find a local story of the Confederates arresting the flames in Wrightsville. I found a regional account of the burning of the bridge that day in a booklet printed for the celebration of the Columbia Civil War Centennial (1863-1963):

Some quarter of an hour passed, and a column of smoke, at first barely detectable, then rapidly growing and traveling downwind made it apparent to all that the bridge was afire. In minutes the group who had entered with their task of destruction appeared, and soon the word passed rapidly through the crowd. They set it on fire. The link between eastern and western shore was now blocked by a wall of flame which spread rapidly, more rapidly toward the Wrightsville side for a fairly strong northwest wind carried the flames in the direction of that town.

Now the fire increased in intensity and spread toward the Columbia end, sending huge billows of smoke swirling downstream and high in the air, making visibility of the west shore difficult owing to the smoke pall that swept low over the stream. The roar of the flames grew louder as the fire swept eastward, and the town of Columbia mustered the firemen and their engines to guard against spread of the flames to river shore structures and thence to Front Street, and perhaps to the remainder of the town with a resulting general conflagration.

Wrightsville, now occupied by the Confederate forces, did not fare so well. The wind, as previously mentioned, was from the northwest driving the flames diagonally downstream in the direction of the town. Several structures adjacent to river and bridge end took fire almost simultaneously, the flames spreading rapidly. The situation looked very serious from the onset. General Gordon, however, ordered two regiments of his men to form bucket brigades from the river; and with the help of a small hand pumper from the town, the flames were prevented from spreading generally throughout the houses of the small community. This gracious act was long remembered by the citizens, who realized that their town had been spared through the efforts of the enemy at the orders of their Commander.

I started to drive back in the direction of Gettysburg. Shannon piped up and said, "Don't you want to go across the bridge?" From the back seat Samantha added, "Yeah! Don't you want to get to the other side ***this time***?" I thought for a very short moment and then said, "Yes, yes I do." Swinging the car around we headed across the river to Columbia on the far side. Driving back across this modern bridge of concrete and steel, I checked the odometer to see just how long it was. Over one mile of bridge spans the river between the two towns. What a sight it must have been in 1863 to see that large wooden bridge become engulfed in flames and disappear into the river. Crossing the river had given me what appeared to be a belated feeling of satisfaction and I relished it as we traveled back to Gettysburg.

For me, the first day of the battle of Gettysburg, July 1, 1863 is very poignant. There are three reasons for this:

First, it is the third and final of my tales of what might have been.

The second reason involves a story of General Gordon's conduct that day.

Lastly, it brings some of my relatives into play.

On that hot July 1, 1863, Lee's Army of Northern Virginia and Meade's Army of the Potomac were engaged in heavy fighting West and North of the little town of Gettysburg. General Early's division arrived on the field of battle on the afternoon of the first. Their arrival was one of those instances of being in the right place at the right time. The right flank of the Union army (11th Corps) was on a knoll overlooking Rock Creek.

Early's men were in a perfect position to execute an attack on the exposed Union flank. At approximately 3:15 P.M., Gordon's Brigade was ordered to launch their attack. The Confederates succeeded in pushing the Union troops back through the town and up onto Culp's Hill and Cemetery Ridge. This is where they remained. The successful route of the Union troops was not followed up. The army of the Potomac retained the high ground and the rest was literally history. There have been many theories attaching blame to many different people. Had the momentum of the first days' battle been pushed up to and over Cemetery Ridge, the outcome may have been disastrous for the Union. This event, or should we say lack of action, has been debated, studied and dissected for more than a century. Most likely it will continue ad infinitum.

In command on the small knoll that now bears his name, was Union Brigadier General Francis Channing Barlow. It was Barlow's men who bore the brunt of Gordon's brigade attack. The Gordon/Barlow story of Gettysburg is one of the most endearing stories to come out of the War Between the States. Through one of those quirks of fate, I stumbled onto a book. The title: *Blood Is Thicker Than Water: A Few Days Among Our Southern Brethren.* The book was written in 1886 by Henry M. Field, DD (Years later Gen. Gordon and Mr. Fields would co-introduce Mrs. Jackson's book on her late husband, Stonewall Jackson). Mr. Fields, a Presbyterian minister, describes his travels in the South with companions that nowadays would be described as "Movers and Shakers": Mr. John H. Inman and Mr. Cornelius N. Bliss, both cotton merchants; Mr. J.A. Bostwick one of the founders of the Standard Oil Company; Mr. H.O. Armour of Armour foods; Mr. Thomas Rutter and Mr. Harles H. Bosher, both railroad directors with the Louisville and Nashville Railroad. While in Atlanta, Georgia, they were treated royally and given a wonderful dinner reception. Attendees of the dinner included the Mayor of Atlanta, the Governor of Georgia and Henry Grady, Editor of the "Atlanta Constitution" (Grady, at the time, was a good friend of John B Gordon). During the evening's festivities, the speakers were being most kind to their northern visitors. Dr. Field seized the opportunity to convey a story of compassion on the battlefield. He leads into the story by speaking of General Grant's funeral in New York at which he represented the Presbyterians. The following is copied just as Dr. Field wrote it, even the italics are his:

> In the procession of that day rode a Southern officer, of whom (as his home is here in Atlanta) it seems not inappropriate to tell a story in harmony with the spirit of the hour. As it has been related to me by *both* the actors in the scene described, I can vouch for its literal accuracy. I give it as nearly as I can in the very words of that gallant soldier of Georgia, General John B. Gordon:
>
> "It was the first day of Gettysburg. The battle was in progress when I came into it with my division, and struck the Federal line at an angle, which caused it to break, doubling on itself, so that it was driven back in some disorder. As it was retreating, and our line advancing, in crossing a field I saw an officer lying on the ground, and dismounted to see if I could render him any assistance. Raising him up, the blood spurted from him, and I thought that he must be

mortally wounded. To my inquiry for his name, he answered that he was General Barlow of New York. I asked him if I could be of any service to him. He said 'No,' and told me to leave him and go and do my duty. But on my pressing the offer of assistance, he asked me to send word to his wife, who was in the rear of General Meade's army. I answered that I would not only send to her, but send *for* her. I called for bearers, who were coming on the field to pick up the wounded, to bring a stretcher. They took him up and carried him back to 'the branch' (the name given at the South to a stream), on which a camp hospital had been improvised; and I sent an aide with a flag of truce to the lines to forward the message to the wife of the wounded and, as I supposed, dying officer. The message reached its destination, although Mrs. Barlow was seventeen miles back from the front, and at two o'clock in the morning word was brought to me that she was at the lines. I sent word to have her immediately passed through, but bade the messenger tell her that her husband was 'desperately wounded.' I had no idea that she would find him alive.

The next morning the battle was resumed, and all that had passed was forgotten in the great struggle. It was nearly two years more to the close of the war. I remained in the army to the last, and was with General Lee when he surrendered at Appomattox. When all was over I returned home to help restore the fortunes of my State, if anything were left to her in the general ruin. Years passed on, and I was chosen United States Senator from Georgia. When in Washington, I was invited one evening to dine at Mr. Clarkson N. Potter's. I did not arrive till the guests were seated. Among the others to whom I was introduced I heard the name of Barlow, but took no notice of it till there was a pause in the conversation, when I turned to the gentleman so designated and said, 'Pray, sir, may I ask if you are a relative of the General Barlow who was killed at Gettysburg?' Imagine my astonishment at the answer: 'I am the man!' 'And you, sir,' he asked in reply—'are you the General Gordon who picked me up on the field?' I could not deny it. At this point he sprang to his feet, and I thought would have leaped over the table. And then he told the story of the scene in which we had met before, at which not only the ladies, but the men round the table, found it difficult to control their emotion."[50]

I recently came into possession of a newspaper article from *The New York Times* dated July 4, 1888. It was during this time period that the celebration of the 25th anniversary of the Battle of Gettysburg was being held. Generals Gordon and Barlow met once again on that small hill North of Gettysburg. I quote from the article: "The two men met for the second time in 25 years and the meeting was rather affecting. Gen. Barlow was left upon the field on the first day's fight. He was found by Gen. Gordon, who not only saw that he was taken care of, but allowed Mrs. Barlow to come through the lines to nurse her husband."

At Barlow's Knoll, there is a monument to the 17th Connecticut Volunteer Infantry. This unit was made up of men from around the Fairfield County area of Connecticut (Fairfield County is where I have lived all of my life.) On one side of the large gray stone is a list of names of those killed from this unit. As my eyes scanned down the names, one stood out, Joseph Whitlock. My mind flashed back to a few months earlier; the scene was an old graveyard near the boarder of Ridgefield and Danbury, Connecticut. My uncle, Joseph Knapp, took me to this small family cemetery. Without his help I never could have found it. Stone walls surrounded the graves, an area of approximately 75 feet by 50 feet. Many headstones were missing, while others were half-imbedded in the trunks of mature trees. We were there seeking the grave of my Great-Great-Grandmother, Charity Stacy Whitlock. Information supplied by my great-aunt, Auntie Mae, stated that Charity Stacy Whitlock (her Christian name) was a Susquahanock Indian. We could not find her stone, but we came across other Whitlocks. Two stones stood side by side, on the upper most portion of each are the words "CIVIL WAR Co. C 17th CT VOL. INF." One stone bore the name Nephi Whitlock and the other Joseph H. Whitlock. Because of the date of death on Joseph's stone, July 16, 1863, I made mention to my Uncle Joe that he died around the time of the battle of Gettysburg. From the book, *Connecticut Yankees at Gettysburg,* I was able to verify that Joseph Whitlock was mortally wounded July 1, 1863 and was interred in Ridgefield, Connecticut. Nephi Whitlock likewise was wounded that day, but survived. It was Gordon's brigade that came in contact with the 17th CT.

> The fighting now grew fierce as Gordon's troops closed in. At one point a color bearer of the 17th was banging his flagstaff against the flagstaff of one of the Georgia regiments, an episode rare enough to be specifically commented on afterwards.[51]

I marveled to think that it was Gordon's men who killed one of my distant relatives. It is indeed a small world.

Anna and I planned a trip to Washington, D.C. and the surrounding areas. Anna made a phone call to her friend Jane Smith, who lives in Maryland. Anna thought it would be nice to see her old college roommate as we passed through on our way to Washington. Jane invited us to stay with her a while. Anna said, "Oh, Jeff's into Civil War things so we will probably be zipping all over the countryside." Jane said, "Anna, don't you remember what my major in college was?" Anna said, "No." "Political Science," Jane replied and added that the Civil War period had always been one of her passions. Anna said, "Jeff's not into the Civil War the same way you are; he's interested in it for a far different reason." She went on to explain a little about the John Gordon story. Jane said, "Becky (Jane's daughter) reads Tarot cards." Anna said, "Oh, good, if we stay with you, I might as well sit in the corner with my thumb up my butt." We stayed with Jane on the trip and it never became necessary for Anna to assume the uncomfortable position she had described. It was amusing, though, to watch Jane sitting between the two of us, alternating conversations about the Civil War and stories of the good old college days. Jane and her husband, Lee, were kind enough to let us use their house as a base of operations while we visited the surrounding countryside. During one side trip, we went to Thomas Jefferson's home, Monticello. Being a stone's throw away from the Shenandoah Valley, I took Anna over the mountains and into the valley. The weather was not cooperating and heavy rain made the driving difficult. We decided to spend the night at the Days Inn motel in New Market. The motel is built on part of the old New Market battlefield. In the morning, Anna said, "I was worried about you last night. I couldn't tell if you were breathing. I thought some of your old friends came and got you." I laughed and said, "I'm safe; Gordon wasn't at the battle of New Market."

When Anna and I visited Washington D. C., we toured the regular tourist stops, including Arlington Cemetery, the Smithsonian and so on. We scurried past the Wall. I did not care to linger here or read the names of those who had died during the Vietnam conflict, for fear of recognizing some of the names. The Air Force Hospitals where I was stationed processed many men and women from their tours of duty in Vietnam.

I told Anna before we went to Washington that there was one stop I had to make, the Library of Congress. Standing just inside the entrance to the main building of the library were rows of computers. I fumbled through the instructions and was pleasantly surprised to find what I was looking for with relative ease. I wrote down the floor and room number, and we were off. One elevator ride and a few twisting hallways later, Anna and I found ourselves in the Photographic Section. There are multiple forms to fill out and identification to show before one is allowed entrance to the files. Having done this, I was escorted in, leaving Anna behind in a small fenced-in waiting area. I was given a pair of small, white gloves that are required when handling the photos. I saw an opportunity I could not pass up. Returning to the small waiting area, I called to Anna as I knelt with one knee on the floor, gloves raised doing an Al Jolson impression. Anna just shook her head (she seems to do this a lot, although I can't fathom why).

One of the women that works in the library escorted me to the proper files I sought. She knelt down and pulled out the bottom drawer of the file cabinet. Finding the file on John B. Gordon, she removed one of the pictures. I heard myself say out loud, "Oh my God." The woman looked up at me with a strange look. Most of the photos I had seen of Gordon were when he was in his early thirties or when he was much older in his sixties. This photo showed a Gordon in his late forties or early fifties, close to my own age. The resemblance between the two of us was more than amazing. I took the photo over to where Anna sat reading. I whistled as I held the photo in front of me. Anna looked up at me then the picture. An amazed look came to her face and once more she shook her head.

I returned to the file to search for more photos. Most I had seen before or already had at home. I found some photos of James B. Gordon, John's kinsman, mixed in with his and some of John's in James' file. I pointed this out to the lady who had helped me. She said, "Would you straighten them out, please?" I did, then took a seat to fill out forms for copies of the photos I had selected. I hand carried the forms to the proper office and paid for them. It took a while for processing and more correspondence by phone to get all the photos. It seems one of the negatives had been loaned out for some special purpose and they were having a hard time locating it. Finally, they were all in my possession. As I sat in my living room studying the new photos, I noticed what appeared to be a dark shadowy area over Gordon's left eye. The area seemed to be indented slightly and showed rather well in that first photo I had seen at the Library of Congress. Maybe his scars were showing more with his progression in age. I checked earlier photos and sure enough, there were dark areas over his left eye. If I had not had this strong desire to investigate this strange mark, I probably would have missed something that turned out to be a most remarkable find. On one of the earlier photos of Gordon, this dark mark took on a most unusual shape, roughly a five-pointed star leaning slightly to his right. A visit to the bathroom mirror showed the same shape, in the same place, over my left eye. I believe I may have received mine in junior high school, by running into a bolt sticking out of the wall. (I am not sure exactly where on my forehead it struck me.) There was a dark recess, where a large door that separated the gymnasium into two halves folded, when not in use. I walked through this dark niche instead of using the door from one side to the other. My reward for this action was running into a bolt in the dark.

A teacher saw me as I emerged and sent me straight to the nurse, though I professed not to be injured. My head injury, bleeding badly, as they do, soon turned me into something from a bad nightmare. The school nurse took one look at me and started to turn white. She cleaned my face and both our complexions returned to normal. But where had Gordon received his wound? I remembered reading something written by Jed Hotchkiss, the mapmaker for General Stonewall Jackson and later General Jubal Early. I went to my bookshelf and removed the book. Hotchkiss, in a letter to his wife, Sara, described seeing Gordon wounded in a skirmish in Virginia. "General Gordon was struck by a glancing ball, in the forehead, and bled profusely, but was not much hurt. He did not get off his horse or stop to have his wound dressed, but pressed on after the enemy, all sprinkled with blood."[52]

Now a total of three areas on Gordon's face and mine matched, the small star over the left eye, the area of the bullet entry wound under the left eye, and the jagged line from the right ear across the right cheek. I needed no more proof of my relationship to Gordon, but I continued to be amazed by it when it appeared. Most skeptics would probably chalk all these things up to coincidence or, worse yet, fraud. To coincidence, I say let them sit down with a calculator and figure out the mathematical odds of these occurrences. To fraud, I reply thank you, for giving me enough credit and foreknowledge to mark up my face in adolescence and preadolescence in such a way as to mimic those of someone long dead. Better yet, they may say I doctored the photos. Well, they are welcome to visit the National Archives or the Library of Congress and view the photos for themselves. I have witnessed the security at both of these establishments first-hand and have seen measures used to maintain their collections. They are especially protective of their glass plate negatives for, if broken, they are irreplaceable. Stiff penalties and harsh fines await anyone tampering with items in their charge.

Once while passing through Gettysburg with my mother, I purchased a book titled, *Women of Gettysburg,* and a poster-sized picture of John Gordon. When we stopped for the night, I stood the picture of Gordon upright on the dresser, leaning it against the wall. In this enlarged photo it was easy to see the deep dent under Gordon's left eye. I said, "Some dimple, huh?" nodding in the direction of the photo. My mother confirmed my assessment of the damage and added how amazing it was that he survived such a horrendous wound. I settled down with my new book. It contained a short story on Mrs. Gordon's life. Though Fanny Gordon had not been at Gettysburg, the book was paying tribute to the women of the day. I turned the pages to the story of Fanny. At the top of the page it read, "Frances Haralson Gordon." It stopped me cold. This was the first time I had seen her referred to as Frances.

I sat looking down at the back of my left hand and what I saw there transported me back to my Junior High School days. I was around age 13 and in the midst of a silent crush on a classmate. She was one of the sweetest people I have ever met; helpful, kind, never saying a bad word about anyone. Her manner and dress seemed to be that of an earlier era. Being young and not concerned with such things as disfigurement or infections, I found myself scratching the back of my hand with the end of a paper clip. A large letter appeared, the first letter of her name. The raised welt became darker and darker until blood flowed. As time passed, a scab formed followed by a scar. My mother asked me, at the time, why I had done that to my hand. I replied, "I don't know." At the time I did not know why; it had just happened. Now, more than thirty-five years later, maybe I have found the answer. The scarring has faded, but remnants still linger. She never knew how I felt about her, but I remember. All I have to do is look at the remainder of the scar that formed the letter F, for her name was Frances.

A short way into the story on Mrs. Gordon it tells of Fanny referring to John's facial wound as his "Yankee dimple." I laughed, recalling how a short time before opening the book, I had used the word dimple in describing Gordon's wound.

One section of the book tells of a collision between two trains, one carrying John and Fanny Gordon. Both were unhurt. Fanny attended to the wounded while General Gordon supervised the removal of the debris to rescue the injured and remove the dead. Being a shift commander of Fire/Rescue units, I know all too well the aftermath of pain and suffering from high speed crashes.

The story continues, telling of Mrs. Gordon's ministering to wounded troops and of her near capture at the third Battle of Winchester. The end of the story gives a brief summary of her life with John. They were married for just short of fifty years. The author included a quote from *Holland's Magazine,* February 1938, that seems out of place with the rest of the story and would be of little interest to the reader. Speaking about General Gordon, Mrs. Gordon says, "Every Spring he planted cape-jasmine. Every winter they died." This quote seemed to have been placed there just for me. When Anna and I moved into our new home to begin our life together, having hardly any furnishings, the rooms were rather sparse and barren. On an outing one day Anna spied a small plant on a shelf and called me over to see it. The plant was about five inches tall and seemed lost among the other larger plants in the nursery. We decided to give it a home. Over the years the plant has grown and now stands almost six feet tall. It is still in a pot, although one much larger than the original. Every spring we carry the plant outside, then return it to the indoor as the cool winds of winter approach. Sometimes when it blooms, Anna will pick a few of the delicate white blossoms and drop them over my shoulder onto the table next to me as I work. The wonderful fragrance drifts up to greet my nose. I do so love the smell of Jasmine.

CHAPTER TEN

Synchronicity Plus

ON ONE FORAY DOWN SOUTH, I ran across a string of what one might call synchronistic happenings. The first happened when, instead of taking my normal route through Tennessee, I swung east across the Blue Ridge Mountains and into North Carolina. Shortly after crossing the North Carolina border into South Carolina, I saw signs for Kings Mountain. I said to my mother, "I wonder if that's the same Kings Mountain I read about." I pulled the car over to the side of the road and went to the trunk. Checking one of my books on John Gordon, I came across a story on ancestors of Gordon's fighting at King Mountain during the Revolutionary War. The battle was fought on October 7, 1780. Of particular note that day was the hand-to-hand combat between an English officer and Charles Gordon, Jr.

> Making "a quick, bold movement into the midst of the enemy," he seized the officer by his queue and began dragging him down the mountain, when the Englishman drew his pistol and shot his attacker in the left arm. Seizing his sword, young Gordon killed the officer outright.[53]

The location in the book was the same, so we made a slight detour and drove to Kings Mountain. It was early in the morning and the park was not yet open. Spotting a park employee, I went to talk to him. He said they would not be open for another 40 minutes, but we could go ahead and walk around.

Since time was not a luxury this day, we quickly followed the path around the battle site and after a short visit to the gift shop; we were back on the road to Georgia again.

We stopped at the University of Georgia in Athens. At the library, I perused a collection of papers donated by the Gordon family. I could have spent a year there, but I pried myself away after placing an order for copies of some of the documents. One in particular was worth the trip. A love letter to Fanny from John. It was written during one of those rare periods when Fanny Gordon was not with him as he traveled with the Army of Northern Virginia. John was lonely and missed his wife very much. The letter was a long declaration of his love for her and his sons. After reading so many stories about John Gordon the General, Senator and Governor, it was refreshing to see John Gordon the husband. On the last page of the letter at the bottom in the left hand corner, two words in large script stood out, "Big Kiss."

My next stop was the Main Library in Atlanta. In the research section I talked to a lady at the desk. I told her I wanted a copy of a boyhood sketch Gordon had done for Youth Companion Magazine. She could find nothing in her file. I told her that in a book I had read, it stated that this library had the only copy. As we talked, three or four other reference employees gathered nearby. The lady I was talking to told me that the library had been renovated in the early part of the 20th century and what I sought was probably lost. I informed her that the book I referred to was written in 1955. In a flash all of the reference people disappeared like knights-errant in search of the grail. Ten minutes went by, then twenty, then thirty. Forty minutes later, they all returned as quickly as they had departed. The girl I had spoken to originally stood before me with a big grin and an outstretched hand. "Here it is," she said, "If you had come here yesterday, you would have been out of luck. We found it in a room that had been locked for eons and we just got the key for the room this morning." I made copies and started off on the final leg of our journey to Lafayette. My run of luck, if you care to think of it as luck, was not over yet, not by a long shot.

Early in the afternoon, we arrived in Lafayette. I had unpacked what few things I had and went for a walk. I planned to stay one day and then return to Connecticut. While walking in the back yard, my nephew Justin came walking up the driveway, on his way home from school. When he saw me, he yelled, "Hey, Uncle Jeff, have I got the deal of the century for you!" Justin could be a pint-sized con man at times, so I waited for the follow-up. There was none. I had judged him too quickly. What came out of his mouth next stopped me dead in my tracks. He said, "My class is going on a tour of the Marsh House and Gordon Hall tomorrow. Do you want to go with us?" Bright and early the next morning, I found myself standing in the seventh grade classroom of Mrs. Davis. Justin asked his teacher for permission for me to attend the tour. I told Mrs. Davis I was writing a book and that one of the main characters was John Gordon. I explained that I had many photos with me and would be glad to answer any questions if I could. She said they would be happy to have me come along, but they were not leaving on the tour for about an hour. I told her I would meet them at Gordon Hall.

I drove to Gordon Hall and waited outside. In a short while, a man appeared. He was from the Chamber of Commerce and was there to unlock the building. He unlocked the door and then asked me if I would take charge of the building, because he had to leave. "Sure!" I said. On my first visit I had to settle on peeking in the windows, now I was "In charge" of the building. What a turnabout. I walked inside and looked around. The main room appeared to have a fresh coat of light blue paint. Over the fireplace hung an oil painting of Gen. Gordon. I found a table on which to lay out my collection of photos for the children to view. I walked back outside, where I met a pretty lady from the Woman's Club. She was the one who was giving the tour of Gordon Hall. Now I had been relieved of command; my time of being "In charge" had been short-lived. A little while later, we could see in the distance the entire 7th grade class from

Lafayette Middle School marching down Main Street like good little soldiers. The class was quite large, so the teachers divided it into groups. I went with the first group to Marsh House. The Marsh House is owned by Mr. and Mrs. Clement. Mrs. Clement was our tour guide on the trip through their beautiful home. In one room she pointed out a picture of John Gordon and made reference to the fact that he boarded there while attending school at Gordon Hall.

In the main hallway, I noticed a cannonball mounted on a plaque. It was sitting on top of a table that was shoved back under the staircase. I walked over and took a closer look. On the wooden base there was a brass plate stating that this was a Union cannonball that had been fired into Petersburg, Virginia, during the siege. Mr. Clement stood nearby and I matter-of-factly said, "My great-grandfather, Lewis Knapp, was with the 1st Connecticut Heavy Artillery at Petersburg and may have fired this very cannonball into the city." There was a deafening silence followed by a less than enthusiastic two-word reply from Mr. Clement when he said, "Oh really." I hurried to catch up with the tour group; safety in numbers I figured.

On the second floor, Mrs. Clement pointed out a pane of glass in the hall window that still retains a bullet-hole from one of the battles fought around the house. Many bullets are still embedded in the exterior of this battle-scarred home. As I moved down the hall, to an area just outside one of the bedrooms, just at the bottom of the attic stairs, a strange feeling ran through me. It was much like the sensations you feel when you sneeze, but without the sneeze. I wondered if this had been the very room shared by John and his brother Chapman? I hung back, as the group descended the staircase to the first floor. I attempted to linger a moment, but only a moment, keeping in mind that I was no longer a renter.

The house tour completed, we returned outside and crossed the lawn to the old schoolhouse. It did not take long to complete our excursion through Gordon Hall. The building consists mainly of two rooms, an open floor plan with one room over the other. I watched the children file past the table covered with

Gordon photos and occasionally answered questions about John and Fanny.

It was now noon and the class sat on the grass eating lunch. They were scattered about around the gnarled base of a large and very old oak tree. The tree's leafy arms covered a span of sixty feet or more with the schoolchildren beneath intertwined with the shade and sunlight. It truly was an ideal scene for a painter. One of the teachers approached me, to ask if I would talk to the children about General Gordon after they finished their lunches. I asked, "How long would you like me to speak?" She said, "About fifteen minutes." I said, " I can do that." Just then my nephew Justin, who had been listening to the conversation, interrupted with, "Uncle Jeff are you going to tell them about reincar..." I quickly placed my hand over the child's mouth before he could finish the word reincarnation. I said, "I will tell them what I feel they should know, Justin." After all the food had been devoured, I was introduced to the children. I began by telling them about John Gordon's early life with his family on Taylor's Ridge, just outside Lafayette. I spoke about the men from the Raccoon Mountains going off to war and the many battles they fought. They were intrigued by the story of Gordon's five wounds received at Antietam and Mrs. Gordon nursing him back to health. So the young ladies would not feel left out of all the action stories, I told them about Fanny Gordon's near capture at the 3rd Battle of Winchester. When I finished, there was a question and answer period before it became time for them to return to school. Later that day when Justin came home from school, I explained why I had hushed him when I was speaking to the teacher at Gordon Hall. I said, "It was not the proper forum in which to discuss reincarnation." I also reminded him that we were in the "Bible Belt" and that it would not be too pleasant to see his Uncle Jeff hanging from a tree with flammable liquids all over him.

On my return trip home, I planned my route so I would pass through Lynchburg, Virginia. Driving along one of this city's streets, I spotted a sign out of the corner of my eye. It was a large sign attached to an archway connecting two, long red brick walls. Fort Early, the sign read. Parking the car, I grabbed my camera and walked over to the old fort. It was late in the day and the building in the enclosure was closed.

After the Battle of Cold Harbor, Early and his men were being sent to the Shenandoah Valley via Lynchburg. Upon reaching Lynchburg, they found the Union forces under General David Hunter were no more than two miles away. General Hunter was known as Black Dave, because of his liberal use of the torch in the Shenandoah Valley. Private homes, mills, barns and even The Virginia Military Institute in Lexington were set ablaze by Hunter and his men. Fort Early remains as a symbol of the Battle of Lynchburg. Early was not only successful in his defense of the city, but chased Hunter and his men over the mountains and away from the Shenandoah Valley. After taking a few pictures of the fort, I continued my journey in the direction of Petersburg, Virginia. I had not intended to stop there, but just as so many other times on this trip, Mr. Destiny would step in. In Tankersley's book on Gordon, there is a chapter called "Retreat from Petersburg." In this section, he mentions the home of James Pinckney as being the house where Fanny Gordon and the newborn John B. Gordon Jr. were left, when the Confederate Army pulled out. A note at the bottom of the page states, "The house is still standing and located at 17 South Market Street."[54] The book had been written in 1955. I wondered if there was a possibility of the house still being there forty years later? I decided to find out.

I had never been in the city of Petersburg proper, nor had I any maps. I figured I would drive into the City and ask someone for directions. On the interstate, a sign appeared "Petersburg next 5 exits." I randomly picked an exit. At the bottom of the exit ramp something told me to turn left. It was now around 10:30 PM, the streets were dark and almost devoid of life. I figured I was on the right track, because the road I was on appeared to be the dividing line for the northern and southern roads. Driving along, I checked each street sign as it came into view. Suddenly, my brain said **TURN BACK**; so I did. I turned left and left again, in an attempt to backtrack, but at the next stop sign, my journey ended. I sat staring at the street sign that stood before me. The three words written on it reverberated in my head: **South Market Street**. Driving along, I checked the houses for numbers. The last two houses on the odd numbered side had no numbers on them that I could see. I parked my car and walked down the street to see if I could find the numbers on the last two houses. The house nearest the corner was of pre-Civil War construction and beautifully maintained. A large wrought iron fence and gate separated it from the sidewalk. There was an air of familiarity about it, but I found myself standing and staring at a parking lot to the left of this house. The parking lot was for a large commercial building on the corner of South Market Street. I walked back up the street to a fire station a block away. Two firefighters were sitting in the dispatch room. I walked in and said, "Could you guys help a brother firefighter?" They said, "Sure, what do you need?" I told them I was trying to find #17 South Market Street, but could not find the numbers on the last house. Neither one of them knew offhand where #17 was. They got out a street directory and looked for it, but there was no #17 listed. The younger of the two men got up and said, "Let's go see if we can find it." We left the firehouse, and as we passed the window to the firefighters' dayroom he yelled inside, "I'll be right back, I'm going down the street." The firefighter explained that over the years the numbering system had changed. We stood once more in front of the house with the wrought iron gate, but still could not see a number anywhere on the house. It was now past 11 o'clock at night and my hopes were fading fast. Something that I had always known was shortly to be reinforced; all firemen are a little crazy. The firefighter said, "I'll find out the number for you." Before I could stop him, he was through the gate and bounding up the large stone steps to the front porch. He rang the doorbell and knocked on the door. A dog started barking inside the previously quiet home. The young man on the porch turned around so the occupant of the house could see the words Petersburg Fire Dept printed on the back of his shirt. The door opened slightly and he talked to the woman inside, all the while pointing to me standing on the sidewalk. The two of them walked down to where I stood. The lady informed me the house was #29. I told her why I sought #17. She said that she had some old papers on the house and knew some general had stayed there, but she was not sure which general it had been. I thanked her and left one of my cards with her, just in case she found mention of General Gordon in her paperwork. The firefighter cheerfully invited the woman to bring her dog to the firehouse and have his picture taken on one of the fire engines (turns out that the dog was a Dalmatian). I talked with the young man for a while and thanked him for all his assistance. Returning to my car, I was on my way home once more. At home, I made a phone call to Mr. Chris M. Calkins, author of many books on the Civil War and a historian at Petersburg Battlefield. He confirmed my fears; the parking lot on South Market Street was indeed the location where #17 previously stood. Mr. Calkins was kind enough to send me a picture of the house taken from an old Petersburg High School yearbook. The yearbook had been dedicated to Petersburg's Civil War history. Contemplating my second journey to Lafayette Georgia and the return trip home, I continue to be amazed at all that took place: King's Mountain, the key episode at the Atlanta Library, touring Gordon Hall and Marsh House. Most remarkable of all was the trip to South Market Street in Petersburg. The wonders never cease. In the dark of night in a strange city of forty-five square miles, I picked one of five exits (the correct one) and drove to the street I was looking for. How had I managed such a feat? If I did not receive any help from without, that only leaves one other possibility—guidance from within.

CHAPTER ELEVEN

Thoughts and Presentiments

In September of 1996 I treated myself to an early birthday present. I drove to Fredericksburg, Virginia, for a two-day walking tour of the Wilderness Battlefield. The tour guides for the event were Professor Gary Gallagher of Pennsylvania State University and Robert K. Krick of Fredericksburg, who is a leading authority on the Army of Northern Virginia. The first morning of the tour found us on the west end of the Wilderness Battlefield in the high winds and heavy rains of hurricane Fran. The two buses we traveled in would stop at predetermined points of interest and undauntedly, we would disembark and traipse through the rain-drenched woodlands. One stop took us to the area of Gordon's flank attack of May 6th, 1864. It felt strange to hear two highly respected historians banter back and forth about General Gordon on the very spot of one of the high points of his military career. The group emerged from the woods into a large open area known as Saunders Field. We attempted to seek cover under a three-sided shelter near the roadway. The shelter was just short of sufficient size to contain the huddled mass of time travelers. Just outside the enclosure stood Mr. Krick, attempting to shield his papers from the incessant rain. He related stories of what had transpired in Saunder's Field during the two-day battle. As the wind gained in intensity, Mr. Krick's voice escalated in volume. In a short time, he was to the point of shouting. He lead into one story by saying, "All of you are probably familiar with General George Patton's idiosyncrasy or insanity, depending on how you look at it, regarding his belief in reincarnation." My ears perked up. What followed was a story from the book, *The Pattons,* and the setting was the very field in which we stood. The story goes like this: General Patton was touring the Wilderness Battlefield along with his wife and two children. With them this day was a German military attaché, General Friedrich Von Boetticher. Von Boetticher was a Civil War buff. Patton described the troop deployment, and the sway of the battle back and forth across Saunder's Field. He placed his two children as Confederate units and his wife (being a Yankee) as the Union line. Patton stood on a nearby rise where he declared General Jubal Early had directed the battle. Von Boetticher disagreed with Patton and a loud argument followed. An old man that had been with a tour group overheard the conversation and approached the two men. "The other gentleman is right," he told Von Boetticher. "General Early was on that rise. I was at this battle as a boy." George was pleased. He'd had a feeling he'd been there before; now it was confirmed. "Of course Early stood there," he declared in triumph. "I saw it myself!"[55] I had to chuckle as we boarded the bus.

I am fortunate in that my job schedule affords me the time to travel. Retracing the battles of the Army of Northern Virginia has taken me to many places where history has left its mark—places with mysterious names like the White Oak swamp, Massanutten Mountain or Opequon Church. I have crossed the Rappahannock, Monocacy, Rapidan and Susquehanna rivers; I have traveled over beautiful mountains such as the Blue Ridge and into enchanting valleys like the Shenandoah. These places stood as midwives to the birth of our nation, a birth wracked with pain and suffering. Who was right and who was wrong is still in dispute. Many continue to argue the cause of it all. I feel that if these blessed grounds were given voice, they would all say the same thing. The message would be short: never again the bloodshed or sorrow: learn, grow and move on. The past is filled with lessons from which we should learn. To discount these events, we run the hazard of repetition. I have reached out and touched history, and it has touched me back, both as a spectator and as a participant. I feel as if an unseen hand has come out of the past and guided me, much like a chess piece being moved from square to square. We all need to stop for a moment and listen to the world around us, and in us. Don't just listen with your ears, but use your heart as well. Open your mind and bring all your senses into play. With a little practice and patience you may be rewarded by the gifts that come your way. You may find something; a something that has been talked about, denied, debated and ignored by many peoples for countless years. That something is a soul, your soul. After you have found it, keep in mind what Thomas Jefferson said: "The care of every man's soul belongs to himself." Another brilliant man, Plato, was right on the money centuries ago. Plato's contention was that the soul exists in its own right, that it not only survives the body, but pre-exists it as well. Moreover, Plato declared that the soul, not the body, forms the real or true person.

No one can make you believe in the soul's existence; it comes with a *Knowing.* Pause for a moment and contemplate what the world would be like if reincarnation were proven to be a fact of life. How would we then treat others? When dealing with family, friends or acquaintances, we would need to ask ourselves some questions like: Who are these souls? What is their relationship to me? Am I to learn something from them, or am I to be the Teacher? The possibilities are endless. We all live in the same house and that house grows smaller every day. This planet has become the "Global Village." No longer does it take the written word to tell of events on the other side of the earth. With the flick of a switch, we can sit and watch as events unfold. Every country affects all the others with their finances, pollution problems and their petty hostilities. Now more than ever everyone needs to change his or her way of thinking: no more **I**, but **US**—no more **THEM**, but **WE**. We leave our mark on ourselves and those around us; so let us strive to use a gentle touch.

I long for a return to old values and virtues. Things like honor, courage and moral fortitude. I am not speaking of a soldier's life, for in my ideal world there would be no need of soldiers. The most heroic battles are not fought on the battlefield, but in everyday life. We are here to learn through experience and to put those experiences to work for us. Many times our greatest strides forward come after we muddle our way through some of life's difficulties. There are no free rides. For many years, I thought it ironic that we go through life gathering information, and when we are able to understand much of what these life lessons have taught us, we die and the knowledge is lost. I see now this is not the case. The experiences of this lifetime have brought me to the conclusion that we are both the archer and the target, the deceased and the heir. People worry about the legacy we are leaving our children and grandchildren. What kind of world should we leave them as their inheritance? It should be a world that we would enjoy living in, for it might just come to pass. The purpose of my writing this book was to get people to think, to start them on a path of self-discovery and assist them in finding their true identity. Hopefully they will notice in others not just their differences, but their sameness, and maybe some day their oneness.

Strange things continue to happen to me in the month of September. On my last birthday (49th), I sat reading in my back yard. Anna joined me and pointed out a lone monarch butterfly sitting in the grass, about six feet from where I sat. I held out my left hand, palm up, and continued reading. The butterfly flew straight to me and perched on my open hand. This beautiful creature stayed there for about five minutes, slowly moving its brightly colored wings up and down. I found this visitation much more pleasant than the trip to the hospital on my 30th birthday.

Parallels also continue to appear. In Tankersley's book, he mentions Congressman Elihu Washburne attending the formal surrender formalities at Appomattox Court House on April 12, 1865. After the surrender, many Confederates soldiers stood around rather dejected. A crowd gathered around General Gordon to bid him farewell. In a short time, what started out as a small group grew to several thousand. Gordon mounted his horse and addressed the throng that now included Federal soldiers, along with Congressman Washburne. Tankersley writes, "In conclusion, he advised them to go home in peace, to obey the laws, and to rebuild and work for the future of a reunited nation."[56] The Congressman personally congratulated Gordon on his speech and the spirit of reconciliation it expressed. In May of 1996, I gave a short speech during a memorial service for four fallen brother firefighters who died in the line of duty in 1946. The service was held in a local church with a reception afterward in the church courtyard. A gentleman sought me out to tell me how much he liked my speech and to request a written copy. I mailed a copy to his office and received a letter in return. The last two lines read: "As I told you before, your statement was right on target, and particularly moving and inspiring." The letter was signed Christopher Shays, Member of Congress, 4th District Connecticut.

Recently, I reread a chapter in General Gordon's *Reminiscences of the Civil War*, a chapter devoted to stories of "presentiments." These tales of prophetic foresight or premonitions were not uncommon during the Civil War. Gordon heard many such stories from other officers both North and South. Gordon witnessed a number for himself. He tells one about his friend, Colonel Tennant Lomax. Approaching Gordon just before riding into battle, Lomax stopped and extended his hand to Gordon saying, "Give me your hand, Gordon, and let me bid you good-by. I am going to be killed in this battle. I shall be dead in a half an hour." Gordon writes,

> "I endeavored to remove this impression from his mind, but nothing I could say changed or appeared to modify it in any degree. I was grieved to have him go into the fight with such a burden upon him, but there was no tremor in his voice, no hesitation in his words, no doubt on his mind. The genial smile that made his face so attractive was still upon it, but he insisted that he would be dead in half an hour, and that it was 'all right.' The half-hour had scarcely passed when the fatal bullet had numbered him with the dead."[57]

Gordon tells of his younger brother Augustus Gordon,

> "A youth of scarcely twenty-one years, he was in command of the Sixth Regiment of Alabama. Before going into the fight in the Wilderness, he quietly said: 'My hour has come.' I joked and chided him. I told him that he must not permit such impressions to affect or take hold upon his imagination. He quickly and firmly replied: 'You need not doubt me. I will be at my post. But this is our last meeting.' Riding at the head of his regiment, with his sword above him, the fire of battle in his eyes and words of cheer for his men on his lips, the fatal grape-shot plunged through his manly heart, and the noble youth slept his last sleep in that woeful Wilderness."[58]

Finishing up the chapter Gordon ponders:

> It would require a volume simply to record without comment the hundreds of such presentiments in both the Union and Confederate armies during the war. The few here noted will suffice, however, to raise the inquiry as to what they meant.... They were perceptions. There was about them no element of speculation. Their conspicuous characteristic was certainty. The knowledge seemed so firmly fixed that no argument as to possible mistake, no persuasion, could shake it. Where did that knowledge come from? It seems to me there can be but one answer, and that answer is another argument for immortality. It was the whispering of the Infinite beyond us to the Infinite within us—a whispering inaudible to the natural ear, but louder than the roar of battle to the spirit that heard it.[59]

Reading this, I sat nodding my head in affirmation. From my present vantage point, I could look back and say, "Yes John, you were right"—we are immortal, timeless, ageless spirits. All that I have seen, heard and felt confirmed it. Sometime in the future, would I find myself once again reading books that I had written under different names, answering questions then posed? I smiled as I closed the book and laid it aside.

I sat looking at the pictures and memorabilia gathered from my many trips through the South, names flashed before me, Antietam, Petersburg, Spotsylvania. Places with peculiar names like: The Mule Shoe and Bloody Lane. My gaze came to rest on a tiny picture at the bottom center of one of the wooden frames. It's a photo of a cold gray stone, a tombstone with letters and numbers carved into it nearly a century ago. "John B. Gordon" it reads. My eyes moved to the second date under John's name, the date of his death, January 9, 1904. As I looked at this date two words came to mind: **Not Yet**, followed closely by two more, **Not Ever**.

Author at gravesite of John B. Gordon

General John B. Gordon Monument at Capitol, Atlanta, Georgia

Photo first viewed by author in magazine
(Valentine Richmond History Center)

Old broadside from author's collection

John B. Gordon and Frances (Fanny) Haralson Gordon

Photo from front Page of Connecticut Post, *June 17, 1994*

Photo by George Cardozo

Author (in white) at work during a structure fire caused by a propane gas explosion

Wilkeson's guns at Barlow's Knoll

General Gordon raising up General Barlow on the battle-field
from *Blood Is Thicker Than Water* by Henry M. Field (1886)

Wrightsville, Pennsylvania, bridge razed by Union soldiers to prevent Gordon's troops from crossing

Photo by Michael Warner

Graves of Whitlocks wounded at Barlow's Knoll on July 1, 1863 (Joeseph mortally)

Brady cabinet photo of Gordon from author's collection

Asst. Chief Jeffrey J. Keene, 1998

Senator John B. Gordon, 1873

Gordon family plot, Oakland Cemetery, Georgia

Gordon Hall, Lafayette, Georgia

John B. Gordon *Jeffrey J. Keene*

Sutherland House, General Gordon's home at Kirkwood, near Atlanta

Gordon statue on the capitol grounds, Atlanta, Georgia

PART II

CHAPTER TWELVE

A Return to the South

I STARTED WRITING MY BOOK (although I was not aware of it at the time) in long-hand in 1992. Since the completion of the first portion of the book, many things have happened. My girls have finished college. Shannon graduated from Dickinson College and continued on to graduate from Boston College Law School. Samantha received her degree in business at Keene State in Keene, New Hampshire (I used to kid Samantha about her choice of Keene State by saying, "I guess if you get drunk you will always remember the name of the town you live in and the school you attend"). Anna quit her job and went back to school at the Culinary Institute of America in Hyde Park, New York and I have gained weight.

In July of 1998 I sat in front of a new computer in my office at work, a "babe in the woods" of the electronic age. I decided to try a search on the Internet. With my usual two-fingered style, I typed in the word REINCARNATION and came up with 49,000 hits. Because I was writing a book, I picked a website that mentioned a book on reincarnation. The story at this website was not very interesting. Before leaving that site I spotted a reference to another site dealing with a documentary on reincarnation. One click of the mouse and I was there: "IN ANOTHER LIFE: How Americans Approach Reincarnation" read the title. The website talked about a documentary-in-progress and "exploring current attitudes towards reincarnation in the United States." Two things struck me in the first paragraph. One was the mention of interviews with people "who have had direct and verifiable experiences relating to reincarnation." The other was the location of the production company, Atlanta, Georgia. I caught myself thinking out loud, "Boy are they in a great place for a Gordon story." Anyone caring to contribute to this project was asked to contact Steve Sakellarios at Gold Thread Video Productions. On July 4th, 1998, I called and left a message on Steve's phone giving him the "Readers Digest" version of my story and asking him for his mailing address so I might send him some information. Even though it was a holiday (and a Saturday), two hours later I received a return phone call. Steve was very enthusiastic about my story and I sent him the first few chapters of my book along with some newspaper clippings. A week later I received a letter from Steve saying he was definitely interested in including my story in his documentary. He made the suggestion in his letter that he fly to Connecticut to film an interview with me. I think I surprised Steve when I called him and offered to fly down to Georgia for the interview. This would give me a chance to visit Gordon's grave once again and afford Steve a better photographic backdrop for the interviews.

On August 4, 1998 Anna and I flew to Atlanta, Georgia. I called Steve to set up the schedule for the next four days. The following morning I drove to Steve's office. It was nice to finally put a face to the voice on the phone. We used Steve's car to drive to Oakland Cemetery and parked a short distance from Gen. Gordon's grave. I walked over to the gravesite while Steve unloaded his video equipment from the car. It looked like nature was going to supply us with perfect weather for filming. Steve checked out the location and he then placed me in a squatting position just downhill and slightly to the left of Gordon's headstone. Steve wanted to film me with Gordon's grave visible over my left shoulder. Steve made a few adjustments to the camera, did a sound check, and we were ready to film. I did a reprise of my experience at Antietam, the Halloween party, and some of the discoveries that followed. Things were moving along fine until one of the groundskeepers started up a leaf blower. Steve stopped filming and went over to the man. They talked for a while, then the man kindly moved off to a distant part of the cemetery. Steve returned and we started the whole process all over again. When Steve was satisfied with the end product, we moved to the site of the Gordon family plot. Steve filmed as we walked and I retold the story of my mother and I finding the family plot on our first visit to this cemetery. With filming completed, we walked back towards the car. I noticed some women moving among the graves picking up sticks and other debris. I approached a woman standing in the roadway not that far from Gordon's grave. She appeared to be the leader of this group of feminine caretakers. I said, "Hello, are you ladies members of the United Daughters of the Confederacy?" My assumption was correct and I asked if they were the ones responsible for the cleanliness of General Gordon's grave. The woman said, "Why, yes; he was a fine gentleman." I thanked her for the fine job they were doing. She said, "We're glad to do it." As I turned to walk away, a curious look came over her face. Afterward, I wondered what this woman would have thought had she known that she had been talking to an Oakland Cemetery resident.

Steve had arranged two separate psychic readings for me. The first was with numerologist Michael Ferniany. We met Michael at his condominium. After introductions, I was shown to a couch while Michael sat down in a chair nearby. Steve started filming from across the room. For the second time in two days Steve's filming was interrupted, this time by a noisy pet bird. Michael got up, covered his bird, and once again there was quiet. Michael had been given only my name, birth date, and where I was born. Themes of authority, leadership, and responsibility came up repeatedly. Most of the reading appeared to have been about my present life. I could see Steve was becoming a little "down in the mouth." I know he was hoping for some mention of the American Civil War, Georgia, or any hint of a past life as a military figure. As the session was coming to a close, I asked Michael about past lives and their effects on my present life. He reaffirmed the leadership theme and followed it by saying, "You have had great responsibility; in past lifetimes, you were like a general." With the mention of the word "General," I could see a big, wide, grin appear on Steve's face.

The reading Michael did for me that night was very much on an intellectual level. The next reading was strictly on a more emotional level, like a punch to the heart.

The second appointment Steve arranged was with clairvoyant Candace Zellner. Once again the only information given was my name and birthday. Steve wrote about my session with Candice on his website and I will quote his observations.

> In Candace's reading, the first thing out of her mouth after her opening prayer, was to describe images of Jeff as a soldier, including a general or an officer with great responsibility ... but most of this appeared not to relate to John Gordon, but to Jeff's most recent past life as a British special forces officer. Jeff has had two other psychics (also without any pre-knowledge) describe this latter lifetime, and he wrote about it in the manuscript of his book, which I had already read. So, as she was giving this material, I could see that it closely paralleled his manuscript.[60]

I sat in a chair next to Candace. With her eyes closed, Candace asked out loud to see my last three lifetimes. There was a pause and then she said, "Immediately Jeff, let me tell you something; I see you on a battlefield, in a war, and I'm trying to see what war it is. This is in another country. You're either in France or Germany, and boy, do I feel it's France. You are in charge here leading this group of men." Candace continued, "You carry such a sense of responsibility for these men in this lifetime that I would think that it would be overwhelming to you and that you would still carry that trait more than normal in this lifetime." During the reading Candace mentioned, "Black men speaking French." She said, " I kept feeling something French. I don't understand this, I want to say French black men, it's the weirdest thing." All this would fit in well with the fusilier's lifetime. In North Africa, especially in the French Algiers area, you would have no problem finding black men speaking French. A little later on Candace got right to the heart of the matter, literally. She said, "You're so concerned about these men it just puts a lot of pressure on you. You know what, Jeff? This is so interesting. You're not fearing the battle; oh, this is going to make me cry." I said, " I know what you are going to say." Candace continued and what followed took both of us on an emotional sled ride, downhill fast. She said, "You're fearing the loss. You're leading these men into battle and you're just praying, 'Dear God, dear God, don't let anything happen to these men'; you don't care about the gunfire, you don't care about the hand grenades, you don't care about the bombs, you don't care about any of it. All you care about is the connection and responsibility you have for these men. I see you going forward with this burden on you. I can't see what happens after that, I don't know what happens. It's just like it lifted; it's just like all that pain just lifted. There was such pain and grief and so much responsibility you carried." By this time both our faces were quite wet. She saw the soldier surviving this battle and being decorated for his actions.

One of the highlights of my trip to Georgia was meeting Steve Smith. Steve Sakellarios had been doing his research on reincarnation and wanted to contact Patricia Hayes (author of *The Gatekeepers)*, at Delphi University. A young man named Steve Smith had answered his repeated phone calls. After a few unsuccessful attempts to reach Ms. Hayes, the two Steve's started conversing, and in their conversation my case was mentioned. When Steve Smith heard that I believed I had been Confederate General John B. Gordon, his immediate response was, "Oh, Gordon was my great-great uncle!" It was arranged for Steve Smith and I to meet at the Atlanta Capitol building. Steve Sakellarios introduced us and told us not to pay any attention to him, that he would just be a "fly on the wall." Steve filmed us getting to know one another in front of Gordon's equestrian statue on the northwest corner of the Capital grounds. Later he filmed us under a painting of Governor John Gordon that hangs inside the Capitol building. At first, Steve Smith seemed a little standoffish; but, after our two-hour talk, he appeared to be convinced of my sincerity. We had fun trading family stories and sharing the information we both had gathered, he from family, I from my life (and past life) experiences. I asked Steve what he thought when he heard my story of reincarnation involving Gen. Gordon. Steve said, "It was a first for me, I almost dropped the phone and my teeth dropped out." I asked, "Do you think it was a coincidence that Steve Sakellarios called you?" His reply was, "No, it was supposed to happen, there's a reason for it." He asked what my experiences had taught me. I told him about the deep soul-searching and that it has been a wondrous journey with few dull moments. I told him, "I've learned that the earth is a schoolroom, sometimes we are the students, while at other times, the teacher. I've found that the "***meaning of life***" is the ***experiencing of life*** itself. I got a warm feeling inside when Steve Smith said to me, "I consider this a unique honor to know of my relatives and to get to meet you in your search and discovery."

The three of us moved across the street to the First Presbyterian Church; the same church where John B. Gordon's funeral had been held in 1904. As we walked into the old sanctuary, Steve Sakellarios asked me if I felt anything. I said, "Yes, just before we walked in here my heart started beating like a bass drum." It had first started when we entered the church by way of a newer addition, one that had been added long after Gordon's death. We entered the vestibule from the left side. As I stood in the center of the foyer, looking down the steps that led to the street, my heart started beating faster. The beating built in intensity until it felt as though I was being punched in the chest, but from the inside. This pounding stayed with me during our tour of the church and continued until we were back out on the street. We wandered back across the street to the grounds of the Capitol building. Steve Smith told me he had never read General Gordon's book. Before we parted, I took down his address and later sent him a copy of *Reminiscences of the Civil War.* I inscribed the book, "To Steve Smith, from your Uncle?" I hope he gets a chuckle every time he reads it.

I received no monetary compensation for the filming for the documentary *In Another Life*; just a promise from Steve

Sakellarios that he would feature my story on his web site. Steve kept his promise and a short time later, not only my story, but also pictures and film clips became a permanent fixture on his web site. Steve was planning a trip to Philadelphia to interview Carol Bowman, author of *Children's Past Lives* and *Returned from Heaven.* These two books deal with the past lives of children and relatives reincarnated within the same family. After hearing of his plans, I suggested he hold off on his trip until September, 1998 when I would be at Sharpsburg, Maryland for a two-day walking tour of Antietam battlefield. This would allow him to "kill two birds with one stone," interview Carol Bowman and film some footage of me at the Sunken Road. Some strange things happened during Steve's trip, but I will let him tell it in his own words:

Steve Sakellarios wrote the following. It was taken from the update section (dated 9/13/98) on his **In Another Life** web site (www.ial.goldthread.com):

> Carolyn and Steve Bowman were very gracious, down-to-earth hosts. Steve and I talked website construction, and Carol was patient with the technical set up and handled the interview expertly. Afterwards I was invited to a late breakfast with her son Chase, now in high school (it was Chase, as a young boy, who started it all with his memory of being a black Civil War soldier killed on the battlefield), and some of his friends.
>
> Then I drove to Sharpsburg to meet with Jeff Keene at Antietam Battlefield Park. While there, I had two fascinating coincidences (although Jeff insists there is no such thing as a "coincidence").
>
> Having taped Carol Bowman just the day before talking about children recalling their past lives, I was in the dimly lit Antietam Battlefield museum trying to capture a shot of a sword handle, when I heard a little boy behind me on the stairs leading to the room exclaim, "I know that man!" He was referring to a photo of John A. Thompkins, about 24 feet in front of him (I paced it off later). His mother and father didn't take it seriously. But as he came running up to the photo next to me, I asked him, "Who is it?" He answered, "It's John." Then I asked him, trying to keep the question vague and nonleading, "What did he do?" The boy answered, "He killed the bad people." This was all he had to say about it, but he had been very definite about these two statements. His mother told me that at age 5, he doesn't read yet, or at best he

only reads very simple words. His father simply shook his head and said quietly, "He wouldn't have been able to read that."

Before going on this trip, my mother had told me I had an ancestor, Fidello Biddle, who had fought at Antietam. I happened to be talking about it with Jeff in the parking lot. Now, Jeff was with a Civil War group. Two members of the tour were walking by, a younger man and older one, and when I said "Fidello Biddle," they stopped frozen in their tracks and stared at me! To make a long story short, they were my relatives—Joe Biddle Sr. and Joe Biddle Jr.; Joe Sr. is my mom's cousin—his parents (as my mom told me afterward when I called her) were her favorite aunt and uncle whom she often visited as a child.

Just think of the odds that I would happen to speak Fidello Biddle's name out loud at exactly the moment when these two men were within earshot. Given that I didn't interact much with the tour, it's unlikely that I would have seen the name tags and made the connection otherwise, and they certainly wouldn't have known who I was.[61]*

I kidded with Steve about his experiences. I said, "Here you are in Maryland, a long way from Georgia, you mentioned a Civil War ancestor's name in the middle of a parking lot, and the only two people within range of hearing are relatives of yours. You interview Carol Bowman, who deals with children's past lives and then you run into a little five-year-old boy who, in a past life, had been friends with a Union Lt. Col. whose picture you just happened to be standing next to. Coincidence, right?"

Having my story on Steve's web site began to pay off in ways I had not expected. I thought the exposure might help to get my book published. On August 9th, 1999, Steve Sakellarios e-mailed me saying, " A representative of Arts and Entertainment has contacted me asking for contacts for a segment they are doing on reincarnation." Steve said they were interested in getting in touch with me, but he did not want to give them my e-mail address without my permission. I gave Steve the okay to give them my telephone number and e-mail address. The very same day I received an e-mail from Actuality Productions with

---

*It was later discovered that Fidello Biddle became ill and did not actually participate in the Battle of Antietam.

information regarding the documentary. The e-mail stated: We are making a two-hour A&E special which will take a balanced, academic look at the concepts and beliefs regarding the afterlife. It is still in the development process, but right now we are planning to explore near-death experiences (positive and negative), after-death communications/dreams, reincarnation, ghosts, mediums, etc. What followed was an impressive list of doctors and professors from all around the United States. After many rounds of correspondence and signing release forms, a date was set for filming my segment of the program. The filming was done on September first and second of 1999. They filmed an interview at my home, and then the crew followed me to work at the firehouse during one of my night shifts. They did some filming in my office, on the apparatus floor, and even interviewed some of the firefighters. I knew ahead of time that they would be speaking to some of the people I worked with. I did not know what questions they would be asked; the only thing I could tell them beforehand was to answer honestly. With the filming completed, the crew disappeared, leaving me to wonder what the finished product would look like. The production company continued to e-mail me with many questions such as, "Are you aware of any famous people who believed in reincarnation?" My reply follows:

> Maybe you should put me on the payroll? In the book *Reincarnation the Second Chance,*[62] there are many famous people mentioned as professing a belief in or leaning toward the theory of reincarnation. I list a few: Spinoza, Voltaire, Ben Franklin, Beethoven, Kant, Goethe, George Santayana, William Blake, William Wordsworth, Napoleon, Schopenhauer, Shelley, Balzac, Victor Hugo, Ralph Waldo Emerson, John Greenleaf Whittier, Poe, Wagner, Thoreau, Gustav Flaubert, Leo Tolstoy, Gustav Mahler, Rudolph Steiner, Henry Ford, H. G. Wells, Kipling, William Butler Yeats, Jack London, James Joyce, Henry Miller, Salvador Dali....
>
> In another book, *Reincarnation, the Phoenix Fire Mystery,* some of the same people show up plus others like, John Milton, Henry More, Frederick the Great, Sir Walter Scott, George Sand (reborn as Taylor Caldwell), Walt Whitman, Elizabeth and Robert Browning, Louisa May (and her father Bronson) Alcott, Emily Dickinson.... Seems I am in pretty good company.

I leave you with this: *"Love is a thing to be learned, through centuries of patient effort."* —D. H. Lawrence

The documentary "Beyond Death" aired for the first time on April 30th, 2000. I was pleasantly surprised by how well the program had been done. My segment followed Carol Bowman's on children's past lives. They used a good bit of footage that had been filmed by Steve Sakellarios at Oakland Cemetery in Georgia and the Sunken Road in Sharpsburg, Maryland. Along with the narration and my interview they used some file footage of a palm reader at a Halloween party. I worked at the firehouse the night of April 30th and the guys got a kick out of seeing their fire station and apparatus on TV. I was also pleasantly surprised at the interviews with two of the firefighters that I had worked with for over 20 years. Firefighter Denis Duffy said, "At first we kidded about it saying, Oh here comes General Gordon and stuff like that." He finished by saying, "Then it started to be believable." Lt. Gene Maloney, when asked what he thought of my story said, "The way he is, his actions, his words, the way he treats people, in a way it's out of another time. That's what adds to the plausibility of his story."

I much admire the work Carol Bowman has done over the years in the field of reincarnation. Of the two books she has written, the one I enjoyed the most was *Return from Heaven: Beloved Relatives Reincarnated within Your Family.* The reason for this is that she delves into the intricate workings of reincarnation. Every case that she presents gives us insight into some of the reasons why we return time and time again. Carol and I have much in common. We both are referred to in Steve Sakellerios's website, "In Another Life." Carol's story was the segment just before mine on the A&E documentary, "Beyond Death." Last, and most importantly, is that we are attempting (and I hope succeeding) to bring the realization of reincarnation to the masses. Though in Carol's work she focuses on cases involving children, adults are also drawn into the dance of life.

In Carol's first book, *Children's Past Lives,* she showed us sign-posts to use as a guide when a child is attempting to communicate to us events from a past life. I will list them for you.

- Matter-of-fact Tone
- Consistency of Detail
- Knowledge beyond Experience
- Memory of Death
- Behavior and Phobias
- The Age Window [usually between the ages of 2 and 7]

The last one, The Age Window, is what you could call the closing of act one. It is when the veil or curtain between here and the other side thickens, and the child's thoughts and memories begin to reside more here, in the present. I've seen, and heard, of that veil being pierced, many times. Remember the little boy in the bookstore who blurted out "Samurai"? What about Steve's encounter in the battlefield museum with a young man who recognized the picture of his friend the Colonel? These episodes were spontaneous, but they can be brought to the surface by a little stealth and cunning. I offer to you the following with the suggestion that you try it for yourself. Be advised though; use the technique sparingly and at the appropriate time. If your timing is off, wait for another time. If your timing is right, you may be very surprised at the outcome. The old saying is true, "Out of the mouths of babes ofttimes come gems."

One day, as I sat by myself watching television, one of Anna's granddaughters came in from outside. At the time she was approaching the ripe old age of 5. She had been sent inside to fetch her shoes. Finding her shoes, she picked them up and ran outside. As happens often these days, there was nothing much on television worth watching. I decided to go out and get some fresh air. I came across the aforementioned child attempting to put on her shoes. She was not having much success. It seems that there is a phenomenon common among children; they pull their shoes off without untying them and then strain to shove their feet back into them. She asked me for help in putting on her shoes. I said, "Do you know how to tie your shoes"? She said she did not, so I told her to sit on the stairs and I would tie them for her. I took the opportunity to try something. I untied the shoes, knelt down in front of her and pushed her feet into them one at a time. While I did so, I said, "Did you know how to tie your shoes when you used to be big"? She stared off into the distance. I was delighted to discover just how far she was seeing. She said, "Yes, they were white shoes" and then leaned over and pointed to an area on her leg about three or four inches above one ankle. She said, "They were different, they came up to here." She continued by explaining how the shoes were fastened from the bottom all away up to the top. As she spoke, I had no trouble at all envisioning a young lady from the Victorian era struggling with a buttonhook while putting on her high-top shoes. She paused for a moment, and once more stared off into space. Suddenly the little girl before me returned. Abruptly, and a bit gruffly, she said, "I don't want to talk about it any more." The spell had been broken. Off she ran like a modern-day Alice hot on the trail of the white rabbit.

While on the subject of children, I watched a story on the television program, *Sightings,* about an amazing young man; his name is Doron Blake. As a newborn, Doron could mark time to classical music with his hands. By age 2, he was using a computer. By kindergarten, he was reading *Hamlet* and learning algebra. At age 6, his IQ measured over 180. (The test was unfinished because Doron was "bored with it.") Also, at age six, Doron typed out the original draft of his book about a dinosaur named George.[63] At ten he edited and put the book on computer. This delightful children's story was published in March of 1994. Doron qualified for a Los Angeles school for the gifted and followed that up by winning a full scholarship to Phillips Exeter in New Hampshire, one of the nation's best high schools.

Doron is a product of the Repository for Germinal Choice, an institution founded in Southern California in 1980 and better remembered as the "Genius Sperm Bank." Mr. Blake's father was known only as Batch 28 to his mother, Afton. As the first boy born of this Sperm Bank, he has appeared on numerous television shows such as *48 Hours, Inside Edition, Hard Copy, Donahue, The Other Side* and the previously mentioned *Sightings.*

What I found most remarkable about this boy were his tales of reincarnation. At three years old, he said to his mother, "Do you remembered the time you and I lived in California? We lived in huts made of wood, but that time I was your wife." He remembers two lifetimes in Afghanistan, a lifetime in Egypt as a healer, and being in William Shakespeare's actors' guild. Doron does not put a lot of stock in genes. He believes much of his knowledge and intellect springs from these past life experiences. He expressed a desire to some day write a book that will explore the connection between intelligence and reincarnation.

Arts & Entertainment's "Beyond Death" had some wonderful aftereffects. A man from Canada contacted me. When he saw me on the television set, he kept telling his daughter, "I know that man, I know that man." He was so unnerved by seeing me in the program and hearing the retelling of the Battle of the Sunken Road that he paced the floor most of the night. He felt impelled to get in touch with me. He called the Westport Fire Department and spoke to a secretary. The secretaries are not allowed to give out employees' home phone numbers, so she took his phone number and told him I would get the message that he wanted to speak to me. I wrote down the number and then placed the long distance call to Canada. The man on the other end of the phone thanked me for calling him back and proceeded to tell me a most amazing story. He believes he had been a 16-year-old Confederate soldier, one of Gordon's men that had been killed at the Sunken Road. He has had many memories come to him in dreams. He said at that time Gen. Gordon called him "Sonny" and that he would often send the young man on errands. Then he even gave me what he thought was the proper name of this soldier, John Allen Cutler. The gentleman spoke with an unusual rhythm to his speech. I asked if he was a native, meaning a native of Canada. He said, "Yes" and started talking about the Manitoba area of Canada. As he talked, it dawned on me from the way he was speaking and the subject matter he was covering that he was a Native American. He paused long enough for me to ask him if he was Inuit.[64] The Inuit people are big believers in reincarnation. I have read many stories about Inuit men telling their families, just before dying, that they would be reborn into their own families as a grandson or great-grandson. When the newborns arrived, sure enough, they bore birthmarks or scars that corresponded to wounds that the dear departed had suffered during his lifetime. It turns out the man on the phone was half Cree Indian. We talked for quite a while. He had never been to the Antietam Battlefield and did not have much information on the battle. I sent him a few website addresses on the battle and a copy of Gordon's *Reminiscences of the Civil War.* After doing a little research in the roster for the Sixth Alabama Regiment, I came across a close name match. The name was Cutner (CUTNER—Private, Company?, 6th Alabama Infantry Regiment. Adjutant). No first name, but with the mention of the job title "Adjutant" a little more credence was added to the find. There is no doubt that during the Civil War adjutants ran errands. Could this man in Canada have been a one-time member of the Sixth Alabama Regiment, indeed, possibly one of Gordon's "Raccoon Roughs"? With no way of proving or disproving his story, I was left to ponder the question; had I spoken to "One of the Boys"? I hope so.

In early May of 2000, I checked my mailbox at work to find an envelope postmarked Memphis, Tenn. I found it strange that it had reached me at all. Under my name was simply "Assistant Chief, Fire Department, Westport, CT. No street address or ZIP code. I read the enclosed letter. It was from a woman who had been born in Little Rock, Arkansas, and raised in Germantown, Tennessee. She had watched "Beyond Death" and caught the segment about my experiences with reincarnation. She wanted to give me a little history concerning General John Gordon. The information contained within gave me her family's lineage back to her grandmother's mother whom, she stated, was a daughter of John B. Gordon. She finished with; "Do any of these names ring a bell? Maybe in your family background there's a connection. I would appreciate hearing from you." (Small aside: some people believe there is the possibility of some type of genetic memory.) The last page of the letter bore a telephone number and e-mail address. At the first opportunity I phoned and explained that from all the research that I had done, I could not find any connection through my family tree to General Gordon's. I said, "From what you wrote in your letter it would appear that you are one of John Gordon's great great-granddaughters. Do you know which one of his daughters was your great-grandmother?" She was not sure of her name, but knew she had passed away when her grandmother was three months old. From this information I could tell there was only one answer to my question. Her great-grandmother had to have been Carolyn Gordon. I knew this because Gordon only had two daughters that survived to marriage age. His daughter Francis Gordon was still alive long after the birth of this woman's maternal grandmother. We talked for a while, but before hanging up she surprised me by asking for my home mailing address. A short time later I received a letter from her. She opened with, "Dear, (How do I address you 'Grandfather')." This tickled me somewhat coming from a woman nearing the 80-year mark. She had enclosed a picture of her grandmother, John Gordon's granddaughter. The picture was approximately 3 by 5, black and white; with a woman standing next to a large flowerpot. She appeared to be around 40 years old. There seemed to be a sadness about her. After reading further on in the letter, I learned what may have brought about this unhappy facade. At the age of 13, she and the boy next door ran away from home and married. All this was done in an attempt to get away from her stepmother who had been very unkind to her. The letter also revealed that John Gordon had been mentioned twice in the original *Gone with the Wind,* a fact that I was not aware of. I did not know it at the time, but this little tidbit would come in handy a little farther down the road, when I would meet the author of the book. The letter closed with "Always glad to hear from you. Love, Bettye." There was a P.S. "Sure hope you can read this." She had added this little note because she is legally blind and thinks her writing is not too legible. Little does she know that her handwriting is better than mine. I make it a point to use large type in my correspondence to her. I have enjoyed my phone conversations with Bettye. Though 25 years her junior, I guess it's okay for me to call her by her first name, after all, she calls me grandfather.

One night at work the dispatcher paged me saying I had a long distance call. I took the call in my office. The woman on the other end of the line introduced herself. I told her that her name sounded familiar to me. She told me she had seen the A&E program "Beyond Death" and that her family are descendants of John B. Gordon. She was calling from Chickamauga, Georgia. She said it was not too far from Lafayette. She got a kick out of it when I told her, "My mother and sister live in Lafayette." I told her how I had visited the area, while doing research. I mentioned a few places like Gordon Hall, Gordon Springs and Taylor's Ridge. She said, "You do know about things down here!" She said, "My father has a store out near Taylor's Ridge. Then it struck me why her name sounded familiar. I had driven by her father's store and remembered seeing the name. I told her about doing research at the Cherokee library in Lafayette. She said, "I have a cousin that works at that library." I said, "A girl in the Georgia Room by the name of Dannette would always help me." She yelled, "That's her! That's my cousin." We talked for quite a while and when we'd finished, she invited me to visit the next time I was in Georgia saying, "Stop by sometime, we'll treat you like family."

Another man from Canada wrote me a seven-page letter. I will paraphrase it for you here:

> Dear Mr. Keene,
> My name is Bradley Gordon Paul Langton. I am 41 years old and reside in a suburb of Vancouver, British Columbia. I'm writing to you in regards to the program on A&E Sunday July 30th, 2000. It has taken me a great deal of thought whether I should write you or not. As I watched the program about you and General John Gordon I became very overwhelmed with what I was watching. Though your face I did not recognize, I surely did recognize General John B. Gordon's face. It was like an old friend who I would see occasionally in my dreams or thoughts, but I felt as though I did know this person, perhaps in another life. I must first explain the events that lead me to write you in the first place.
>
> All my life, mostly from about age 2 to 15 years old, I felt very out of place living in British Columbia. I yearned for and was very

drawn to the South; Southern music, Southern food, anything to do with the Southern culture. I was very drawn to the Civil War. Being a teen and confused anyway, I just enjoyed my own little world without understanding the why of it. As a teen in school, I never liked Canadian history or politics; I am still not interested even today. I've been told that I am different in my way of life and views on politics and other issues. There have been times in my life when I just knew I had been in the American Civil War. As long as I could remember I would get very angry with anyone who put down Southern people, the Confederate flag or their culture. I would voice my opinion to them, which was usually in the form of very colorful metaphors. I've always gotten very teary-eyed when it comes to the Civil War. The first time I cried was when I was very young watching The Good the Bad and the Ugly. There was one scene of a Confederate prisoner of war camp where a Federal soldier told some Confederate musicians to "Play." The tune was very sad and I still remember it to this day. The first time Gettysburg was playing at the picture show I went to see it. My emotions ran circles inside my head. I was saddened beyond belief, joyous, and at the same time, proud inside my heart. I tried to suppress my feelings, but always needed an answer as to why I felt this way.

My mom phoned me very excited but cautious about what she was about to tell me. My mom had just had an experience. Over the years, I have come to understand that she is a receiver of information. This information comes from a "Higher Power" if you will. Mom knew my passion for southern culture and the Civil War. She said, "Brad you better sit down" and then began to describe the chain of events and information she had received. She said she had been told that I had been a young boy named John Paul Verdun, born in 1850. She was not sure where, but thought it may have been Missouri. She said, "He was a 14 or 15-year-old Confederate soldier killed somewhere between Dec. 1864 and April 1865." I could not believe what I was hearing. I do not go to church, but I do have some faith. I was unsure if I believed in reincarnation or not. My mother said that John Verdun had been killed by a sword or bayonet that went through his back and into his heart. There is a mole [or birthmark] on my back and on occasion I get a sharp pain through that area. After a while the pain goes away.

One night I was channel surfing and this program came on A&E called "Beyond Death." I changed the channel, but something inside me said to go back. I was blown away by this show and phoned my mom the next day to tell her about you and General Gordon. Today mom phoned and said she had more information.

> She [mom] told me that she asked if John Verdun knew General John Gordon and the answer was "Yes." She also said, "Gordon wanted the boy to go home, but John Verdun refused and wanted to keep fighting." According to mom's notes, General Gordon was like a father figure and tried to watch out for the boy as best he could. General Gordon gave something to John Verdun, a piece of cloth, perhaps colors to put around his neck. After John Verdun was killed, General Gordon was very upset that the young boy had not gone home.
>
> This is the only information I have, it has lessened my yearning for answers, but I have a need to find out more. I feel that there may be some kind of mention in General Gordon's memoirs of a young boy. In my heart, I know, because the feelings have grown stronger each day. Aside from my mom, and you, I have told no one else of my story. I am very exhausted from all this excitement. I hope you enjoy my experiences, though yours are quite different from mine. Some would think that we are kooks, crackpots, but some would understand. I personally don't care what anyone thinks of me. I know I am of sound mind. Having some answers to the "whys" has been a great feeling to my soul and I'm sure I will find more answers some day. I would like to thank you for listening to my story and I enjoyed your program on A&E. Feel free to contact me if you wish by letter or phone. I understand that this is a lot of beans to swallow, but I know what I feel inside and it will forever be with me.

As I read the letter, a picture came to mind. The same picture that so haunted me that I felt it necessary to write about it earlier in this book. It was the photo of a young boy, approximately 14 years old, lying dead in the bottom of a trench at Petersburg, Virginia. I called Bradley on the phone and during our conversation I mentioned this photo to him. I told him I would do some research to see if I could find out exactly where in Petersburg the photo had been taken. After doing so I would send him a copy of the photo. After posing the question of the photo to Robert E. L. Krick of Petersburg, Virginia, I received my answer in the form of a letter a short time later. The results follow:

> Dear Jeff,
>
> Regarding the forlorn dead Confederate, I am surprised to have found that the evidence is fairly clear about the troops defending that stretch of line on April 2, 1865. Bryan Grimes's emaciated division of the Second Corps ran right through there, fresh from its

participation at Fort Stedman the week before. One source places the 53rd North Carolina actually inside Fort Mahone, but other accounts that seem to be more reliable have the 3rd Alabama Infantry as the unit driven out of the fort. Of course everything around Fort Mahone was a network of dirt embankments, and it is possible that the photograph was taken at some adjacent site. There was a series of more than twenty similar shots ("death studies") taken on April 3, 1865, by T. C. Roche. The original caption for the one that you are interested in is as follows:

"This view was taken in the trenches of the rebel Fort Mahone, called by the soldiers 'Fort Damnation,' the morning after the storming of Petersburgh, Va., April 2d, 1865. It shows a boy about 14 years, who must have been asleep when the attack was made, as he is but partially dressed; he was killed as he came out from a bomb proof; he has on the rebel grey uniform."

The site of Fort Mahone today is on the west side of the Jerusalem Plank Road; about over where the enormously tall Pennsylvania Monument is, just west of the marker for Colonel Gowan of the 48th Pennsylvania. It is developed beyond recognition, as you doubtless know.

After receiving the photo, Bradley called me on the phone. He was astounded by the similarity between the boy in the picture and himself at that age. His mother, after seeing the photo, was so unnerved that he said, "She cried for two days." In a subsequent letter from Bradley I was to discover another synchronistic event in his life. He wrote, did you know my birthday is April. 9, 1959? To most, this date would not mean much, but to anyone with a slight interest in the Civil War it rings a very big bell. Apr. 9, 1865 was the day that General Robert E. Lee surrendered the Army of Northern Virginia to General Ulysses S. Grant.

The song that Bradley had mentioned from the movie *The Good, the Bad and the Ugly* had affected me in the same way. I first saw the movie in early '70s long before the start of my reincarnation adventures. I ran right out to buy the record (33.1/3 RPM) of the soundtrack.[65] The song that Bradley talked about is titled "Story of a Soldier." I found the song so haunting that I would play it over and over again. I even said to my first wife,

Bridget, "I'd like to have that song played at my funeral." When long-playing records fell from vogue I went out and purchased a copy of the same album in compact disc.

Next to come along was an old "comrade-in-arms." The postmark this time was Virginia, a little closer to my home and to my heart. The letter read:

> Dear Mr. Keene,
> Last night I watched "Beyond Death" on A&E and heard your particular story. "At last," I thought, "someone has had the same experience as I have had!" My story began in October 1993. Until then, I'd never had any special interest in the Civil War despite the fact that I was living in an area where much of it took place and in an antebellum home. The confluence of three things changed all that: I saw the movie *Gettysburg,* read the book that it is based on called *The Killer Angels,* and lastly was having my house painted by a young man who was a keen Civil War enthusiast. It was at his suggestion that I read the book when I told him I had seen the film. Suddenly, almost overnight, I became a raging fanatic about the war. I subscribed to all the magazines, took books from the library, joined the Civil War Roundtable in my area. At this point in [it was May 1994], I went to my first re-enactment in Orange, VA. They were doing the battle of the "Mule Shoe" which was part of the Spotsylvania campaign in 1864. And I was very deeply moved by the sight of the tents, cannons, horses, men in uniform, and ladies in hoop skirts. I began to wonder if perhaps I might have lived through those times, but, in truth, I could not remember anything like that. This reenactment was held on May 8th, but the actual battle of the "Mule Shoe" took place on May 12th. I was sitting at home on the 11th of May, 1994, thinking about the reenactment and also the fact that on May 11th, 1864, J. E. B. Stuart had been mortally wounded at Yellow Tavern—a direct result of the Spotsylvania campaign. The word "Nemesis" came into my head, much like the words "Not yet" came into yours. I found myself thinking of how Phil Sheridan had certainly been Stuart's nemesis on May 11th, and then I realized that a man named Sheridan had also been my nemesis in my life. In the next instant, I found myself remembering the movie *Gettysburg* and of how Robert E. Lee felt disappointed and let down by Stuart. I then thought of the Lee in my life who, although very fond of me, could not get over his anger at my divorce [for reasons that are irrelevant here]. Lee and Sheridan in both lifetimes I thought to myself. But it was the 11th

> of May when these thoughts came to me. At first, I thought they might be coincidence, but as time went on I realize that so much in my life paralleled his; my lifelong devotion to horses, my love of Irish music of the sort played during the war, my fascination with West Point [I love books set there such as *Dress Gray*], and a number of other things too numerous to mention. As time went on, I began to keep a journal and I could identify people in my life as people from his. I wrote an 80-page account of all of it and it was crystal clear that my life was indeed an echo of his life including certain physical characteristics, although perhaps not as pronounced as your cheek. I've traveled to many battlefields with tour groups and it is amazing how often the subject of reincarnation will come up. Most people confess that they do not know what to believe, but you, I, and others like us do know. Jeb Stuart is always with me as John B. Gordon is with you. They want us to be aware of them and of their lives. That is why they chose to make us aware of their presence. I would love to hear from you on the subject but, life goes on, and you're a busy man. I told my three sons about my story and I think two of them believe me and one does not. I suppose it is like that for all of us experiencing this.

There was a phone number at the bottom of the letter. I called, and to make a long story short, made arrangements to meet up with her at an upcoming Civil War tour. I spent two enjoyable days touring Virginia battlefields with this woman who claimed to have once been Confederate General J. E. B. Stuart. She was charming and sincere, had a great sense of humor and walked with the swaggering gait common to one who was "born to the saddle." We shared some old stories and some new ones. I learned that she had spent a good part of her life working for the U.S. Government and that her job had taken her to many different countries. When she told me the name of the agency, I just looked at her and said, "Still doing reconnaissance, huh?" The weekend came to a close all too soon. I hugged my new old friend and kissed her on the cheek. It was not a good-bye; it reminded me more of the old cavalry parting phrase "Until the next post." As I walked away, a thought popped into my head, "Did I just kiss Jeb Stuart?" Well, at least no beard this time.

CHAPTER THIRTEEN

Many Happy Returns

SO IT WENT, people entering my life with stories of having been with me in past lives. What many of these people had in common was a strong urge to contact me, to share their stories. Why? Because they knew I would understand. They could see within my story their own. They had found a kindred spirit, a kinsman on this long and sometimes confusing journey called life. Many of them expressed feelings that I knew well, feelings of lonliness, wonder, doubt, fear, longing, joy, sorrow, amazement, pain. The list could go on and on.

Once again I received a call from the chief's secretary. This time she gave me a phone number for a Dr. Walter Semkiw. She said he wanted to get in touch with me regarding the "Beyond Death" program. Dr. Semkiw had been sent a film clip of my segment from "Beyond Death." I did not recognize the area code. I dialed the number and Dr. Semkiw answered. The first thing I asked was, "Where are you located?" He said, "San Francisco, give me your number and I will call you back." I liked him already; he was picking up the tab for a coast-to-coast call. He explained the research he was doing into reincarnation and that someone had sent him a clip of my portion of the A&E documentary. He gave me a little of his background, his education, jobs he has held and so on. Then he caught me by surprise when he told me he believed he had been John Adams (second president of the United States). Now I knew what it was like to be on the receiving end. I thought this must be the reaction many people get when I tell them my story. Being open minded, I decided to listen to the story from this man "bringing coals to Newcastle." Dr. Semkiw went on to tell me how his story of reincarnation started:

> My story begins in 1984 when I went to a medium who had the ability to channel one's spiritual guides. I had never gone to a psychic or medium before, but reasoned that for the $50 fee, the experience should be entertaining at the very least. As the guides spoke, the medium's voice and facial expressions changed. At first, with surprising accuracy, the guides discussed my family and professional life. Later on, they told me about a lifetime in Revolutionary America. The guides stated that had I signed my name on parchment and in doing so, helped secure new ideals for humanity. At the end of the session, they told me that in this past era, I was John Adams. The guides told me that if I researched Adams, I would see myself.
>
> Of course, I didn't believe that I was John Adams. I had heard that psychics routinely tell people that they were someone famous, for that is what people want to hear. I largely dismissed the past life information conveyed. Instead, I pursued my medical career, taking a position as medical director of Unocal 76, an oil company whose slogan happens to be "The Spirit of 1776." The years passed until quite unexpectedly, in 1996, I had an extremely strong intuition to study the life of John Adams and to research astrology. 1996, coincidentally, marked the bicentennial of the start of John Adams' presidency.
>
> As I researched Adams and reviewed portraits of his family and friends, I found that I did see myself in John Adams. Personality traits were uncannily similar and there was a physical resemblance.[66]

Physical resemblance is what brought him to seek me out. At the time he was finishing up his book titled, *Return of the Revolutionaries* and wanted to include my story [which he did].

In a three-year span Dr. Semkiw had accumulated more than fifty past-life cases. He saw in these cases some startling similarities. He observed three principles at work.

> People look the same from lifetime to lifetime. *Facial architecture*, the shape of the hands and even body postures are remarkably consistent from one lifetime to another.
>
> *Personality traits persist*. A person's demeanor and habits of thought stay the same. Spiritually, we seem to pick up where we left off before. Indeed, the work that I am doing now is a continuation of the spiritual thought of John Adams.
>
> *We come into life in groups*, based on shared karma, emotional attachments and joint projects. We come back with friends, loved ones and work associates from before.
>
> I utilize the three criteria cited above to establish past life matches. In the future, I believe there will be a fourth criterion, that of DNA analysis. Since people look the same from lifetime to lifetime, I believe that a correlate or marker in a person's DNA may be found.[67]

I have no doubts as to most of Dr. Semkiw's findings (I will leave the DNA to the scientist). As to people returning in groups, retaining their personality traits and physical features, I can give testament:

First, I shall submit here two short stories, one from the present, the other from long ago. The reason for doing so is to illustrate "personally traits" of the group I am with today as compared to yesteryear. An added bonus is to confirm the old adage, "The more things change, the more they stay the same."

Over the years, I have often wondered if the people I work with were with me during those tumultuous times back in the 1860s. Sometimes their action and deeds caused me to ponder. I will relate a conversation that took place one night at fire headquarters. This type of banter is not uncommon during confrontation of a verbal nature. I am a bit of a chocoholic, so one night I brought in two large chocolate bars and put them in the platoon locker. One hour later I returned to the locker to find only one bar remaining. I asked in a loud voice, "Who ate my chocolate bar?" There was quiet in the dayroom. Nearby stood Firefighter Mike Kronick, his head turning to look at everybody else in the room but me. I said, "Mr. Kronick, did you eat my candy bar?" He turned his head to face me and said, "I ate half of it." I said, "Well then, who ate the other half?" Once again he looked around the room at his brother firefighters with a half-pleading look in his eyes. With no help forthcoming he turned back to me and related the saga of the candy bar. He said, "I ate half the bar and then put the other half on top of the kitchen table. The next time I came by the table it was still there, so I ate that half too." What could I do but laugh. Next time (and there will be a next time) I will have to phrase my question differently to get the whole story instead of a half at a time.

Compare this encounter with one written by John Gordon about an incident that took place at Gettysburg, Pennsylvania in 1863.

> Going into camp in an open country and after dark, it was ascertained that there was no wood to be had for even the limited amount of necessary cooking, and I was appealed to by the men for permission to use a few rails from an old-fashioned fence near the camp. I agreed that they might take the top layer of rails, as the fence would still be high enough to answer the farmer's purpose. When morning came the fence had nearly all disappeared, and each man declared that he had taken only the top rail! The authorized(?) destruction of that fence is not difficult to understand! It was a case of adherence to the letter and neglect of the spirit; but there was no alternative except good-naturedly to admit that my men had gotten the better of me that time.[68]

Second, I offer six photos. Three are of men I work with; the remaining three are Civil War generals. The three firefighters have no recollections of any past lives and have not expressed to me, one way or another, their beliefs in reincarnation. They were kind enough to let me use their pictures. Look for yourself at the three side by side comparison, then you decide if they could be the same people photographed more than one hundred years apart. I have come across more than six different photos of Civil War era soldiers that bear a striking resemblance to people I work with today, or have worked with in the recent past. Not only the photos, but also the description of their personalities, then and now, are consistent.

Union Gen. Wesley Merritt

Firefighters
Wm. Dingee and Rob Yost

Compare the face, bone structure and the hand on the hip of firefighter Rob Yost (above far right) to that of Gen. Wesley Merritt. The pose of Mr. Yost was not staged. It is a picture that was taken on top of Mt. Washington with firefighter William Dingee (see Wm. Dingee, next page). In real life, the similarities of looks between Gen. Merritt and firefighter Yost is even greater than displayed in the photos above.

Firefighter Wm. Dingee

Confederate Gen.
Edward Porter Alexander

Another set of photos above show once again a similarity of bone structure and looks between firefighter William Dingee and Confederate General Edward Porter Alexander. Firefighters are not allowed to wear beards so I used a photo of Mr. Dingee while he was on vacation and enjoying a reprieve from shaving.

Confederate Gen.
Cadmus Wilcox

Firefighter Wayne R. Zaleta

The most amazing resemblance of the three is that of firefighter Wayne R. Zaleta to Gen. Cadmus Wilcox. You will note a darkened area on Wayne's left cheek that runs from the tip of his mustache up towards his ear. In the photo of Gen. Wilcox the markings in this area is much more apparent. None of the pictures have been retouched.

They say, "We pass this way but once." We do not live the same life twice, that is true, so I guess what they say is correct. All one can hope for is to do the journey in good company. It appears that I'm doing it this time back amongst the best.

I sent Dr. Semkiw information on my story, a copy of my manuscript and photos. A short time later my case was included on his website along with two cases on published authors.

Police Captain Robert Snow, who wrote *Looking for Carroll Beckwith.* This Indianapolis Police Captain in charge of Homicide Division, went to a past life regression on a dare and experienced profound memories of a lifetime as a portrait artist. He remembered 28 specific facts in the regression, including painting a portrait of a hunchback woman. Captain Snow didn't believe in reincarnation and tried to find an alternate explanation for the experience, such as the possibility that he viewed the portrait in a book or museum. After searching for a year, Captain Snow was not able to locate the portrait in books or museum collections. While on vacation in New Orleans, Captain Snow coincidentally ran into the portrait of the hunchback woman in a gallery. From the painting he was able to derive his past life identity and confirm 26 of the 28 facts from the regression. Captain Snow also looks like his past life identity, Carroll Beckwith.

William Barnes, who describes his lifetime as the designer of the Titanic, in "Tommie Andrews, Voyage into History." William Barnes started having spontaneous memories of the Titanic at age four and told his mother his name was Tommie, not William. Later on, he was able to deduce that he designed the Titanic and died on her maiden voyage.

Westport Connecticut Assistant Fire Chief Jeffrey Keene, who wrote "Not Yet"[69] which documents his discovery of a past life as Civil War Confederate General John B. Gordon. Chief Keene had an unexpected profound emotional experience when he visited a portion of Antietam battlefield called Sunken Road. He later was able to derive that he was a Confederate soldier, John B. Gordon, who was almost killed at that very spot. The resemblance between Gordon and Keene is termed "scary" by many who have seen the comparisons.[70]

On the weekend of April 27th, 28th and 29th, 2000, I traveled with Dr. Semkiw to a conference being held in Sturbridge, Massachusetts. The International Association of Regression Research Therapies put on the weekend of lectures and classes. Dr. Semkiw was one of the lecturers that weekend. He presented many case studies of past lives, including his own as John Adams. I was to be Dr. Semkiw's guest during his reincarnation lecture and I acted as sort of a "Show And Tell" when it came time for my story.

Dr. Semkiw had forewarned me that one of the attendees would be Dianne Seaman, a woman who believes she had been

Margaret Mitchell, author of the best-selling book of all-time (after the Bible) *Gone with the Wind.* Dianne had not made this past life story known to the general public, but kept it among close friends and trusted associates. What little I knew of Ms. Mitchell, I did know one thing for sure, her last resting place is in Oakland Cemetery, the same Cemetery as General John Gordon. Conducting a search on the Internet, I found a web site called Find a Grave. Find a Grave is "A resource for finding the final resting places of notable people." You can search by name, location or claim to fame. The page dedicated to Margaret Mitchell contained a short biography and a few photographs.

Margaret Munnerlyn Mitchell
Birth: Nov. 8, 1900
Atlanta
Georgia, USA
Death: Aug. 16, 1949

> Writer, author of *Gone with the Wind.* She began working as a journalist, using the name of Peggy Mitchell for the *Atlanta Journal* as a feature writer. That same year, Mitchell married Berrien Kinnard Upshaw. The marriage lasted only a few months, but the couple was not officially divorced until 1924. In 1925, Mitchell married John Marsh. Ms. Mitchell shocked Atlanta society by keeping her own name, "Margaret Mitchell" for professional purposes. (In private life, she was known as Peggy Marsh.) It took her ten years to write *Gone with The Wind,* then titled *Tomorrow Is Another Day.* She also changed the name of the heroine, a beautiful and manipulative Southern belle, from her original choice of Pansy to the more evocative Scarlett. In addition to its staggering sales, the novel won both the Pulitzer Prize and the National Book Award in 1937. Just one month after the release of the book, the film rights were sold to David O. Selznick for the then highest paid fee ever—$50,000. Mitchell wanted no part in the movie, and had a clause written into her contract absolving her from any more work on the project. The film won eight Academy Awards, including best picture for 1939, arguably one of the greatest years for film. Apart from a lively correspondence, she personally answered a good deal of her millions of fan letters. Mitchell never wrote again. On August 16, 1949, Margaret Mitchell was struck by a taxicab on Atlanta's Peachtree Street while on her way to a movie

with her husband. She died five days later at the age of 49. As of 1998, *Gone with the Wind* was the best-selling book of all time, after the Bible, with a total of 23 million copies sold worldwide. In 1996, figures indicated that almost 200 million people had seen the Selznick film version of *Gone with the Wind*; a gala re-release of a remastered version in 1998 undoubtedly pushed those numbers even higher.

Burial:
Oakland Cemetery
Atlanta (Fulton County), Georgia, USA[71]

One of the photos showed a coquettish Mitchell somewhere in her early 20s. Her face was posed in a three-quarter view with her eyes casting a glance to one side. I made a copy of the photo and bio to take to Massachusetts. Upon arrival at Sturbridge, Dr. Semkiw and I checked into the Public House Historic Inn. We were just in time to attend a meeting being held in one of the large conference rooms in the Inn. As we sat listening to the speaker, I asked Dr. Semkiw to point out Diane Seaman. In my hand at the time was the picture of Margaret Mitchell I had copied from the Internet. Dianne was pointed out to me, but she sat with her back towards us, so I could not see her face. A moment later she turned to talk to another person at her table. I compared the photo to the person sitting across the room. Dianne's face was in three-quarter view, eyes looking to one side, just as in the photo. I leaned towards Dr. Semkiw and pointed to the photo saying, "That's her, even the same pose." When the meeting was over, Dr. Semkiw and I walked around the room speaking with some of the other people attending the conference. We finally met up with Dianne Seaman. Dr. Semkiw introduced me to her. I said, "We have something in common." She gave me a quizzical look. I handed her a copy of the page from Find-a-Grave adding "Real estate in Oakland Cemetery." Dr. Semkiw explained a little about my past life as General John B. Gordon. Diane had to confess that at the mention of the words "Oakland Cemetery" she got goosebumps. She, too, had experienced first-hand what it is like to stand next to one's own grave. After spending some time together that weekend, Dianne and I developed a friendship and traded addresses. After Dr. Semkiw's lecture and listening to me speak, Dianne decided it was time for her to stand up in front of the assembled group and tell her story of the Margaret Mitchell past life. I enjoyed watching and listening to her story; we even had a little fun with the fact that General Gordon and Ms. Mitchell were "sleeping together." It is nice to have a fellow traveler walking the same road. One can become lonely moving along the highway of self-discovery. Now I had gained another travel companion. In the coming months, Dianne and I would lend support to each other. I e-mailed Dianne copies of rejections of my book that I had received from publishers. She wrote back "If I may pass on some lessons I have learned from rejections... [1] don't take it personally and [2] do not get attached to the fruits of your labors. You have my permission to remind me of these when I am in need of it!!" I found this to be sage advice. One time I came across a quote from an article Margaret Mitchell had written when she was a writer for the *Atlanta Journal*. Her profile of General Gordon appeared in the *Journal's* magazine section of November 29,1925 it read in part:

> General John Brown Gordon, the "Bayard of the Confederacy," whose statue now guards the entrance to the State Capitol and after whom Gordon Street in Atlanta was named, was a handsome man, pleasant of smile and possessed of great dignity and bearing. He was magnetic, drawing all hearts and eyes to him and when he spoke, all others were silent to listen. A stranger coming into his presence could not but realize that he stood before a great man.

Though Mitchell was only a toddler when General Gordon died, she wrote some very kind words about him. I e-mailed a belated thank you to Dianne and received in return an e-mail stating "You're Welcome." Dianne had not been aware of the Gordon article and wrote "... this in part reinforces why, whenever I think of you, I place you in Georgia and have to force myself to think of you in Connecticut.... That far north in Yankee territory!!" Dianne is also in the process of writing her story. She sent me a two-page excerpt that described her first visit to the house where Margaret Mitchell penned her epic novel, *Gone with the Wind.* Though only two typewritten pages in length, it took me a while to read through to the end. Twice I was brought to tears. Many of the things Dianne wrote vividly described feelings I had felt at Sunken Road and other places I have passed on my journey into this world of reincarnation. She wrote about her perception of time changing; being hit with many different feelings simultaneously. She wrote about bursting into tears, being scared, and questioning her sanity and finally a feeling of total exhaustion. I knew these feelings well; I've been through them myself. I had even written many of the same things down in my book, although not as eloquently as Dianne had expressed them. I reread the two pages one last time and then went outside to sit on the front porch and gather my thoughts. Many emotions had arisen in me from the description of Dianne's encounter with her past life. After a while these were replaced by the warm, peaceful feeling of knowing you are not alone.

I owe Dr. Semkiw a debt of gratitude for many reasons—being included in his book, on his website, and being allowed to travel with him to conferences. He set up radio interviews and recommended me to a literary agent. The first radio show I did was Uri Geller's *Parascience and Beyond.* You may remember Mr. Geller from his mental spoon-bending days back in the 60s and 70s. The next show was a real treat. The good doctor booked us on Jill Lawrence's show, *Jill and Friends,* broadcast by Wisdom Radio. Capt. Snow, Bill Barnes, Dr. Semkiw and I spent a delightful two hours discussing our stories with Jill.

Dr. Semkiw was intrigued with my writing style when he read my manuscript. He noticed what he thought were similarities between Gordon's style and my own.

> In *Not Yet,* Jeff includes documents that show similarities between his writing style and Gordon's. In his later years, General Gordon wrote a book called *Reminiscences of the Civil War,* which provides material for such analysis. Let us compare two passages, one from Gordon's book, describing the efforts of his men to put out a fire in Wrightsville, Pennsylvania, and one from Keene regarding his fire

department's response to an emergency incident. My observation is that the two documents seem to be written in the same 'voice.' Linguistic analysis may allow us to better define common traits between the passages.[72]

A linguist from the University of California, Berkley did an evaluation that uncovered common traits in six areas. What follows are the results of that evaluation:

Writing Sample One: General John B. Gordon (from *Reminiscences of the Civil War)*

With great energy my men labored to save the bridge. I called on the citizens of Wrightsville for buckets and pails, but none were to be found. There was no lack of buckets and pails a little while later, when the town was on fire ... My men labored as earnestly and bravely to save the town as they did to save the bridge. In the absence of fire-engines or other appliances, the only chance to arrest the progress of the flames was to form my men around the burning district, with the flank resting on the river's edge, and pass rapidly from hand to hand the pails of water. Thus, and thus only, was the advancing, raging fire met, and at a late hour of the night checked and conquered.

Writing Sample Two: Assistant Chief Jeffrey Keene (from a letter to Fire Chief)

With my radio restored, man power and apparatus were brought in and put under the guidance of Acting Lieutenant Christopher Ackley. While setting up a plan of action, Lieutenant Ackley displayed good common sense, knowledge, training and a deep concern for the safety of firefighters under his command. A large amount of gas entered the structure by way of a open window. Though we tried to remove all possible sources of ignition, we were able to remove all but two. The owner informed us that the house contained an oil-fired furnace and a hot water heater. There was no way to shut them off from the inside or outside. Using metering devices, a positive pressure fan and opening and closing windows, the hazard was removed.

Findings of Linguistic Analysis:

Close in average number of words per sentence: Gordon-21, Keene-18

Use of compound sentences: Gordon—"the only chance to arrest the progress of flames was to form my men around the burning district, with the flank resting on the river's edge, and pass rapidly from hand to hand the pails of water." Keene—"While setting up a plan of action, Lieutenant Ackley displayed good common sense, knowledge, training and a deep concern for the safety of firefighters under his command."

Use of preposed clauses in complex sentences: Gordon—"In the absence of fire engines," Keene—"While setting up a plan of action."

Use of existential-there sentence with negation: Gordon—"There was no lack of buckets." Keene—"There was no way to shut them off."

Adverbial clauses at beginning of sentence: Gordon—"With great energy," "In the absence of fire-engines." Keene—"With my radio restored."

Most of text is in active voice except at the end. In both passages, paragraphs end in passive voice, as if the success came about without the intervention of those involved. Excitement is achieved by altering expected word order, separating two parts of the verb. Gordon—"was the advancing, raging fire met, and at a late hour of the night checked and conquered." Keene—"Using metering devices, ... the hazard was removed."

I had never given any thought to the possibility of a correlation between Gordon's writing style and my own. Dr. Semkiw told me that the linguist who did the report stated, "Similarities in writing style definitely did exist, though it is not proof that the authors are the same."[73]

It would be impossible for anyone to compare two handwriting samples and say with absolute certainty that the authors were one and the same person. It would appear though, that the results of the linguistic analysis of these two small samplings gives some credence to Dr. Semkiw's hypothesis of the same "voice."

CHAPTER FOURTEEN

Joy and Sorrow

ON AUG. 11TH, 2001, my daughter Shannon was married just north of Newport, Rhode Island. The wedding ceremony was held in a house built in the 1920s to resemble a French chateau. After the reception dinner, I walked into the ballroom to find the dance floor completely empty. I'm not much of a dancer but, I am mostly Irish, and having consumed a few drinks I decided it was time to get the party going. I asked the disc jockey to play "What'll I do," a song that I often sang to Shannon when she was an infant. Of the 70,000 songs this man had in his collection that song was not one he brought with him that night. I asked if he had Tony Bennett's "I Left My Heart in San Francisco." He did and I told him to put it on next. I found Shannon near the front door and hurriedly dragged her to the ballroom. We were far from San Francisco but this song is a very special one. Shannon's great-uncle Marty Manning had won a Grammy for his arrangement and her grandfather Arthur (Buddy) Brennan was playing the well-known melodious piano notes. I took the opportunity, while dancing with Shannon, to pass on some of the things I had learned in my fifty plus years of life. I said, "You know, no one ever truly dies, not the way most people think of death. Everyone that you have ever loved or that has ever loved you still exists. All the things that I have seen, felt, and experienced tell me this is true. Your grandmother Fran, your grandfathers, and all the rest are watching here today and sharing in your happiness." With this the tears started flowing down Shannon's cheeks. Shannon knew what I was saying was the truth. I had made a similar statement during my interview for A&E's "Beyond Death" right after being asked the question "What have all your years of discoveries taught you?" For whatever reason, they chose not to include my answer in the finished documentary.

Slowly more couples moved onto the dance floor. Next I sought out my daughter, Samantha. She had jettisoned the high heels from her bridesmaid's apparel and was now wandering around barefoot. She claimed not to know how to slow dance. She wasn't going to get away that easily. I said, "Stand on my feet like you did when you were a little girl." Samantha placed her feet gently on mine and we started to dance. It must have been a sight, for the photographer took several pictures of us dancing and a few close-ups of her bare feet on top of my tuxedo shoes. The music changed to a faster rock-and-roll beat and I now was forced to adapt my 60s dance steps to a new century's music. I fared pretty well, so much so, I was later given the *nom de soirée,* "Dancing Boy." My reply to that was to ask, "How many people were dancing before I started"? The answer was "None." I then asked, "How many people were dancing after I started dancing?" The answer to this was "Everyone." I rested my case.

Late in the evening I moved outside to get some fresh air. While standing in the courtyard I talked with the police officer that had been hired for the night. Anna appeared at the front door and yelled, "Hey! Why aren't you dancing"? At this, the policeman held out his arms and he and I proceeded to dance around the courtyard. Anna shook her head and said, "No! I meant in here!" It was a beautiful wedding and a fun reception. The phrase "A good time was had by all" comes to mind. In attendance that day was my brother Joel, his wife Cindy and her son Joe. They were up from Jacksonville, Florida and wanted to do some sight-seeing while in the Northeast. I had not seen my little brother in nearly ten years, so we made arrangements to visit New York City on Monday, August 13th. The four of us took the train to Grand Central Station and walked the few blocks to the Empire State Building. On top of the one-time world's tallest building we found that our view was limited because of weather conditions. I pointed out some landmarks: the Statue of Liberty, the Chrysler Building and the Twin Towers of the World Trade Center. We returned to street level and made our way up Fifth Avenue, all the while Joe laughing at my stupid jokes and Cindy shaking her head (I don't know why, but women seem to do that a lot when they're around me). We stopped at Rockefeller Center and St. Patrick's Cathedral. From the look on Cindy's face I could see St. Patrick's would be the highlight of her trip to New York. It is hard for anyone not to be taken aback by the beauty of this structure, both inside and out. There was a mass in progress and Cindy asked if we had time for her and Joe to take communion. Joel and I stood in the back of the church while the two of them moved down the center aisle to receive communion. They walked back and sat for a while in one of the last pews on the right hand side. Less than two months later, I would sit in the same area, not as a visitor, but as a mourner.

September 11th 2001

On the morning of September 11th, 2001, I, like countless other Americans, stood transfixed in front of the television as the tragic events of the day unfolded. A plane had hit one of the World Trade Center's towers. At first, it appeared to be a freak accident, but as the second plane came into view, it left little doubt as to what was happening. As the first 110-story tower collapsed to the ground, I turned to Anna and said, "The New York fire department just lost a large number of men." I was aware of how they handled fire operations in high-rise buildings. Firefighters are sent to the areas where the building's occupants are in the most danger, staging areas for manpower and equipment are set up on the floors below. Command and Control centers are put into operation on other floors. All this requires a large amount of personnel, even in normal size buildings. I could only imagine the number required for one of the tallest buildings ever built. Then, I watched the second tower come down like a curtain on a bad play. Only smoke, dust and sky were left where these two majestic buildings had once stood. I called the Westport Fire Department and suggested we send some men with Rescue #8, a vehicle that contains rescue tools, cribbing and a generator for lighting. I was put on the list of members volunteering to respond to New York. A call came later that day to be ready to go with only 10 minutes notice. My fire-fighting gear was in my car along with a plastic trash bag containing blue jeans, socks and other hastily assembled bits of clothing that might be needed for a prolonged stay.

Days passed and it became apparent that our department was not sending anyone to New York City. Some members took it upon themselves to go. Like old fire horses that have answered thousands of calls, their feet started moving to the sound of the alarm. It is difficult to rein in people whose physical nature and character is one of action. I know, because it is one of the most difficult aspects of my job. I must keep careful watch over this strange breed of humans, to stop them from going beyond their limits, because at times, they feel limitless. Early one morning they met at the railroad station for the trip to New York. The Westport crew was put to work setting up a warehouse for rescue equipment near the Engine #10 Truck #10 firehouse (this fire station was the closest to the World Trade Center). A one-time delicatessen was transformed into a supply house for rescue saws with metal cutting blades needed to cut through the heavy beams. They helped comprise one of the human chains that formed to clear away debris from the huge piles of rubble. At one point they were called off the piles and asked to stand behind some barrier tape. They soon learned the reason; it was the first visit of President George W. Bush to "Ground Zero." With him that day were Sen. Hillary Clinton, Gov. George Pataki, Mayor Rudolph Giuliani and Fire Commissioner, Thomas Von Essen.[74] These dignitaries passed along the line of barrier tape, shaking hands with the rescuers. While President Bush held Westport firefighter Lisa Ruot's hand, he pulled her forward to whisper something in her ear. He said, "When we find the hole the bastards are hiding in, we'll take care of them." The department did not give these members the go-ahead; they went of their own volition. I felt especially proud of them. They had some amazing stories to tell upon their return. It seems the people of New York City took very good care of them with free train rides, food, and even rubbed and powdered their feet while they changed their socks for them. Civilians lined the street to cheer the rescue workers going to and from the scene. People stopped them on the street to shake their hands and pat them on the back.

Television coverage continued to show rescue efforts, but as the days went by it became obvious there was no one left to rescue. 343 firefighters perished. With the discovery of each firefighter's body came a somber and touching sight. There is a tradition in the fire service that the department takes care of their own. All the machinery comes to a stop and the rescue workers form lines. Firefighters are sent in to remove the body of their fallen brother. They drape the American flag over the departed and carry him back down off the pile of debris to his final rest. As they passed the long lines of workers, some would doff their headgear and bow their heads while others would salute. With the sorrowful task completed, the men and machines return to work. This scene was to be repeated many times over the days and months that followed September 11th.

On the morning of Thursday, October 4, 2001, the uniformed emergency services formed ranks down the center of Fifth Avenue. The assemblage covered only a one-block area directly in front of the beautiful St. Patrick's Cathedral. Not so long ago, a single line-of-duty death would have brought out block after block of uniform personnel. Now, thinned by the tragedy of September 11th and longer shifts, there were too many funerals and not enough people able to attend. The New York City Fire Department made a plea to anyone who could do so, to please attend the funerals and memorial services for their fallen brothers. The fire service personnel were centered at the main door of the church. A short while later everyone was brought to attention. The coffin carrying one of New York's Bravest was lifted down from the hose-bed of the fire engine parked in the roadway. The marking on the truck was that of Rescue Company One. The bagpipers struck up the familiar old hymn "Amazing Grace," the song that is always reserved for playing when a coffin enters the church. Though some consider the sound of bagpipes annoying, for others the quality is almost mystical. Bagpipes hold the unique distinction of once having been classified as an "Instrument of War." For three centuries a Scotsman ran the risk of death just for having pipes in his possession. There are large numbers of men in the fire service with Irish, English or Scottish ancestry. One would be hard pressed to find a dry eye among them when the pipes are playing, especially a song as near and dear to their hearts as "Amazing Grace." As the final strains of the pipes died away, the formation moved from the street up the stairs and into the building.

I sat in St. Patrick's Cathedral attending the funeral of 41-year-old Captain Terence S. Hatton. Capt. Hatton was with Rescue Company 1 of the New York Fire Department. He received 19 commendations during his 21 years on the department, a hero among heroes. At six-foot four and good-looking, he reminded many of the film star, Gary Cooper. He was known for his coolness while under fire, literally. If you watch the films of the World Trade Center taken on Sept. 11th, you can see a light gray colored smoke coming from a portion of the first tower hit. It appears at the lower portion of the massive plume of black smoke. All firefighters know that this is an indication of water being applied to a fire. When you consider that some elevators could not be used and that the men had to walk up all those flights of stairs laden with heavy equipment, it was a remarkable feat. It is believed that it was Capt. Hatton and his men that did just that. They died attempting to hold back the fire in an effort to give others the needed time to escape.

The funeral service was quite lengthy with an impressive list of eulogizers:

Joseph M. Allbaugh, Director of Federal Emergency Management Agency
Lieutenant Michael Pena, Rescue Co. No. 1
Timothy Brown, Supervisor of the Office of Emergency Management
Kenneth Hatton, Deputy Chief [Retired] (Father of Capt. Hatton)
Fire Commissioner Thomas Von Essen
Hon. Governor George E. Pataki, New York State
Hon. Mayor Rudolph W. Giuliani, City of New York

When Mayor Giuliani spoke, you could hear the emotional impact creeping into his voice. This was a personal loss for him. Captain Hatton's wife, Beth, is one of the Mayor's aides and Mayor Giuliani presided over their wedding. It was shortly after September 11th that Beth learned she was pregnant. Capt. Hatton perished along with 10 other members of Rescue 1. They, along with all the other departed emergency workers, had died doing the jobs they had trained for and dedicated their lives to.

I'd like to share with you a quote that is framed and hangs on the wall at the central firehouse in Westport, Connecticut. My guess is that it hangs in many other firehouses also.

> I have no ambition in this world but one, and that is to be a firefighter. The position, in the eyes of some, may appear to be a lowly one; but we who know the work which a firefighter has to do believe it is a noble calling.
>
> Our proudest moment is to save lives... Under the impulse of such thoughts, the nobility of the occupation thrills us and stimulates us to deeds of daring ... even of supreme sacrifice.
>
> Edward F. Crocker,
> Chief of Department, F.D.N.Y.
> 1899–1911

After the funeral ceremony was completed inside St. Patrick's, we formed up outside in front. The coffin was carried down the steps of the cathedral and placed once more atop the fire engine. A final salute was given and the funeral procession moved off down Fifth Avenue to the sound of the drums beating out a final tattoo. Month after month, the mournful sound of pipe and drum would echo through scores of cities and towns in the tri-state area.

Moving along the streets of New York City I experienced firsthand some of the things I had only heard about from others. As we moved south on Fifth Ave., in our dress uniforms, people would come up and shake our hands and pat us on the back. They would say things like, "You guys are my hero" and "Thank you for the job that you do." I would say, "Thank you" in absentia for those whose voices had been silenced. The pretty girls smiled, while others just met your eyes with a look of extreme sadness. The city was a kinder, gentler city. Seldom would you hear a car horn, an old New York City trademark. Like a wounded animal the city was suffering in silence. I knew that it would take time, there would be a recovery, maybe not a full healing, but a recovery nonetheless. The rescue workers digging at "Ground Zero" worked on bent knees but their backs were never straighter. Fathers searching for sons, sons for fathers, brothers for brothers. When the pall of smoke and dust lifted, we all stood a little taller. The wound would heal but the scars on our hearts would remain. Our antagonists had no victory, no triumph; they had only caused an awakening.

I felt compelled to return to New York City and go to "Ground Zero," to see firsthand what others could only try to describe. My travel companions were Lieut. Robert Kepchar and firefighter Denis Duffy. We took the train to Grand Central station, then walked west across Manhattan. Our first stop was Rescue Co. No. 1 to pay our respects. I explained to Bob and Denis that we should keep our visit brief. After we exchanged pleasantries and condolences with the men of this elite rescue unit, I turned over the 18 dozen cookies Anna had baked for them. We were offered coffee [a firehouse staple] and then sat around a large oak table talking. Their pain was palpable. Though we tried to stay off the subject of the World Trade Center, it would keep creeping into the conversation. One of the

Rescue One members talked about the noise the first tower made as it fell to the ground. He said, "I will never forget that sound." Another one of the members across the table from him just stared at the tabletop and said, "I didn't hear a thing." It is strange how people perceive things differently during times of crisis. Where one hears a horrible din, another perceives only silence. I felt for these men, they had suffered much. Their suffering continued through the actions of well-meaning people. The department was not sending them on their usual number of calls. They were more or less being held in reserve, which allowed them more time to contemplate the events on September 11th. They were being bombarded day and night by well-wishers knocking on their door. When they were called out, it was usually to Ground Zero to aid in the search. On their days off, they would be hit with the added dilemma of having to decide which friend's funeral to attend. In spite of all this, there was something wonderful about these men. They were not victims; at least not "victims" as it is normally defined. They were tools that wanted to be used. They had a strong desire to get back to work. Instead of standing around they wanted to be busy helping others. If the World Trade Center incident was to be repeated, I have no doubt they would all answer the call once again.

The three of us rode to lower Manhattan as far as the cab could take us. After making our way to West Street we headed south along the river. We passed long lines of trucks carrying their huge cargoes of debris to the barges waiting dockside. As we drew closer to "Ground Zero," the devastation grew in magnitude. Trucks watered the highway to keep down the omnipresent gray dust. All along the way, heavyhearted police officers and soldiers stood guard. Almost every intersection and side street had checkpoints. Once pristine skyscrapers now bore the scars of broken windows and blackened façades. Fires continued to burn everywhere underground. Where once stood towering skyscrapers, now there were only voids and smoldering ruins. Dante could not have imagined a more dismal and ravaged landscape. The scene truly defies description because of the enormity of the destruction and the knowledge of the humanity intertwined with the wreckage. Between the three of us we had almost 90 years of accumulated service in fire rescue, but never had we ever seen anything to compare with this. The sights, sounds and smells that assault the viewer strike within them a chord, one that will resonate forever. One other time I have had close to the same feelings. It was while standing on the Arizona Memorial at Pearl Harbor in Hawaii. But that was different, that was past history, this was present. Even standing there it was hard to believe. I did not want to believe it, but, there were just too many empty helmets resting on coffins, or clutched in the hands of sons and daughters for the truth to be denied.

Photo by Lieutenant Robert Kepchar

CHAPTER FIFTEEN

Then, Now and the Future

MANY YEARS AGO, back in 1992, I awoke one morning with a phrase repeating in my head. "What once was, will be again." I was not certain what this ambiguous statement referred to, but I thought it was something concerning the American Civil War. Another Civil War in America? Highly unlikely I thought. I filed the incident away in my memory bank and that was the end of that, I thought. As reporters gave their stories on the tragedy of September 11th, certain comparisons were being made. The attack on the World Trade Center itself by planes was likened to the sneak attack on Pearl Harbor. The raising of a flag by firefighters at Ground Zero was compared to the flag raising on Iwo Jima during the World War II. Then I heard one news reporter say that this had been the bloodiest day in our nation's history in the past 140 years. It wasn't too hard for me to do the math. What the reporter had alluded to was the battle of Antietam. The casualty statistics for the battle of Antietam is approximately 23,000 killed, wounded and missing. Though the total number for the World Trade Center attack did not approach this figure, the death toll for September 11th made it the second bloodiest day on America soil.

During the 60th anniversary of the attack on Pearl Harbor reporters asked survivors to give their impressions of what it was like "being there." A person walking in on this conversation without seeing the screen would undoubtedly have thought they were talking about the September 11th attack at the World Trade Center. The Pearl Harbor veterans described "disbelieving" what was unfolding before them. Others said, "It was like I was watching a movie." Watching film footage from September 11th, 2001, especially when the second plane crashed into the second tower, one could easily envision a production from Hollywood. As we know now though, it was all too real.

While standing at Ground Zero, my senses attempted to take in all of my surroundings. Flashes of news footage replayed in my head, scenes of firefighters rushing into the Trade Center buildings, policemen helping the injured and civilians rushing to get away. So many people caught up in a common nightmare. Horrible scenes of death and destruction interspersed with acts of courage and compassion. In my mind's eye I had no trouble placing these individuals at other events in other times. I could see many of them back on the flaming deck of the battleship Arizona or struggling to raise the American flag over Iwo Jima. Then again, I could see still others lying motionless in a little country lane in Sharpsburg, Maryland. It seems I always find myself back among the soldiery. Once I was in gray, the next time khaki, this time blue.

Our history of aggression has moved from conflicts with sticks and stones to guns and planes. It has continued to escalate all the way to up to nuclear weapons that threaten the earth itself. We have now entered a New Age; an age where airliners filled with fuel, trucks containing explosives, even a letter in the mail can be turned against us. No longer is war restricted to far-off battlefields or knights in single combat. The global village has become the global battlefield. Huge armies are no longer needed. A devastating amount of damage can be done by a single person crossing a border from one country to the next or by buying a ticket on a plane whose destination will be determined in-flight. Hopefully, some day, we will come to the understanding that killing is not an acceptable form of communication.

Once Albert Einstein was asked what type of weapons he thought would be used in World War Three. To this question he had no answer but replied that he knew what weapons would be used in World War Four—"*Stones*." With the passage of time my purpose in life has become clearer. One life task being the completion and printing of this book. It has fallen to me, in this lifetime, to bring what I have experienced and learned to as many other people as possible. One author wrote that John B. Gordon had been one of the most important people in the U.S. in the last half of the 19th century. This was not because of his war record but because of his political and social record after the War Between the States. Gordon used his posts as Governor and Senator of Georgia to help rebuild the South during reconstruction. He used his position as Commander-in-Chief of the United Confederate Veterans and his popularity as a lecturer to rebuild the human wreckage of war and reconcile the onetime combatants to a greater sense of brotherhood. This was no small feat, when you consider the amount of damage done in the loss of lives alone (620,000 dead). Gordon's book, *Reminiscences of the Civil War,* and his lecture, "Last Days of the Confederacy," were very well received both in the South and North. In the late 1890s Maj. Gen. Joshua Lawrence Chamberlain, Medal of Honor winner, the same man that had saluted the Army of Northern Virginia at Appomattox Courthouse, proposed a joint lecture tour with John Gordon.[75] Through all the intervening years these two men had remained like-minded when it came to the reunification of a war-torn nation. Their shared venture never materialized, but still, until their deaths, these two distinguished men of war, remained two prominent men of peace.

More and more people will be telling stories similar to mine in the years to come. To what end? They will tell them until we, all of us who occupy this big blue marble floating in space, realize not ***who***, but ***what*** we are. The stories will continue to take root, to grow and branch out until people take the time to sit down with the program and read it from cover to cover. Some people will grasp the "Master Plan" sooner than others will. We all learn at different rates. We learn from our successes as well as our mistakes, or at least we should. How many times do you have to smash your face before you open the door and walk through the opening?

I will tell you some of the things I have learned and maybe we can speed up the evolutionary process a bit. I give you free rein. You can agree with what I tell you, disagree, or just shrug your shoulders and say, "I don't know, I will have to give it some thought." Those are pretty much the only three choices you can make anyway. There is a fourth choice, but that would be to have a closed mind on the subject of reincarnation, and anyone with a closed mind would not be reading this book. So, here we go with what I will call universal truths.

You choose if you will reincarnate or not. We help choose lifetimes and situations that will give us the best opportunity to learn the lessons needed for our soul's development.

William Shakespeare wrote, "All the world's a stage, and all the men and women in it merely players. They have their exits and their entrances; and one man in his time plays many parts." I wonder if he realized, when he wrote these words, that he was speaking the unadulterated truth? Maybe he did, but did he mean until death or could he see past that final curtain? We help choreograph our own dance; we have input in writing our own life's script, even to the point as, Shakespeare puts it, of our exits and entrances (birth/death). From one lifetime to the next, the roles are ever changing, one day a king, the next a jester, sometimes a hero, at other times a villain. Which is the greater part? Everyone loves a hero, but what about the villain? No play would be complete without a scoundrel. If for no other purpose, they serve to make us look better. But really, protagonists are a necessary part of the learning process. They put things into motion. Many will listen to the tale (and web) they spin and join them in their dance. Others will observe from a safe distance and cluck their tongues. While still others will be stirred to action because they understand there is no safe distance. A cancer left unchecked will consume the body. We should not judge any man because we are not able to ascertain the role he plays nor the script he follows. What is proper, is to judge their acts. Earth can be compared to a schoolroom; some people are first-timers—I guess you could equate it to being in Kindergarten—while others are going for their master's degrees and have been here many times before.

We come back in groups, people we have spent eons with. Many of the people you are with in this life have been with you before. This makes sense. Why start all over with strangers, or should I say, fellow actors that we have never worked with before? Would it not be easier and more enjoyable to progress with other souls we have worked with over many lifetimes? These others could play off us and each other to bring about the present script, which may even involve the scripts of former lifetimes. As a matter of fact, we are so involved (or evolved) with many of these other souls that, if you drew their comings and goings in our lives, it would look like vines on a tree.

We learn, here on earth, by gaining knowledge in three different areas. I give them in no particular order.

- ***Intellectual Knowledge***: This is gained through schools, reading or observing etc.
- ***Physical Knowledge***: We get this by way of experiencing through the body itself.
- ***Emotional Knowledge***: This is feeling our feelings, anger, love, sadness, and joy....

I will walk you through the process and give examples of each of the three types of knowledge I have mentioned:

I studied Fire Science at a state technical college before joining the Fire Department. We read books that contain facts; such as, during structure fires ceiling temperatures can reach temperatures above two thousand degrees Fahrenheit. No one would disagree that this is a very hot situation indeed, but we still only have an "**Intellectual Knowledge**" of how hot it can get during a structure fire.

You are wearing all the proper protective gear (helmet, coat, boots, gloves, breathing apparatus...) as you enter a structure under fire conditions. As you advance a hose-line, you are in a stooped position. Your surroundings are getting hotter, so now you go into a crouching posture. The temperature above you is still climbing and your gear is heating up. (Remember that fire-fighting gear is flame resistant, not fireproof. There is a *BIG* difference). You are on your knees now and you can feel the heat of the floor through your clothes. Where your skin is exposed (neck, ears and around your wrists where there is a separation between the gloves and coat sleeves), you can really feel it starting to hurt. This would be the good time to stand up with a thermometer and check the ceiling temperature to see by how many degrees the professor had been off. You decide to take his word for it, because now you have the **Physical Knowledge** of how hot it can get inside a burning house.

Now you are lying on the floor and the smoke has dropped down to your level. You literally can no longer see your hand in front of your face. Your heart beats faster. The whole length of your body is heating up both from above and below. Your brain starts conjuring up pictures of a hotdog on a barbecue grill. The facepiece fogs up from the moisture evaporating off your face. It's you and Mr. Hose against a red devil that is growing in strength every second. Mr. Hose does not seem quite up to the task. Now enters old Mother Nature with her "Fight or Flight" syndrome. With heart pounding and ears burning, you turn around and quickly use the hose-line to find your way back to the door you came in. All of a sudden it becomes very bright, even though you still cannot see through the water vapor covering the facepiece, you are remarkably happy to find yourself outside. You scramble down the front steps to the lawn and even though it is eighty-five degrees that day, it feels as if you just crawled into a walk-in freezer. You now have an **Emotional Knowledge** of what it feels like to be inside a structure under fire conditions.

The education process is complete; you have all three legs of what we will call the ***tripod of knowledge***. These three elements are essential for a **Complete Knowledge** of any subject.

How we respond to these learning methods will determine if we have learned our lessons and gained a greater mastery over ourselves. During adverse situations our thoughts and actions will display our progression through this process and determine whether we may need to repeat any or all portions of that particular lesson.

We are guided: Guidance is always there in some form, **thoughts** for one. I have found myself at times giving advice to people on many different subjects—life, death and other problems we face on an almost everyday basis. On more than one occasion I've noticed tears in the eyes of the person I have been talking to. Every time this happens, I find myself taken aback a bit when I realize the effect my words have had on them. I also understand that those words came through me, not from me.

Guidance can come at any time, any place. We only need to heed that wee small voice. Driving home from work one morning I heard that small voice in my head saying, "You should get some carrots for the horses." At the time I was driving past some homes that did have horses, but I didn't think the owners would appreciate someone else feeding their animals. I continued driving. Once again the voice said, "You should get some carrots for the horses." I shook the message off again as I applied the brakes for the approaching stop sign ahead. I made a right-hand turn and, there, dead ahead of me, in the middle of the road, stood two riderless horses. A man was attempting to get them off the road, so I stopped to help. The man told me he had found the horses in the roadway and they were not cooperating one bit with his attempts at guiding them to a safer location. Together we were successful in getting them onto the grounds of a nearby estate. Other people were now arriving to lend assistance, a young lady (who I later learned was the wife of one of the firefighters I work with), a policeman and the husband of the horses' owner. Every time the horses were approached, they would take off running willy-nilly wherever they felt like going. The two of them were having a grand time with the new-found freedom. The owner's husband went home and returned with a couple of buckets of oats. Every time he would get near the horses they would run 100 yards or so and then stop and look back as if to say, "We're not falling for the old oats trick." The pony show (pardon the pun) continued for an hour until someone came along with a big bunch of carrots and had no trouble at all getting the horses follow them. The police blocked the street while the two horses were led the half-mile back to the safety of their barn. As I continued my trek home, I thought about how much time could have been saved if I had just stopped and bought some carrots when the suggestion was first made to me.

KARMA: When Dr. Einstein said, "Man is not capable of knowing the full results of his actions." I do not believe he factored in reincarnation. Reincarnation makes it possible for a man to see the effects of his actions on others through the passage of time. He may even be the recipient of something he himself authored and placed in motion. Some would describe this as karma. Karma is often thought of in the negative sense. So that there is no misunderstanding, we will substitute the word *Experience* for *Karma*. We can experience what we perceive as good or bad, but who's to say which is which? We are pretty sure at the time it is happening to us, which is which, but in retrospect we may come away with a broader understanding of what has transpired. You sometimes hear people tell a horrendous personal story, the type of story that would send most of us screaming off into the sunset. When the listener sympathizes with the person, they are sometimes met with the phrase, "It was one of the best things that ever happened to me." They go on to explain how being in a motor vehicle accident placed them in the hospital in a bed right next to a long-lost relative. Or how the physical exam in the hospital disclosed an ailment that, left untreated, may have led to their demise. Many times an aliment or injury will cause a person to be suddenly forced into spending some time with themselves. This could result in "taking stock" or becoming more reflective on how they have conducted life. They may discover what is really important in this life—not material things like big houses and fancy cars. These things are transient. You cannot own anything. Most of the time these items own us during our stay here, what with mortgages and car payments.

To "**Reap what you sow**" can be carried out in many different ways. If you have wronged someone, you may decide to right that wrong in many different ways. You could experience the same misdeed first-hand or as a second party to the action, whereby you watch a loved one suffer the fate you bestowed on another. Retribution does not have to be punitive. Past actions can be met and understood not just by experiencing them in the form of punishment, but by love and understanding. Let's say you were a murderer one lifetime. Now you have returned to experience what you had forced on others. It is very difficult to teach someone a lesson by killing them, so instead of being a murder victim you become a family member of a murder victim to better understand what this type of behavior does to others. You may find yourself working in the prison system dealing with murderers all day long while attempting to help them make something of their lives. You might very well come back as a doctor, policeman or fireman and save lives instead of taking them. The possibilities are boundless.

One of the greatest gifts God gives us is "**Free Will**." How would we ever learn, if each and every time that something unpleasant crossed our path, we were spared going through it? This goes for anything from falling off a bicycle and skinning our knee, to watching the ones we love leave us when it is time for them to return home. At a very early age we are all cognizant of the fact that bad things happen. In this world there is no shortage of scenes of great sorrow, death and destruction. Many have wondered why these bad things happen. People always ask, "Why did God do this," or "Why did God allow this to happen?" The answer to the first question is God did not do it. We do these things to ourselves or, I should say, we allow these things to happen for our own edification or as lessons to others. The second statement is true: God did allow it to happen. God must allow things to happen in order for us to learn.

Evil is of man and not God. We should always keep in mind what Edmund Burke said, "All that is needed for the forces of evil to succeed is for enough good men to remain silent."

Unlike God, we can interfere with processes here on Earth. We can use our goodness (or Godness) to intervene, to change things for the better. I was recently reminded of the story I'd heard many years ago. In the year 1914 it was not all quiet on the western front. The first four months of World War I had brought about over one million casualties. In some places the enemy trenches were less than 60 yards apart. On Christmas Eve the sound of singing was heard drifting across from the German lines. The German regiments had just received shipments of Christmas trees, which set the mood for the singing of such songs as Silent Night and O'Tannenbaum. Some of the Allied soldiers decided to crawl over to investigate. Halfway across in "no man's land" they discovered German soldiers crawling in the opposite direction. After meeting up with them, a discussion followed, and it was decided that at dawn the next day the opposing armies would exchange Christmas presents. This one event was to lead to other meetings and it became common for the two sides to play football games between the trench lines. When the fighting was ordered to resume it was difficult to get the soldiers to shoot at one another. They often fired into the air over their enemies' heads in the hopes that no one would be hit. Even with the influx of new recruits this impromptu policy remained in effect. This is a true story, it really happened. Just think about it for a while: they gave a war and peace broke out.

I have often thought about what the possible effects would be on mankind if reincarnation were somehow, miraculously, proven beyond any doubt, to be fact. Can you picture millions of people coming to the realization that everyone of us has been many different races during our earthly incarnations? **Our true nature is spirit**. We come from the same place, we return to the same place. We were born from the same energy, from the same source. I will refer to this source as God. You may use whatever term you feel comfortable with. Coming from God makes us part of God, therefore, our lineage from our creator makes us gods [small g]. We are powerful spiritual beings with the ability to create or destroy; it all boils down to our intentions. We are only renting these fleshy vehicles we inhabit; we have no true earthly ancestry. We are human chameleons with the ability to blend into our surrounding. Our camouflage is so perfect that we are able to hide from others of our own kind and at times ourselves. I wonder how people would act when presented with the truth that we are in actuality ageless, timeless beings whose true nature is race-less (or all-races). When faced with the reality that we are truly brothers and sisters [in the literal sense], what would they think? How would they act?

We should all take a lesson from September 11th, 2001. As those survivors, those ashen specters rose up from the remains of that dastardly act, there was a commonality. As they stumbled into the sunlight, there was no race, no yellow, black, white or any other skin tone, just gray. There are miles of film footage and tons of photos showing people helping and caring for one another. This touching display of concern should stand as a model to all of us. It should not take the worst to bring us to our best. Instead of looking at what makes us different, we need to start understanding what makes us the same, those common threads that run through us all.

I have left the best two observations for last. They are simple and need not be delved into at great length: **No one ever dies** (at least not in the way many perceive death here on Earth), and **Love lasts forever.**

My vision for this book was (and is) to get it into the hands of as many people as possible. I believe telling my story is one of my main missions in this life. The world is in an awakening period and I feel strongly the need to poke it in the ribs, so, dear reader, if you have gotten this far, consider yourself poked.

My journey of discovery has been long and extraordinary. It has taken me on forays into the distant past, which led to an introspective analysis of myself and a good look at our world today. I have some hopeful visions for the future, but it all depends on the willingness of everyone to work together. Like Anne Frank, I too believe, in spite of everything, people are really good at heart. I have already begun my excursion toward a better tomorrow, and it all started with someone else's yesterday.

The Cloak

What fools we be, that cannot see, the truth that lay within.

There in the dark, that eternal spark, that makes us kith and kin.

Push on I say, and find a way, to let the traveler roam.

Given free rein, though he suffer some pain, the pathway will lead him back home.

Jeffrey J. Keene
(A gift from an in-between time)

History Restored

Myth no more:
Proof of the Gordon/Barlow story of Gettysburg

It seems in recent years there has been a movement afoot to rewrite history. Many long-standing beliefs, stories and even legends have been questioned to the point where the story will be completely negated.

Case in point is the well known and much loved Gordon/ Barlow story of Gettysburg. Confederate General John B. Gordon tells in his lecture, "Last Days of the Confederacy," and book, *Reminiscences of the Civil War,* a story of coming across Union General Francis C. Barlow wounded on the battlefield that hot July 1st, 1863. Though the story has been embellished over the years, the least elaborate still remains Gordon's own version from his book. Gordon tells of stopping to inquire as to Gen. Barlow's wounds and having him removed to the Confederate rear. At that time Gen. Gordon believed Gen. Barlow's wounds to be fatal. Barlow, however, recovered and returned to service with the Army of the Potomac. Gen. Barlow later read of a Gen. J. B. Gordon being killed and believed this to be the Gen. Gordon who had succored him at Gettysburg. In truth the deceased General was James B. Gordon, a kinsman of John B. Gordon. During John Gordon's second term in the U.S. Senate (almost fifteen years after Gettysburg) Gordon and Barlow attended the same dinner party at Rep. Clarkson Potter's house and discovered their mutual resurrections. Gordon used the story as the centerpiece of his lectures, illuminating it like a beacon to light the way to reconciliation between North and South. The Gordon/Barlow story stood unchallenged for more than a century.

In May of 1985 *Civil War Times Illustrated* carried a story written by William Hanna titled, "A Gettysburg Myth Exploded." This story claimed to debunk the Gordon/Barlow story, stating that General Gordon never came in contact with General Barlow. Mr. Hanna writes, "After careful examination of all verifiable facts, the story cannot stand up under the weight of the evidence against it." The article does not display "evidence against" but a lack of evidence supporting the story. Good investigation requires an opposing point of view, seeking out any evidence for, instead of a lack of evidence supporting a story.

To accumulate facts showing the story to be more likely true than false would have nullified the "Myth Exploded" article all together. Mr. Hanna states, "There is no evidence, incidentally, that General Barlow, who died in 1896 ever knew of the legend." By using the same sources quoted by Mr. Hanna, along with others readily available to him at the time, we will show the high likelihood of the story being true. As a scale for weighing the evidence let us use the same determining factors that apply in civil court cases. To prove a case, what must be displayed is a preponderance of the evidence. The Rosetta Stone for unraveling the Gordon/Barlow story rests mainly on Barlow's own letter (which Hanna admits is missing some pages) written to his mother on July 7th, 1863. He uses this not as proof, but as lack of evidence because Gordon is not mentioned (in reading the letter I found no mention of Mrs. Barlow being present in Gettysburg, but by July 7th she most assuredly was). In a court of law this would be known as trying to prove a negative and would be swiftly thrown out of the courtroom. The following items are based on fact:

1. Gordon first delivered "Last Days of the Confederacy" at the Tabernacle of Brooklyn in New York City on November 17, 1893. The lecture was so well received that Gordon was persuaded to repeat it a week later at Carnegie Music Hall. The tale was retold in periodicals like *The New Haven Evening Register*; *McClure's Magazine* and the book, *Campfires and Battlefields.* This shows that the Gordon/Barlow story was not only heard, but also seen in print in New York as early as November of 1893.
2. In the May 1894 issue of *Confederate Veteran* magazine there is an interesting quote. "Gen. Miller, the Department Commander of the Grand Army of the Republic of Alabama, who was there with a token of regard for Gen. Gordon, who saved the life of Gen. Francis C. Barlow. Commander Miller presented, in the typical manner of an American soldier, a cane cut from the place which is known as Barlow's Hill, to Gen. Gordon." *Confederate Veteran* magazine was the official publication of the United Confederate Veterans (UCV). Commander Miller was a member of the Grand Army of the Republic (GAR), a Union veteran's organization. This demonstrates that Union and Confederate veterans alike knew the story.
3. The book *Warrior Generals* gives us some insight into Barlow's life after the war;
   (a) Secretary of State for New York
   (b) U.S. Marshal for the Southern District of New York
   (c) Practiced law in New York City
   (e) Helped found the New York Bar Association
   (f) New York State Attorney General.
   (Barlow's greatest achievement in that capacity was the prosecution and conviction of William M. "BOSS" Tweed of Tammany Hall.)
   (g) Francis C. Barlow died in New York City in 1896.

These facts clearly show that Barlow was a very well known figure both in New York City and New York State.

Gordon gave his lecture in one of the nation's greatest forums, Carnegie Hall, in New York City, long before Barlow's death in 1896. If he were spouting lies, he would have been called on it long before 1985. We see no possible way that Barlow himself, and his family members or friends could have remained ignorant to the fact of General Gordon's inclusion of the Gettysburg story in his speech. These facts tilt the scales of justice in favor of the story being true, but we will not settle for a slight tilt.

Hanna writes of Barlow, "The only Confederate officer credited with helping him on the field was a "Major Pitzera." In this he alluded to Lieutenant A. L. Pitzer, General Early's aide at Gettysburg and throughout the war." Barlow had the name correct, for if you read the letter you can see where a typographical error has been made. The '**a**' is misplaced after Pitzer's name. The statement should read, Major Pitzer, '**a**' staff officer of Gen. Early. Gordon writes, "I summoned several soldiers who were looking after the wounded, and directed them to place him (Barlow) upon a litter and carry him to the shade in the rear." Could not Major Pitzer have been one of these soldiers? Just because Pitzer *was there* it is not an indication that Gordon *was not*.

Looking deeper into Barlow's letter of July 7th, we find what may well be some of the strongest evidence for Gen. Gordon coming in actual physical contact with Gen. Barlow. In his letter Barlow tells of being shot once in the left side and later, as he was being helped from the field, struck a second time by a spent ball in the back "which made quite a bruise." Doctors probed the wound in his side and found that the ball had entered and then "passed downward." Gordon wrote that when he checked Barlow's wound on the battlefield he found "the ball had entered his body in front and passed out near the spinal cord," General Gordon was wrong in his assessment of Barlow's wound; what he took for one wound was, in reality, two. A spent ball, powerful enough to make "quite a bruise" as Barlow put it, would also be capable of making quite a welt. Gordon may have mistaken this lump for an exit wound. The likelihood of Gordon knowing about this damage to Barlow's back without being there is highly remote.

At the time of the attack on Blocher's Knoll (as it was known before the battle) Gen. Gordon was riding a beautiful black horse named "Milroy." "He was an immense horse of unusually fine proportions, and had behaved very well under the cannonading; but as we drew nearer the blue lines in front, and their musketry sent the bullets whistling around his ears, he wheeled and fled at such a rate of speed that I was powerless to check him until he had carried me more than a hundred yards to the rear. Fortunately, some of the artillerymen aided me in dismounting, and promptly gave me a more reliable steed, on whose back I rapidly returned in time to redeem my reputation." General Gordon did not mention in his book to which battle this horse reacted so poorly. The question is answered in Robert Stiles's book, *Four Years under Marse Robert*. Stiles paints a glorious picture of Gen. Gordon astride Milroy as they rode off into battle at Gettysburg. There is a footnote that points to a story in *Scribner's Magazine* for June 1903. The article included Gordon's telling of Milroy's flight to the rear. This article prompted Stiles to write in regard to Milroy, "I am glad I did not witness this disgraceful fall. Nothing could have been more superb than his bearing so long as he was under my eye." This tale of the horse (pardon the pun) is mentioned because it shows that Gordon was bringing up the rear rather than being in his usual position among his troops. The incident with the horse may have afforded Gen. Gordon the opportunity to observe the wounded Gen. Barlow. This, coupled with the successful push of the Union troops by Gordon's men, could have allotted him time to stop and render momentary aid to a stricken Union general.

It was a real stroke of luck to come across the book, *Blood is Thicker Than Water: A Few Days Among Our Southern Brethren* by Henry M. Field. To recap from Chapter 9, during the evening festivities in Atlanta the speakers were being most kind to their northern visitors. Dr. Field seized the opportunity to convey a story of compassion on the battlefield. He leads into the story by speaking of General Grant's funeral in New York at which he represented the Presbyterians. The following is copied just as Dr. Field wrote it (even the Italics are his):

> In the procession of that day rode a Southern officer, of whom (as his home is here in Atlanta) it seems not inappropriate to tell a story in harmony with the spirit of the hour. As it has been related to me by *both* the actors in the scene described, I can vouch for its literal accuracy. I give it as nearly as I can in the very words of that gallant soldier of Georgia, General John B. Gordon:
>
> "It was the first day of Gettysburg. The battle was in progress when I came into it with my division, and struck the Federal line at an angle, which caused it to break, doubling on itself, so that it was driven back in some disorder. As it was retreating, and our line advancing, in crossing a field I saw an officer lying on the ground, and dismounted to see if I could render him any assistance. Raising him up, the blood spurted from him, and I thought that he must be mortally wounded. To my inquiry for his name, he answered that he was General Barlow of New York. I asked him if I could be of any service to him. He said 'No,' and told me to leave him and go and do my duty. But on my pressing the offer of assistance, he asked me to send word to his wife, who was in the rear of General Meade's army. I answered that I would not only send to her, but send *for* her. I called for bearers, who were coming on the field to pick up the wounded, to bring a stretcher. They took him up and carried him back to 'the branch' (the name given at the South to a stream), on which a camp hospital had been improvised; and I sent an aid with a flag of truce to the lines to forward the message to the wife of the wounded and, as I supposed, dying officer. The message reached its destination, although Mrs. Barlow was seventeen miles back from the front, and at two o'clock in the morning word was brought to me that she was at the lines. I sent word to have her immediately passed through, but bade the messenger tell her that her husband was 'desperately wounded.' I had no idea that she would find him alive.
>
> "The next morning the battle was resumed, and all that had passed was forgotten in the great struggle. It was nearly two years more to the close of the war. I remained in the army to the last, and was with General Lee when he surrendered at Appomattox. When all was over I returned home to help restore the fortunes of my

> State, if anything were left to her in the general ruin. Years passed on, and I was chosen United States Senator from Georgia. When in Washington, I was invited one evening to dine at Mr. Clarkson N. Potter's. I did not arrive till the guests were seated. Among the others to whom I was introduced I heard the name of Barlow, but took no notice of it till there was a pause in the conversation, when I turned to the gentleman so designated and said, 'Pray, sir, may I ask if you are a relative of the General Barlow who was killed at Gettysburg?' Imagine my astonishment at the answer: 'I am the man!' 'And you, sir,' he asked in reply—'are you the General Gordon who picked me up on the field?' I could not deny it. At this point he sprang to his feet, and I thought would have leaped over the table. And then he told the story of the scene in which we had met before, at which not only the ladies, but the men round the table, found it difficult to control their emotion."

At President Grant's funeral Gen. Gordon rode to the right of Union General Winfield S. Hancock. Gen. Gordon describes an unexpected event.

> It will be remembered that General Hancock was commander of the Department of the East (United States army) at the time of General Grant's death, and was, by reason of his military rank, the chief marshal of that stupendous and most impressive pageant witnessed in New York at General Grant's obsequies. I was included among those ex-Confederate officers who had been specially invited to participate in the honors to be paid to the dead soldier and former President. General Hancock had requested that I should ride with him at the head of the mighty procession, and he had playfully said to the staff that each of us should take his place according to rank. Of course I had no thought of claiming any rank, and I took my place in the rear of the regular staff. General Hancock sent one after another of his immediate staff to request me to ride up to the front, with the message that I must obey orders and report to him at once at the head of the column. When I reached the head of the column General Hancock directed the staff to compare dates and ascertain the ranking officer who should ride on his right. My rank as a Confederate general was higher than that of any other member of his staff and he ordered that I should take the place of honor, As I could not gracefully resist this assignment any longer, I accepted it, saying to the Union generals, who also

> served on General Hancock's staff, that they had overwhelmed me some twenty-odd years before, but that I had them down now. General Fitzhugh Lee was similarly honored.[76]

From all we have covered on Barlow's history with New York it would be logical to assume he was there also. Dr. Field said he heard the story from "*both*" men. He may very well have come in contact with the pair at this time or he may have met Barlow in New York where the good doctor was a newspaper editor.

Given the prominence of the dinner guests and their wide geographical domain, it would be reasonable to take for granted that the Gordon/Barlow story spread to most of the major cities. In that era not many things were more appreciated than a good story. Research at the Gettysburg College microfilm file yielded a real jewel. In July 1888 the celebration of the 25th anniversary of the Battle of Gettysburg was underway. The July 4, 1888 issue of the *New York Times* contains a report that on July 3rd Generals Gordon and Barlow met on Barlow's Knoll. I quote from the column: "The two men met for the second time in 25 years and the meeting was rather affecting. Gen. Barlow was left upon the field on the first day's fight. He was found by Gen. Gordon, who not only saw that he was taken care of, but allowed Mrs. Barlow to come through the lines to nurse her husband."

The earliest written account found to date is one from *The Dublin Post,* Dublin, Georgia, dated Wednesday March 19th, 1879. This date would put the article at the "almost 15 years" mark mentioned by Gen. Gordon in his writings. This "almost 15 years" is the amount of time Gordon said transpired between Gettysburg and the dinner party at Rep. Potter's house. *The Dublin Post* article states that it is a reprint from an even earlier article in the *Boston Transcript,* Boston, Massachusetts, demonstrating that the story had newspaper coverage in a wide geographical area shortly after events unfolded at the dinner party. The article also appeared in the *National Tribune* (March 1879) and in a one-page story in *The Southern Bivouac* (September 1883). What is most interesting is that the anecdote of the

Generals' first meeting on July 1, 1863 was related to those present by *Barlow* and not by Gordon.

In a book titled *Major General Francis C. Barlow at Gettysburg and other Battlefields* written in 1923, there's an address that was given by Col. Lewis R. Stegman during the unveiling ceremonies for Barlow's statue at Barlow's Knoll. Stegman tells the Gordon/ Barlow story followed by, "I, too, have the honor of being counted among General Barlow's friends. I first made his acquaintance when he formed a partnership with my friend George Bliss, and I met him many a time and oft after the war. I heard from his own lips the story of his exploits at this very knoll as well as that near the Bloody Lane, Antietam where he also almost lost his life."

The scales have come full tilt. The facts presented demonstrate that the meeting of the two former adversaries truly took place on that small hill so many years ago. Of that there can be little doubt. Let us hope that others will be as swift to rectify the wrong done, as they were to perpetuate flawed conclusions.

A major problem with the "A Gettysburg Myth Exploded" story was that through lack of investigation it opened a floodgate of misinformation. Others took up the gauntlet and perpetuated what had been initiated. This has happened time and again since the article first appeared. A further consequence has been that, even in books **not** involving Gettysburg, the inference of Gordon being a liar based exclusively on that piece can be found.

Probably the greatest shame and insult is the new introduction in a recent reprint of Gordon's own book. This new introduction precedes Gordon's and replaces a most elegant one written by Confederate General Steven D. Lee (1904 memorial edition). The very first page of the new introduction tells an abbreviated version of the Gordon/Barlow story followed by "Obviously a heart-warming tale, even if fictitious. Recent evidence indicated that the Gordon/Barlow encounter never actually took place and that this story recounted in *Reminiscences* was likely a romantic invention by John B. Gordon."[77] This is followed by a footnote referring to the article in *Civil War Times Illustrated,* May 1985.

Perhaps in the future authors will look back with a kinder eye and investigate thoroughly before throwing out pieces of history like so much jetsam to float forever on a limbo sea. We can only hope that tales of true chivalry and brotherhood born of the sword will not die from the pen.

Thanks go to Mr. Robert Krick of Fredericksburg, VA, Mr. Gary Gallagher of Charlottesville, VA, Mr. Scott Hartwig of Gettysburg, PA, and Mr. Gregory C. White of Canton, GA. Their help and kindness have been invaluable.

A Brief History of the Lawton-Gordon-Evans Brigade (CSA) in the War Between the States

Chris J. Brantley

THE LAWTON-GORDON-EVANS GEORGIA BRIGADE (so-named for its three principal commanders) was one of the premier brigades of Robert E. Lee's Army of Northern Virginia, serving with distinction from the Seven Days battles around Richmond (May-June 1862) until its surrender at Appomattox Court House (April 9, 1865).

The brigade was initially comprised of six regiments (13th, 26th, 31st, 38th, 60th, and 61st Georgia), which were raised at the call of Governor Joe Brown for the defense of the Georgia coast following the bombardment of Fort Sumter.

The 13th Georgia had initially mustered into Confederate service on July 8, 1861 and served briefly with Brig. Gen. John Floyd's brigade in West Virginia, seeing minor action at the Battles of Sewell Mountain and Laurel Hill. They were returned to Georgia due to sickness and lack of clothing suitable for the harsh winter climate in the West Virginia mountains. While on coastal duty, they engaged in a number of skirmishes, including the capture of a gunboat that afterwards bore their name and a brush-up with the 8th Michigan on Whitemarsh Island, Georgia on April 16, 1862.

The six regiments were placed under the command of Brig. Gen. Alexander Lawton, commander of the Georgia Military District, who had proposed formation of an "elite brigade" of

Georgia troops to answer Richmond's call for troops to repel the threat posed by McClellan's advance from Williamsburg on the Confederate capital (i.e. the Peninsula Campaign).

In May 1862, the six regiments, which mustered between 6,000-7,000 men, were moved by rail and foot to Lynchburg and the Shenandoah Valley to reinforce Gen. Stonewall Jackson as part of a deception planned by General Lee to mask his planned offensive against McClellan's forces around Richmond. The regiments arrived just in time to join Jackson's column during its forced march from the Valley to engage in the Seven Days Battles around Richmond. There the Brigade received its baptism of fire at the battle of Gaines Mill (June 27, 1862), suffering 492 killed and wounded out of approximately 3,500 soldiers carried into battle. Spurred on by General Richard Ewell's "Hurrah for Georgia," they formed a line of battle and advanced through heavy woods and marshy stream bottoms until they met the enemy posted on higher ground. On the left, the 31st and 38th Georgia faced Sykes' Brigade of U.S. Regulars, engaging them in a steady exchange of fire until sunset. Then the 38th Georgia, joined by the 5th Virginia and 1st Maryland, charged the Union line, driving back the regulars and overrunning the Hoboken battery. During the balance of the Seven Days Battles, the Georgians maneuvered with Jackson's Corps, drawing fire and taking casualties at Malvern Hill (July 1, 1862) without becoming heavily engaged.

Following the Seven Days Battles around Richmond, General Lee sent Stonewall Jackson northward with half his army to neutralize a second Union army under Gen. John Pope, which was advancing on Richmond. Jackson attacked Pope's advance at Cedar Mountain, where the Georgians guarded Jackson's supply train and saw none of the fighting. Jackson then maneuvered his Corps into the rear of Gen. John Pope's army, skirmishing with rear echelon troops at Bristoe Station and capturing the Union supply depot at Manassas Junction, before concealing his force on a wooded ridge near Groveton. At Brawner's Farm (Aug. 28, 1862), Jackson emerged from hiding to strike King's Union Division on the march to Manassas

Junction. The Georgia Brigade suffered heavy casualties in a prolonged firefight on open ground with the Union Iron Brigade and its Battery B, 4th U.S. Artillery. Georgia Brigade commander Alexander Lawton assumed command of Ewell's division when Ewell was severely wounded. The Georgians were posted in the center of Jackson's line for the subsequent battle of 2nd Manassas (Bull Run) (Aug. 29-30, 1862) but saw little action. They also participated in the pursuit of Pope's retreating forces, suffering light casualties during confused fighting at Chantilly.

After victory at 2nd Manassas, Lee moved his army into Maryland to bring the war to the North. When pressed by the larger Union army under Gen. McClellan, Lee collected his forces near Sharpsburg, Maryland and put them into line along Antietam Creek. On Sept. 17, 1862, the Georgia Brigade was posted at the center of Stonewall Jackson's lines along the fringe of Miller's Cornfield and the East Woods. Under temporary command of Col. Marcellus Douglass, the Georgians blunted the onslaught of Hooker's attacking columns in desperate fighting. Helping to repulse attacks by successive elements of Gibbons', Duryea's, Hartsuff's, and Christian's Union Brigades, the Georgians suffered over 560 killed, wounded, and missing out of the 1100 men who entered the fray in just 45 minutes of hard fighting. Their commanding general (Lawton), their brigade commander (Douglass), and five of the six regimental commanders were either killed or wounded in the fierce conflict. Out of ammunition, and badly frazzled, but not broken, the Brigade was replaced in line by Hood's Texas Brigade during a lull in the fighting and spent the rest of that battle in reserve.

After Antietam, Lee retired to Virginia, taking up positions near Fredericksburg guarding the crossings of the Rappahannock River. On Dec. 13, 1862, the Union Army under Gen. Burnside moved to attack the strong confederate positions on Marye's Heights, making no progress in spite of heavy casualties until George Meade pushed his Federal Division through a swampy gap farther down the Confederate lines and rolled up Gregg's South Carolina Brigade. Major General Jubal Early sent the Georgia Brigade in to plug the hole. Their counterattack was successful and the ardor of the Georgians' charge so great that the 31st, 38th, 60th and 61st Regiments chased Meade's collapsing lines back out on the plains, across the Richmond & Fredericksburg Railroad nearly to the Old Richmond Road, approximately 400 yards from the Rappahannock River. Here their advance was brought up short by Birney's fresh Union division and sixteen guns. Acting brigadier Col. Edmund Atkinson was wounded and fell into Union hands as the Georgians retired.

In the subsequent Chancellorsville Campaign (April 29–May 5, 1863), fighting under new Brigadier General John Brown Gordon, the 13th Georgia helped delay the Union Iron Brigade and its Rappahannock crossing at Fitzhugh's Landing. While Lee faced Hooker at Chancellorsville, Sedgwick's Corps thrust through the Confederate lines at Marye's Heights above Fredericksburg, advancing to threaten Lee's rear until stopped at Salem Church. Sedgwick's Corps was pushed back into a defensive salient. During the subsequent operations, the Georgia Brigade recaptured the lightly defended Marye's Heights and then successfully rolled back the left flank of Sedgwick's Union Sixth Corps, threatening their line of retreat across Banks Ford.

Despite the loss of Stonewall Jackson, General Lee was encouraged by the twin victories at Chancellorsville and Fredericksburg to try a second invasion of the North. Assigned to Early's Division of Ewell's Corps, the Georgia Brigade skirmished with Milroy's Union forces at Winchester (June 13-15, 1863) in the Shenandoah Valley on their way to Maryland and then marched as far north and east as Wrightsville, Pennsylvania before being stopped when fleeing state militia burned the bridge over the Susquehanna River. The Georgians then turned south again to join Lee's army as it concentrated around Gettysburg.

In the afternoon of the first day's fighting at Gettysburg (July 1, 1863), General Gordon led his newly arrived Brigade in a devastating charge that rolled over the far right flank of the Union line, causing the collapse of the Union XI Corps. Aided by the advance of Doles' Brigade of Georgians who struck the Union lines in tandem, Gordon's Brigade closely pressed the disintegrating Union lines, killing or wounding nearly 1500 Union troops and capturing another 1800, against a loss of approximately 400. After the war, General Richard Ewell recalled that "Gordon's Brigade that evening put hors de combat a greater number of the enemy in proportion to its own numbers than any other command on either side ever did, from the beginning to the end of the war." In his reminiscences, Gordon expressed chagrin that his advance was halted and that Ewell later declined his entreaties to attack the confused Federal forces on Cemetery Hill before they could rally and entrench. The Brigade saw little action in the balance of that great battle and served as part of the rear guard in Lee's retreat. The Brigade subsequently participated in several sharp skirmishes as the Union General Meade tested the confederate lines, culminating in his aborted Mine Run Campaign (Nov. 26–Dec. 2, 1863).

The Brigade's next great exploit was at the Battle of the Wilderness (May 5-6, 1864) as the Union army sought to sidestep Lee's army and bring him to battle on open ground near Richmond. Lee moved quickly, striking the Union army in the flank as it passed through the Wilderness. Non-plussed, Union commander U.S. Grant concentrated his forces and struck back hard. Arriving on the field as the Union 5th and 6th Corps bore down on the Ewell's 2nd Corps, Gordon's brigade was launched into the middle of the Union line, penetrating deeply into a gap between the Federal brigades of Cutler and Stone. Apprehensive of being cut off, Gordon formed his regiments in two lines, faced them back to back, and charged again, rolling up the flanks of the Federal brigades in both directions and stalling the Union assault. In the confusion that followed, Major James Van Valkenburgh of the 61st Georgia and several aides single-handedly captured the entire 7th Pennsylvania Regiment by bluff.

Following this successful attack, Gordon's Brigade was shifted to the far left of the Confederate line. Here, early the next day, Gordon determined that the Union right flank was "up in the air" and susceptible to a flanking attack similar to Jackson's masterstroke at Chancellorsville. His division commander Jubal Early refused to believe that the Union lines were unsupported and entreaties to Ewell were unavailing until late in the day when Ewell, under pressure from Lee to mount an attack, authorized Gordon's plan. Attacking as the sun set, Gordon's Georgians and their supports caught the Union troops by surprise, rolling up their lines for nearly a mile, capturing over 600 prisoners and two Brigadier Generals, and apparently causing a near panic among several general officers at Grant's headquarters. Unfortunately for the South, Grant remained unruffled. In his subsequent report and after the war, Gordon argued with much feeling that this attack, if made earlier in the day and with stronger support, would have produced a decisive Confederate victory.

After the Wilderness, the Brigade joined in the race to Spotsylvania Courthouse under the command of new Brigadier General Clement Anselm Evans in a patched-together division created for John Brown Gordon, who was promoted Major General. Held in reserve, they were thrown into the bloody fighting twice on May 10 and May 12, 1864 to plug holes caused by the sudden assaults of Wright's VI Corps and Hancock's II Corps against the so-called Mule Shoe salient, the apex of which was known later as "Bloody Angle." In the second charge, as the fate of the Confederate army stood in the balance, General Lee rode into the center of Gordon's forming line, apparently resolved to lead them in the advance until the cries "General Lee to the rear" by the Georgians and Virginians of Gordon's command compelled him to retire to safer ground.

Evan's Georgia Brigade fought and marched with Lee's army as it was inexorably pushed back on its defensive lines around Richmond and Petersburg during Grant's Overland Campaign. After the Union repulse at Cold Harbor, the Georgians were dispatched with Early's small corps on June 13, 1864 to drive Union forces under Gen. Hunter from the Shenandoah Valley, who were threatening Richmond from the rear and laying waste to the Valley's rich agriculture. After chasing Hunter into West

Virginia, Early's forces raced up the Valley, into Maryland, and towards Washington, DC. Delayed by a day of hard fighting at Monocacy (July 9, 1864), Early's small command reached the suburbs of Washington, D.C. at Fort Stevens just in time to watch reinforcements sent by Grant from Virginia file into the city's fortifications.

Following their disappointment at Washington, Early's command retired into the Shenandoah Valley where they quickly regrouped and aggressively challenged the disjointed Union forces in that region, launching cavalry raids back into northern territory. In August 1864, Gordon's Division was the subject of an inspection report, which noted that "Evans' (Georgia) brigade has lost by casualty so many and such valuable officers as to interfere seriously with its good management." The inspection concluded, however that, "in spite of all defects, the division has fought with conspicuous gallantry and constant success."

Cognizant of the threat posed by Early's still active force, Union Commander-in-Chief U.S. Grant combined all available forces into a new Army of the Shenandoah and assigned command to Gen. Phil Sheridan with orders to begin active operations against Early and destroy the resources of the Shenandoah Valley. Although uncharacteristically tentative in his operations, Sheridan took advantage of his great numerical advantage to inflict embarrassing reverses on the Confederate forces at Winchester, Fisher's Hill, and Cedar Creek.

At Winchester (or Opequon Creek) on Sept. 19, 1864, the Georgia Brigade broke before a surprise Union attack on their line of march, but regrouped and joined the front line, fighting doggedly throughout the day until Early ordered the withdrawal. At Fisher's Hill (Sept. 22, 1864), the Georgia Brigade was posted at the center of Early's line in strong defensive positions, which they were forced to abandon when their line of retreat was threatened by the collapse of Early's lightly guarded left flank. At Cedar Creek (Oct. 19, 1864), the Georgians led the surprise flank attack by Gordon's, Ramseur's and Pegrams Divisions that scattered the Union VIII and XIX Corps, nearly producing a decisive victory. Early, however, failed to press his advantage, allowing Sheridan to rally his men and bring up fresh Union forces that reversed the tide of battle. This defeat caused a falling out between Gordon and Early, who suppressed Gordon's report of the battle and blamed the failure to follow-up the successful attack to disorganization resulting from looting of the overrun Union encampments. The rank and file had lost confidence in Early and longed for Gordon to take command.

Leaving Early with a patchwork force in the Valley, the Georgia brigade returned with Gordon's Division to the Confederate lines at Petersburg. Gordon was given command of Lee's 3rd Corps, Clement Evans was made commander of Gordon's Division, and command of the Georgia Brigade fell on the shoulders of Col. John Baker of the 13th Georgia. The Georgia Brigade fought on in the closing battles of that campaign, including the sharp fighting at Hatcher's Run (Feb. 5-7, 1865) and the forlorn hope attack at Hares Hill or Fort Steadman (March 25, 1865). They helped hold the trenches near Petersburg until the confederate defeat at Five Forks forced Lee to abandon his works. They then served with Gordon's rear guard protecting Lee's army during the retreat toward Appomattox Court House.

Tradition holds that the Georgia Brigade also participated in the last attack made by the Army of Northern Virginia (April 9, 1865), when Gordon's Corps, now in the advance, charged a hastily constructed line of breastworks thrown across their line of march at Appomattox Court House by Sheridan's cavalry corps, carrying the works, capturing two guns and taking prisoners, before Union infantry reinforcements and a flag of truce halted the fighting.

At Appomattox, approximately 750 officers and men of the Georgia brigade were surrendered to Federal authorities, all that was left of a brigade that mustered nearly 7,000 men three years before, and that had been reinforced during the course of the war by another 800 men from the 9th, 12th, and 18th Georgia Battalions. Only the combined Louisiana Brigades of Hays and

Taylor (12 regiments) lost more men than did Lawton-Gordon-Evan's Georgia Brigade during the war.

For further information on the Lawton-Gordon-Evans Brigade, visit the author's web site at http://users.erols.com/brant/GeorgiaBrigade/

Notes

[1] Gallagher, 1987, p. 59.

[2] *Who's Who,* 1903–1905, p. 424.

[3] Gordon, 1903, pp. 87–91.

[4] Gordon, 1903, p. 91.

[5] Bailey, 1984, pp. 96, 107.

[6] Eckert, 1989, p. 50.

[7] Gordon, 1903, p. 92.

[8] Gordon, 1903, p. 102.

[9] Gordon, 1903, pp. 74–75.

[10] Lee, 1915, pp. 94–95.

[11] Gordon, 1903, pp. 147–48.

[12] Gordon, 1903, pp. 321–22.

[13] Eckert, 1989, p. 7.

[14] Eckert, 1989, p. 8.

[15] Gordon, 1903, p. 309.

[16] Gordon, 1903, p. 312.

[17] Worsham, 1912, p. 212.

[18] *The War of the Rebellion: A Compilation of the Official Records of the Union and Confederate Armies*, p. 1035. Here on known as Official Records.

[19] *Official Records,* p. 1035.

[20] *The New American Desk Encyclopedia.*

[21] Gordon, 1903, pp. 322–23.

[22] Gordon, 1903, p. 102.

[23] Gordon, 1903, p. 241.

[24] Pollard, pp. 543–44.

[25] Gordon, 1903, pp. 264–66.

[26] *American Heritage,* 1960, p. 458.

[27] Miller, 1911, pp. 64–66.

[28] Gordon, 1903, pp. 278–79.

[29] Gordon, 1903, pp. 385, 386, 387.

[30] Gordon, 1903, p. 389.

[31] Gordon, 1903, p. 394.

[32] Tankersley, 1955, pp. 183–85.

[33] Chamberlain, 1901.

[34] Gordon, 1900, pp. 15–16.

[35] Gordon, 1903, pp. 318–19.

[36] Tankersley, 1955, pp. 69–70.

[37] Tankersley, 1955, p. 98.

[38] Tankersley, 1955, pp. 94–95.

[39] Tankersley, 1955, p. 99.

[40] Vandiver, 1970, p. 304.

[41] Weiss, 1988, p. 9.

[42] Weiss, 1988, p. 58.

[43] In the book, *Wearing of the Gray* (1867) by John Esten Cooke (of Gen. JEB Stuart's staff), I found that Gen. Gordon enjoyed cigars also. Cooke writes: "We reached General Gordon's and were shown to the General's chamber. General G's cheery voice as he smoked his cigar and discussed the events of the day, did not make my companion smile." Cooke's companion was General Pegram who would die in battle the very next day.

[44] Tankersley, 1955, p. 372.

[45] All quotes in the last two paragraphs, Gordon, 1903, pp. 341–42.

[46] Gordon, 1903, pp. 349–50.

[47] Gordon, 1903, pp. 437–38.

[48] Worsham, 1912, p. 193.

[49] Tankersley, 1965, p. 16.

[50] Field, 1886, p. 33–35.

[51] Jeremiah Williams to John B. Bachelder, 18, June 1880, Bachelder Papers, New Hampshire Historical Society.

[52] Miller, 1993, p. 143.

[53] Tankersley, 1955, pp. 14–15.

[54] Tankersley, 1955, p. 191, note #15.

[55] Patton, 1994, p. 246.

[56] Tankersley, 1955, p. 221 (from *Confederate Military History I,* 704).

[57] Gordon, 1903, pp. 60–61.

[58] Gordon, 1903, pp. 64–65.

[59] Gordon, 1903, p. 65.

[60] From www.ial.goldthread.com

[61] www.ial.goldthread.com

[62] Leek, 1974.

[63] *The Adventure of George the Dinosaur* (LA Adventura De Jorge Il Dinosaurio) by Doron W. Blake, David Gremard (Illustrator), Winafred B. Lucas (Editor)

[64] The Inuit living in the western Canadian Arctic call themselves *"Inuvialuit"* or "real human beings." Their homeland stretches from the Alaskan border east to Amundsen Gulf and the western edge of the Canadian Arctic Islands.

[65] *The Good, The Bad & The Ugly: Original Motion Picture Soundtrack* [soundtrack] Ennio Morricone.

[66] Excerpt from Dr. Semkiw's website, www.johnadams.net

[67] Excerpt from Dr. Semkiw's website, www.johnadams.net

[68] Gordon, 1903, p. 145–46.

[69] "Not Yet" had been the original title of my book.

[70] Excerpt from Dr. Semkiw's website www.johnadams.net

[71] Source: FIND-A-GRAVE www.findagrave.com (Bio by D. Stewart)

[72] Excerpt from Dr. Semkiw's website www.johnadams.net

[73] Linguistic analysis supplied to author by Dr. Walter Semkiw.

[74] Mayor Giuliani received an honorary knighthood from Queen Elizabeth II. Commissioner Von Essen was bestowed with honorary title of Commander of the British Empire.

[75] Golay, 1994.

[76] Gordon, 1903, pp. 35–36.

[77] Gordon, 1993 edition, Introduction.

Bibliography

American Heritage Picture History of the Civil War. New York: American Heritage Publishing Co. Inc. 1960. (Catton, Bruce text).

Bailey, Ronald H. (and the Editor of Time Life Books) *The Civil War; The Bloodiest Day.* Alexandria VA: Time Life Books, 1984.

Chamberlain, Major Gen. Joshua Lawrence, *New York Times,* 5/4/1901.

Early, Gen. Jubal A., *Autobiographical Sketch and Narrative of the War Between the States.* Reprinted by the Nautical and Aviation Publishing Company, 1989.

Eckert, Ralph Lowell, *John Brown Gordon, Soldier, Southerner, American.* Baton Rouge, LA: Louisiana State University Press, 1989.

Evans, Clement A., ed., *Confederate Military History,* Extended Edition. Vol. 7. Georgia. Wilmington, NC: Broadfoot, 1987.

Field, Henry M., *Blood Is Thicker Than Water: A Few Days Among Our Southern Brethren.* New York: George Munro Publisher, 1886.

Gallagher, Gary, "Till the Sun Goes Down or Victory is Won: The Confederate Defense of the Sunken Road at Sharpsburg," *Civil War Quarterly,* Volume IX, June 1987.

Golay, Michael, *To Gettysburg and Beyond.* Sarpedon Publishers, 1994.

Gordon, John B., *Boyhood Sketch, Youth's Companion* LXXIV (1900) 5-16.

Gordon, Gen. John B., *Reminiscences of the Civil War.* New York: Charles Scribner's Sons, 1903; reprinted Louisiana State University Press, 1993.

Johnson, Pharris Deloach, ed., *Under the Southern Cross: Soldier Life with Gordon Bradwell and the 31st Georgia.* Macon, GA: Mercer University Press, Nov. 1999.

Lee, Robert E., *Lee's Dispatches: Unpublished Letters of General Robert E. Lee, C.S.A.* New York, London: G.P. Putnam's Sons, Edited by Douglas Southall Freeman, 1915.

Leek, Sybil, *Reincarnation the Second Chance,* New York: Stein and Day Publishers, 1974.

Miller, Francis Trevelyan, editor in chief, Lanier, Robert S., managing editor, *Photographic History of the Civil War—The Decisive Battles,* Vol. 3,. New York: Patriot Publishing Co., 1911.

Miller, William J., *Mapping for Stonewall.* Washington, DC: Elliott & Clark Publishing, 1993.

Murray, Alton J., *The True Wartime Experiences of the 26th Regiment, Georgia Volunteer Infantry, Lawton-Gordon-Evans Brigade, Confederate States Army.* St. Marys, GA: Alton J. Murray, 1976.

Nichols, Pvt. G. W., *A Soldier's Story of His Regiment (61st Georgia) and Incidentally of the Lawton-Gordon-Evans Brigade, Army of Northern Virginia.* Kennesaw, GA: Continental Book Co, 1961). (E559.5.61st.N53.1961.

Patton, Robert H., *The Pattons: A Personal History of an American Family.* Crown Publishing Group, Inc., 1994.

Pollard, Edward A., *Lee and His Lieutenants.*

Scaife, William R., *The Georgia Brigade.* Atlanta, GA: William R. Scaife, 1988.

Stephens, Robert Grier , Jr., ed., *Intrepid Warrior: Clement Anselm Evans.* Dayton, OH: Morningside House, Inc. 1992.

Tankersley, Allen P., *John B. Gordon: A Study in Gallantry.* Atlanta, GA: Whitehall Press, 1965.

Vandiver, Frank E., *Their Tattered Flags.* New York: Harper & Row, 1970.

The War of the Rebellion: A Compilation of the Official Records of the Union and Confederate Armies (130 Vols.). Washington, DC. 1880-1901. XIX Part 1.

Weiss, Brian L., *Many Lives, Many Masters.* New York: Simon & Schuster Inc., 1988.

White, Gregory C., *This Most Bloody and Cruel Drama: A History of the 31st Georgia Volunteer Infantry.* Baltimore, MD: Butternut & Blue, 1997.

Worsham, John H., *One of Jackson's Foot Cavalry: His Experience and What He Saw During the War 1861-1865.* New York: Neale Publishing Company, 1912.

Who's Who, 1903-1905.

Photo by Liborio Albanese

About the Author

JEFFREY J. KEENE was born in Danbury, Connecticut, in 1947 and grew up in the town of Westport, CT. He joined the Air Force following his graduation in 1965 and specialized as a medic. While serving in Texas, Alabama, Florida, and New Jersey, he rose to the rank of sergeant and received an honorable discharge in 1969.

After returning to Westport, Keene joined the town's fire department in 1976. In his twenty-seven years in the fire service, Keene studied Fire Science at Norwalk State Technical College and attended Delaware State Fire School, where he progressed to the Fire Instructor level. Jeffrey Keene is a decorated firefighter and presently an Assistant Fire Chief with the Westport, Connecticut Fire Department.

An accomplished Civil War researcher and speaker (having visited most of the major battle sites in the North and South), he has lectured on Civil War topics to groups ranging from elementary students to peer experts. His story was featured on the Arts and Entertainment Network's documentary "Beyond Death" and Uri Geller's Talk America Radio show, "Parascience and Beyond." Mr. Keene makes a strong case for reincarnation in *Someone Else's Yesterday.* Through years of research and travel, he has amassed compelling evidence of a former life during the American Civil War—that of Confederate General John B. Gordon. Keene resides with his wife Anna in Trumbull, Connecticut; he has two children and three stepchildren.

Web site: www.ConfederateYankee.net

Someone Else's Yesterday

ISBN: 1-57733-134-6, 256 pp., $17.95

Available from your local bookstore, or
Blue Dolphin Publishing
P.O. Box 8 • Nevada City, CA 95959
(800) 643-0765
(530) 265-6925 • FAX (530) 265-0787
Web: www.bluedolphinpublishing.com
E-mail: bdolphin@netshel.net

Name ______________________________

Address ______________________________

City/State/Zip ______________________________

10% discount for 5 or more books
Please call for additional discounts on quantity orders

Orders: 1-800-643-0765

Payment Method: ❑ MasterCard ❑ Visa ❑ Check

Acct. # ____________________ Exp. Date ________

Signature ______________________________

Add $7.00 s/h for 1st book + $3 each additional book
7.375% tax for Calif. residents

Someone Else's Yesterday	$17.95
(Tax CA only)	1.32
S/H	7.00
(CA Total)	26.27
Non-CA resident Total	24.95

Printed in the United States
88813LV00007B/26/A

9 781577 331346